Core Resource

ACADEMIC STRATEGY

ACADEMIC STRATEGY

The Management Revolution in American Higher Education

GEORGE KELLER

Published in cooperation
with the American Association
for Higher Education

THE JOHNS HOPKINS
UNIVERSITY PRESS
Baltimore and London

LB
2341
K37
1983

This book has been brought to publication with the generous assistance of the Carnegie Corporation. The corporation does not
take responsibility for any statements or views expressed in it.

The Johns Hopkins University Press
Baltimore, Maryland 21218
The Johns Hopkins Press Ltd., London

LIBRARY OF CONGRESS CATALOGING IN PUBLICATION DATA

Keller, George, 1928–
  Academic strategy

  Bibliography: p. 194
  Includes index.
  1. Universities and colleges—United States—Administration
  2. Universities and colleges—United States—Planning. I. Title.
LB2341.K37 1983   378.73   82-4925
ISBN 0-8018-3029-X
ISBN 0-8018-3030-3 (pbk.)

CONTENTS

by
Richard M. Cyert
PRESIDENT,
CARNEGIE-MELLON UNIVERSITY

I T HAS BECOME COMMONPLACE to warn that the next decades will be a time of great change for America's colleges and universities. By the 1990s there will be one-fifth fewer high school graduates, which means greater competition for a decreasing number of college candidates. Higher education costs will probably continue to climb, as in the past decade when they have risen faster than the consumer price index. Universities may have difficulty attracting the most brilliant young people to their faculties because of the decrease in faculty openings. The federal government will likely continue to reduce the flow of federal aid to students and support for university research.

On the more optimistic side, new developments in computing promise to alter the educational process. University research will become more vital to the nation's public health, economic growth, security, and quality of life. Adults will be reentering higher education in unprecedented numbers, and foreign students will continue flocking to our graduate schools.

Thus, we face a new situation in higher education. It holds some novel threats and presents some fresh opportunities. Given the uncertainty of the future, college and university officers cannot allow their organizations to drift. Careful, expert management is now an imperative.

Unfortunately, management in education is still a concept that stimulates a negative reaction from many academics. As a result, organizations in higher education tend to neglect management concepts and practices. But the acute problems of an increasing number of institutions will necessitate an improved style of management.

During the past 30 years many new insights have been contributed by scholars in management. The field has attracted some first-class minds, who have advanced such areas as finance, operations research, decision theory, marketing and market research, social forecasting, strategic planning, and organizational theory.

Strategic planning is a new development of great potential. This type of planning is not the same as the mechanical and deterministic long-range planning that was tried a decade or two ago. Strategic planning deals with a new array of factors: the changing external environment, competitive conditions, the strengths and weaknesses of the organization, and opportunities for growth. Strategic planning is an attempt to give organizations antennae to sense the changing environment. It is a management activity designed to help organizations develop greater quality by capitalizing on the strengths they already have.

Another important development is the notion of participatory management. Developed chiefly by social psychologists, this notion will be especially significant for universities in the future. In order to survive the difficulties ahead, colleges and universities must have more foresighted management. But at the same time, universities must maintain their decentralized form and capitalize on the entrepreneurship and idea-generating abilities of the faculty. Thus, there needs to be more active and decisive campus leadership—but it must seek and include faculty contributions.

Colleges and universities, therefore, are fortunate to have a considerable arsenal of new knowledge available to them precisely at the moment when they need to overhaul their administrative practices. At Carnegie-Mellon University, we have tried to apply the latest management wisdom to our institution. It has enabled us to operate in the black every year, increase our research, and sharpen the focus of our academic programs. Faculty support has been substantial, though certainly not unanimous. We are not alone; other colleges and universities are also adopting a new management style. In American higher education, a major managerial transformation is in process.

This book, based on a national study, is about that managerial transformation. The author, with more than 25 years of experience in teaching, writing, administration, and planning, vividly describes the emerging patterns of higher education management and planning and the reasons for the new patterns. And he points the way for any campus interested in improving its strategic decision making and long-term viability.

The future of our society depends on a strong system of higher education, both public and private. I believe, as does George Keller, that better management and strategic planning are essential to the continued strength of our colleges and universities.

This insightful book, written at a turning point in the history of higher education, is of enormous importance to anyone interested in how to manage change and anyone who cares about maintaining the vigor of American higher education.

A MERICA'S 3,100 COLLEGES and universities are living through a revolution. It is as profound a change as that which crushed the early nineteenth-century world of tiny religious colleges and created the new era of universities, state land-grant colleges, graduate schools, coeducation, research, deans, and postgraduate education for the professional classes at the turn of the century. And it is a shift that is causing unprecedented dismay, confusion, and hand-wringing in higher education circles today.

Two frequently cited causes of this change are the worsening financial conditions at universities and the "birth dearth" of the 1960s and 1970s, which have pushed into motion a deep, sustained decline in the number of traditional students available for college, the first such decline in American educational history. But there are other, more hidden, and equally powerful forces also roaring underneath this revolution.

As the outlines, propellants, and consequences of this upheaval become discernible, and as the survival of hundreds of colleges and universities has suddenly been put in jeopardy, a remarkable counterdevelopment has begun. Dozens of campuses have started to take action against their rising sea of troubles and, by adroit strategy, calm them. What is remarkable is that the chief weapon in this response is modern financial and strategic management, a tool designed largely by business organizations to cope with marketplace threats and opportunities.

Alone among the major institutions in the United States, colleges and universities have steadfastly refused to appropriate the procedures of modern management, even though other nations regard American management as one of the ingenious contributions to the new world of large organizations and rapid change. One distinguished analyst of academic organizations has called campuses "organized anarchies" and likened their management and decision making to that of filling a "garbage can." But now the dogma of colleges as amiable, anarchic, self-correcting collectives of scholars with a small contingent of dignified caretakers at the unavoidable business edge is crumbling. A new era of conscious academic strategy is being born. The modern college and university scene is one that is no longer so fiercely disdainful of sound economics and financial planning or so derisive of strategic management. Professors and campus administrators are now uniting to design plans, programs, priorities, and expenditures in order to insure their futures and to keep American higher education among the world's best.

Like the Germans, who, as Thorstein Veblen noted in his *Imperial Germany and the Industrial Revolution,* benefited by entering the industrial age late, leaving the crude, creaky machinery of early industrialism behind, and like the Japanese, who leaped from quasi-feudal life into electronics, international finance, and robotics, also leaving earlier capital equipment and ideas behind, the colleges and universities are adopting the latest modes of management and planning, which have been honed through decades of often painful and costly trial and error by government and business organizations and by scholarly research. Education's tardy adoption of what business historian Alfred Chandler, Jr., calls "the visible hand" of self-conscious management could conceivably lead universities and colleges into a period of still-greater achievement rather than the expected massive decline.

This book is a description of the management revolution going on at America's campuses. In the first part of the book, the opening section depicts the nature of the revolution that now confronts higher education. Then I describe what I have found to be the new management approaches being tried at the more alert and forward-looking institutions, large and small, public and private. I also present a brief review of the state of planning theory and practice, because planning is not what it used to be, even a few years ago; and it is this newest form of participatory strategic decision making, not the older forms of highly rational administrative science and systems planning, that is being used to deal with higher education's crisis.

In the second part, I try to explain what strategic planning is all about, and how colleges and universities can introduce strategic decision making into their institutional lives, as a few institutions have already installed it in their leafy midsts. I believe strategic decision making is what nearly all colleges and universities will need to practice in the years ahead.

The first half of the book is descriptive, about what is happening and why. The second half is prescriptive, advocating like a physician a useful medicine for suffering campuses.

A small book about a large subject requires some explanation. Though colleges and universities have become central organizations in American society, the study of these institutions, and especially their management, is still primitive. While a few scholars such as David Riesman, James March, and Clark Kerr have demonstrated excellent leadership, the subject of colleges and universities as organizations is a neglected one. Also, study of the operation and management of colleges and universities requires an extraordinary array of equipment: sociology, economics, statistics, psychology, history, and politics as well as the more eclectic disciplines of management science, organizational theory and behavior, marketing, forecasting and futures study, decision theory, computer science, social and organization change, empirical research on government and business planning attempts, financial management, comparative higher education, and planning. Above all, one needs an ardent sensibility toward the peculiar, prickly, and precious mores of scholars, creative people, and professional instructors. The polyglot nature of my bibliographical sources at the end of the book reveals the methodological dilemma.

Yet, as one Nobel laureate is reported to have said about his effort, we need to do our damnedest with whatever is available. So this book is a modest first attempt to tap a nation on the shoulder about a new stirring in the educational forest, and to point the way toward some promising new styles of performance in the field of higher learning management.

The very idea of management in higher education sends shudders into the legs and fury into the veins of many scholars. Certainly a university is no mere business or government agency. But neither can institutions essential to our national vigor, employing a thousand or so teachers, researchers, and aides, operating capital facilities and equipment worth millions, and spending an annual budget of $30 million continue to claim to be akin to a tiny monastic order deserving special dispensation from the rigors of planning, priorities, and management.

Good management is a vital necessity for today's colleges and universities. It has been for decades. But now the profound changes facing higher education no longer allow campuses to evade the necessity. With strategic planning and thoughtfully constructed alterations in governance, colleges and universities can be both more efficient and more effective.

This book has been fermenting for years and has had many counselors, teachers, and contributors as enzymes. At Columbia I had the privilege of learning from scholars such as Daniel Bell, Lawrence Cremin, David Truman, Herbert Deane, Franz Neumann, and Lionel Trilling, the latter two now dead. I have absorbed much from my working association with university leaders such as Samuel Gould, Ernest Boyer, John Toll, and David Adamany.

During my research hundreds of persons across the country were helpful, generous, and informative, giving fresh substance to the threadbare designation "community of scholars." Among them: Fred Balderston, Martin Trow, Aaron Wildavsky, and Stephen Weiner of the University of California, Berkeley; William Massy, Raymond Bacchetti, and Lewis Mayhew of Stanford; Sandy Astin, Burton Clark, Vic Baldridge, and Lewis Solmon of UCLA; Glenn Brooks of Colorado College; Martha Church of Hood College; Richard Cyert, Richard Van Horn, and Herbert Simon of Carnegie-Mellon University; Marvin Peterson and Sue Mims of the University of Michigan; Charles Lindblom of Yale; Joe B. Wyatt of Vanderbilt; Richard Hammermesh and David Riesman of Harvard; Richard Spies of Princeton; Morton Darrow in Princeton, New Jersey; Walter Metzger of Columbia; William Frazer, academic vice-president of the University of California system; Raymond Haas of the University of Virginia; James Hollowood of Boston College; Michael Tierney and Robert Zemsky of the University of Pennsylvania; Theodore Marchese of Barat College, now at the American Association for Higher Education; Carl Adams, Harland Cleveland, Robert Stein, Nils Hasselmo, and Robert Einsweiler of the University of Minnesota; David Breneman of the Brookings Institution; Christopher Jencks and Philip Kotler of Northwestern; Stephen Dresch of the Institute for Demographic and Economic Studies in New Haven, Connecticut; Stephen Trachtenberg and Ted Youn of the University of Hartford; Sister Lawreace Antoun of Villa Maria College; Charles Hofer of the University of Georgia; Alberta Arthurs of Chatham College, now at the Rockefeller Foundation; Charles Levine of the University of Kansas; Robert Hassenger of Empire State College, SUNY; Fred Volkwein of the State University of New York, Albany; Jack Freeman of the University of Pittsburgh; Robert Shirley of Trinity University in San Antonio, Texas; Francis Rourke and William Ascher of the Johns Hopkins University; John Kemeny, David McLaughlin, and Leonard Rieser of Dartmouth; Jack Paton and Burton Sonenstein of Wesleyan University in Connecticut; Rhoda Dorsey of Goucher College; George Ansell, Dorothy Reynolds, and James Morley of Rensselaer Polytechnic Institute; Don Eastman, Homer Fisher, and Robert Landen of the University of Tennessee, Knoxville; and Donald Lelong, director of the University of Texas Institute for Higher Education Management.

Several people in the higher education associations were also very helpful with their perspectives: Irving Spitzberg, general secretary of the AAUP; Virginia Hodgkinson of the National Institute for Independent Colleges and Universities; Robert Gale, president of the Association of Governing Boards; Russ Edgerton, executive director of the AAHE; Daniel Updegrove of EDUCOM; and Kay Hanson and Larry Litten, director and associate director of the Consortium on Financing Higher Education (COFHE) in Boston. George Weathersby, perhaps the finest state commissioner of higher education in the land, shared his views and explained his own computerized monitoring techniques for Indiana with refreshing clarity and daring.

At the University of Maryland numerous of my colleagues in planning, organizational analysis, and education studies submitted gently to my interrogations, often serving up wisdom as well as knowledge: Howell Baum, Robert Berdahl, Colin Burke, Robert Carbone, Morris Freedman, Hugh Graham, Jerald Hage, Melvin Levin, Richard Meisinger, John Robinson, and Frank Schmidtlein. In 1980–81 I had the stimulating task of coproducing a major strategic planning study for the University of Maryland, *The Post–Land Grant University,* with the late Malcolm Moos, whose ability to draw detailed verbal sketches about specific university incidents from his distinguished past was a new form of "that's how we did it" evidence.

I could not have written this book without three groups of people. Alden Dunham, Avery Russell, and the Carnegie Corporation of New York awarded me a grant that permitted me to do research on the subject, travel, and write. The Carnegie Corporation's sustained dedication and innovativeness in helping American education is modern philanthropy at its nudging finest. George LaNoue, professor of political science and director of the Policy Science Graduate Program, and Allan Rosenbaum, associate professor of political science and director of the Institute of Policy Analysis and Research, at the University of Maryland, Baltimore County, provided an appointment as Visiting Scholar and Research Fellow at UMBC in the spring and summer of 1982, as well as personal support and unforgettable dollops of cordiality and concern for my enterprise. George LaNoue also read most of the chapters and made valuable suggestions.

Last, but in some ways first, are my mother and my wife. My mother, who long ago drilled into me the glory and power of learning, kept inquiring, "How's your book going?" My wife, Jane, provided all sorts of assistance and encouragement, and her gentle editorial comments improved the clarity and force of many passages.

My debt is clearly huge. My gratitude, I hope, is correspondingly enormous. The shortcomings of the book though are mine alone, God help me.

Dickeyville, Maryland
September 1982

PART I

CHAPTER ONE

The New Tableau of Higher Education

One thing that is new is the prevalence of newness, the changing scale and scope of change itself, so that the world alters as we walk in it, so that the years of man's life measure not some small growth or rearrangement or moderation of what he learned in childhood, but a great upheaval.... To assail the changes that have un-moored us from the past is futile, and in a deep sense I think it is wicked. We need to recognize the change and learn what resources we have.
ROBERT OPPENHEIMER

Hell is truth seen too late.
G. W. F. HEGEL

I told you I was sick.
TOMBSTONE INSCRIPTION, CONNECTICUT

A SPECTER IS HAUNTING higher education: the specter of decline and bankruptcy. Experts predict that between 10 percent and 30 percent of America's 3,100 colleges and universities will close their doors or merge with other institutions by 1995. On many campuses the fear of imminent contraction or demise is almost palpable.

The number of professors, including hundreds with tenure, that have been let go in the past few years has caused such concern that in May 1982 the American Association of University Professors held a three-day conference in Washington, D.C., to review its position on terminations, tenure, and professorial rights and obligations. There has been a sudden outburst of books and articles on the subject of retrenchment, decline, and realignments in higher education.[1] Every meeting of campus presidents these days is choked with exchanges about financial constriction, declining enrollments, and survival.

The specter lurks in colleges and universities of all sizes, public as well as private, although smaller private colleges and the academically weaker state colleges and community colleges are widely expected to be the worst hit. Indeed, hundreds of colleges and a few universities are already near an end. Wisconsin's Milton College is an example.

Enrollment at Milton College, founded in 1844 by Baptist pioneers, declined from 800 students in 1970 to 210 in 1981–82. Four of the 14 campus buildings were boarded up in 1982, including the 600-seat theater, because the buildings needed renovations costing $250,000, which Milton College did not have. The college owed suppliers and mortgage lenders $3.7 million. Its endowment, never large, had less than $100,000 left in its principal. Salaries for the 24 full-time and part-time members of the faculty were 40 percent below the national average, with a high of only $18,500 a year, and the paychecks were sometimes three weeks late. The college yearbook had not been published since 1974, the campus newspaper since November 1978. In 1981–82 the cost of attending Milton College was $5,800 a year, and many of Milton's students depended on federal grants and loans to pay over half their tuition, room, and food bills. But the federal government was cutting back its swelling aid to students. Four-fifths of the college's $1.9 million annual operating budget came from the receipts from tuition, room, and food charges. Money gifts from alumni and other contributors were frequently used immediately to pay the college's overdue bills or to meet the payroll.[2] Clearly, this institution was in peril, and in May 1982 it did indeed decide to close down its main campus, while still maintaining several off-campus programs.

Milton College is not unusual. The U.S. Office of Education's Loan Management Branch, which took over the administration of the HUD loans to colleges when the Office of Education became a separate executive branch in 1979, reports that as of 1982 some 177 loans, or issues, were seriously delinquent or in default, totaling $22.8 million. Most of these delinquent issues were loans to small, private colleges, a few of which have not been making payments on their federal loans since 1974. Perhaps as many as 1 in 10 of America's colleges and universities may currently be in the same condition as Poland's economy.

The specter is not absent from large universities, including many of the most prestigious in the United States, although their reserves are obviously more ample. New York University and Washington University of St. Louis were recently approaching serious trouble until they received major outside help, N.Y.U. from New York City, Washington University from the Danforth Foundation. Yale, Chicago, Columbia, Cornell, Brown, and Tulane universities, with lax financial and academic management, each ran up large deficits in the 1970s. Columbia was forced to take $50 million from its endowment. Brown, by the late 1970s, had eaten up one-third of its 1972 endowment of approximately $120 million. (Both campuses have in the past few years brought in new financial executives and introduced modern financial management and are now running in the black again.) Stanford had to become a pioneer in financial forecasting and planning to stave off frequent threats that would have resulted in multimillion-dollar annual deficits, a story that two planners have candidly told to the public.[3] Northwestern University suffered a ballooning deficit of nearly $8 million in 1981–82. At the University of Michigan at Ann Arbor, the Regents cut $11.6 million from the 1981–82 budget, and the university faced the forced reduction of its total staff by 600 through layoffs, attrition, and retirements over the succeeding two years. The University of Chicago and Harvard University, with two of the premier graduate schools in the world, have lost nearly one-third of their graduate school enrollment between 1976 and 1983. Princeton University, to prevent possible $10 million annual deficits, has just begun—in the middle of an economic recession—a $275 million fund-raising campaign.

The situation in which American higher education finds itself is both less dramatic and more serious than is widely believed.

What makes it less dramatic is that the colleges and universities have always been pressed to scramble to find adequate funding. America's colleges and universities are a network unique in the world. No other country has so many colleges per capita. None has a system of privately sponsored campuses (though Japan and some western European countries have a few nonstate universities). And none has the tradition of using independent trustees to set policy and oversee affairs, as do the U.S. institutions.

American colleges and universities occupy a special, hazardous zone in society, between the competitive profit-making business sector and the government owned and run state agencies. They are dependent yet free; market-oriented yet outside cultural and intellectual fashions. The faculty are inventors, entrepreneurs, and retailers of knowledge, aesthetics, and sensibility yet professionals like the clergy or physicians. The institutions pay no taxes but are crucial to economic development. They conduct their business much as their European counterparts did in the Renaissance, still proud and pedantic as Rabelais saw those forerunners; yet modern corporations pay them to sniff out the future. They constitute one of the largest industries in the nation but are among the least businesslike and well-managed of all organizations. Whatever, like large animals in a bleak landscape, they are perpetually in search of vital financial nourishment.

In the earliest days, colonial colleges lobbied for state lotteries to support themselves, collected money from church congregations, and cultivated generous friends among successful merchants or pious, prosperous farmers. In the first two-thirds of the nineteenth century, colleges relied on town fathers and boosters, state governments, especially in the South, real estate developers, and ambitious religious sects to help pay their bills. Proud but spindly mendicants, the colleges often feigned more religion than they believed and kept themselves lean and their services cheap, like immigrant peddlers.[4] The 1853 Harvard graduating class of the to-be-famous Harvard president Charles Eliot had only 89 students, and the whole college fewer than 400.[5] Tuition at Yale in 1860 was $39 a year.

Much of the rationale for American higher education, however, was assembled in the nineteenth century. So was the pattern of localism, many competing colleges, and joint private-public support. As education historian David Potts has found, most nineteenth-century colleges received less support from the religious denominations than some people have assumed: "The fundamental element in college-founding was the alliance forged between college promoters and a particular town or county. Initially, this alliance was usually expressed in terms of the promoters agreeing to locate the college in a particular community in return for a sum of money raised within that community."[6] To this day, many colleges carry the name of their communities: Albion, Davidson, Denver, Gettysburg, Ripon, Roanoke, Swarthmore, Whittier.

The presidents, who were seldom scholars but commonly were judges, merchants, editors, ex-governors or ex-senators, and clergymen, usually sought to finance their colleges by borrowing one device from business and one from the churches. From business, they selected the salesman. Most institutions had a "college agent," a combination fund-raiser and admissions officer who was employed to travel extensively throughout his college's region soliciting contributions from leading citizens and the general public and drumming up students for the professors. Their message to the potential contributors: the college would train clergy, lawyers, and teachers; would provide bright and entrepreneurial young people for local business firms; would increase land values in the area; would be a purchaser of building supplies, food, and books and an employer of local help; and would bring culture, civility, lectures, and music to the region. Their message to the potential students: a college education was the crucial step to personal wealth, power, and influence; mental discipline was useful for a swiftly changing, democratically fluid social world; and college learning would open an exciting new world beyond one's family, religion, town, and father's occupation.[7]

In the late nineteenth and early twentieth centuries, colleges and the new universities suddenly found three fresh sources of financial support, sources which launched them into a new era of growth. One was regular solicitation from their own graduates, the device they borrowed from the churches. This is a little like airline companies asking their ex-passengers for annual contributions to help keep the airlines strong—because they once flew you to your dying grandmother hundreds of miles away and because your children will one day also need excellent air transportation. American higher education is still unique in the world in this fund-raising tactic. Williams College, in western Massachusetts, is believed to have formed the first alumni association in 1821. Bowdoin and Columbia followed in 1825, Princeton in 1826, Miami of Ohio and Rutgers in 1832, and the University of Georgia in 1834.[8]

A second new source of financial patronage was the state governments. Though numerous states had created state universities after the early 1800s, when the University of Georgia and the University of North Carolina first opened their classroom doors, most public colleges and universities received little attention or money until the Morrill Land-Grant Act of 1862. Then, in the decades following the Civil War, most states began appropriating money to their state university and to the normal schools and teachers colleges that trained teachers for the boom in public school education.[9] Some states though, notably Pennsylvania and Maryland, preferred to spend their higher education dollars to support the existing private colleges. By the 1920s most of the states outside the Northeast were devoting more than one-tenth of their annual budgets to the support of colleges and universities within their borders.

Third, America's rise to industrial eminence had created hundreds of newly rich families. Beer brewers like Matthew Vassar, railroad investors like Johns Hopkins and Leland Stanford, oil barons like John D. Rockefeller, meat packers, financiers, sugar merchants, real estate tycoons, steel manufacturers, and similar persons of wealth became persuaded that higher education was an honorable pursuit on which to bestow portions of their immense wealth. Some of these industrial leaders founded entire colleges or universities, as at Cornell University, the Johns Hopkins University, and the University of Chicago. The magnates in turn gave rise to an astonishing group of academic entrepreneurs who were as bold as the industrial empire builders themselves—men like Daniel Coit Gilman of Johns Hopkins, Charles Eliot of Harvard, James Angell of Michigan, David Starr Jordan of Stanford, Andrew White of Cornell, Charles Van Hise of Wisconsin, and Nicholas Murray Butler of Columbia. One of their remarkable number was William Rainey Harper, who built the University of Chicago the way Andrew Carnegie built U.S. Steel. "When the University has $50 million, the first step will have been taken," President Harper said, indicating the size of his academic appetite. And he extracted that much from just one of his trustees, John D. Rockefeller.[10]

The institutions of higher learning had to grant places on their boards of trustees to these new benefactors. Alumni began getting seats in the 1870s, and businessmen gradually replaced clergymen on most boards during this period. As for the state universities, they had to battle constantly to keep from being controlled or dominated by elected political leaders.

The history of American higher education institutions has been an unceasing struggle between locating and catering to potential or actual donors who, like modern Medicis, could support the colleges' unusual cultural and intellectual labors, and protecting the colleges' central pursuits and freedom from these frequently powerful and often passionately opinionated patrons. Campus presidents and their boards of trustees in the United States have performed the longest continuing high-wire act in history.

After World War II, universities found three additional benefactors: the large philanthropic foundations, the business firms as corporate or institutional entities, and the federal government, which poured tens of billions of dollars into higher education, especially for research, new facilities, and assistance for the poor and blacks so that they too could attend college. Private institutions received more state and federal aid; public institutions received increased support from alumni, business, foundations, and the newly rich.

Today, all these historic sources of support for higher learning are still in use, even state lotteries again, to supplement the tuitions paid by students and their parents. (Tuition covers about 60 percent of the costs of undergraduate education and about 30 percent of graduate study.) It would seem that this ingeniously woven tapestry of benefactors should not only provide protection against domination and control from any one source but should also be sufficient to give colleges and universities adequate sustenance.

Until recently it did. In fact the 20 years between 1955 and 1974 were the most prosperous years ever for American higher education. Nathan Pusey, who was president of Lawrence College and then Harvard University in this period, recently wrote, "If one will look again, fairly, at what went on in the colleges and universities during these years, the period will be seen, not as one best neglected or forgotten, but rather as one to be remembered happily and gratefully, perhaps even to be celebrated." He went on to call it "American higher education's most fortunate period" and "a golden age of American science."[11]

The statistics on this "golden age" are awesome.

According to federal counts the number of students increased from 2.5 million in 1955 to 8.8 million in 1974, more than tripling in those 20 years. Not only did higher education have to absorb the many young people born in the "baby boom" between 1944 and 1958, but the portion of young people who felt college was necessary expanded. The percentage of 18-to-24-year-olds enrolled for degrees in higher education rose from 17.8 percent in 1955 to 33.5 percent in 1974. The number of black students in college swelled from an estimated 95,000 in 1955 to 814,000 in 1974, an eightfold increase. Students from foreign countries, who rarely studied in the United States in the 1950s, numbered 152,000 by 1974. And the proportion of young women, preparing for general equality, increased from one-third to one-half of all those attending colleges and universities.

To handle this explosion of students, the United States doubled its physical facilities for higher education. More college buildings were built during the 20-year period than during the previous 200 years. State teachers colleges were elevated to colleges of arts and science. Private two-year colleges became four-year institutions. Modest, specialized state universities became large comprehensive campuses. Prestigious private universities spawned new graduate programs and tripled their scientific research. Famous state universities built smaller branches in their regions, or watched huge, new rivals emerge in other parts of their states.

Most significantly, a whole new sector of higher education came into being: the locally sponsored two-year community colleges. In 1955 there were about 400 small community colleges, usually vocationally oriented, enrolling 325,000 students, or approximately 800 students per institution. By 1974 there were 973 two-year colleges, enrolling 3.4 million students, or roughly 3,700 students each. In those 20 years, by building a new two-year college every two weeks, America created a new form of college-going for nearly 40 percent of those in higher education—a form still unique to the United States. The new community college sector shielded the older four-year colleges and universities from many of the rising pressures of vocationalism and job training, from admissions for the less academically qualified, from vast increases in financial aid for the sons and daughters of the poor and minorities, and from much of the new pattern of part-time higher education and adult education.

As for America's faculty members, their numbers increased from 266,000 in 1955 to 633,000 in 1974. To enable this proliferation of professors, graduate programs in arts and science grew swiftly. By 1974 there were more than 850 institutions offering graduate programs. The annual production of M.A. and M.S. degrees rose from 58,000 in 1955 to 278,000 in 1974, the number of doctorates from 8,800 in 1955 to 33,000 in 1974. Such rapid production had its costs. Several recent surveys have indicated that perhaps three-quarters of all current faculty members with a Ph.D. or other doctorate have not published more than one peer-review article in a respected journal or leading magazine in their academic lives. Put another way, only one-fourth of today's more than half-million professors can be counted as producing scholars in the historic sense of the word.

But that one-fourth had become by 1974 the most powerful professoriate in the world. In 1955 it was doing, according to the National Science Foundation, $312 million worth of research and development on all U.S. campuses. By 1974 that sum had rocketed to $3 billion, a tenfold increase in 20 years. American professors have won a lion's share of the Nobel prizes between 1950 and 1981 (93 of 176). The United States is now the leader in the thoughtware field. The federal government, which underwrote 54 percent of the 1955 research, financed 66 percent of the 1974 work. Support from foundations increased 500 percent in the 1955–64 decade alone, and money from alumni and business corporations doubled.[12]

Not surprisingly, it was also the golden age for faculty earnings. Faculty salaries, traditionally below the salaries of other professional groups, have tended to go down less in hard times and rise less in periods of prosperity than the salaries in those groups. During the depression in the 1930s, for instance, a 1937 AAUP survey of 125 colleges and universities found that 84 percent of the institutions had cut faculty salaries at least once between 1930 and 1936—95 percent of the public campuses and 65 percent of the private colleges—but that the purchasing power of these salaries was still 10 percent higher than in 1929–30. As the postwar economy improved, faculty salaries lagged until 1952. Then supply and demand factors and a new public interest in brainpower pushed faculty compensation up faster than the consumer price index and faster than earnings for all workers. Between 1952 and 1970 the earnings of professors rose faster than those of many other professional groups; only the earnings of physicians, lawyers, engineers, local government officials, and members of Congress rose faster. And until 1974, when increases began to slow noticeably, faculty salaries rose faster than the consumer price index, providing greater purchasing power. In addition, fringe benefits for faculty and college staff members, always exceptional, improved further; and earnings from outside activities such as consulting, writing, lecturing, and summer work expanded greatly. By 1977, as one study by Everett Ladd found, 83 percent of all faculty members had outside income, averaging 15 percent of their base salaries. The earnings of productive full professors in the mid-1970s for the first time in U.S. history compared with those of business executives, except for those at the highest levels of corporate and financial leadership.[13]

By the mid-1970s, however, the extraordinary postwar boom in higher education began to fizzle. By 1980 it was clear that at best a decade of hardship and decline lay ahead once again. The student demonstrations and occasional violence and disruptions between 1968 and 1972, and the perceived lack of a firm response by campus administrators and faculty in defense of academic freedom and order, induced a new loss of esteem and confidence on the part of the public. So did the revelations by William Jellema, Earl Cheit, and others that, despite unprecedented increases in financial support for 20 years, many colleges and universities in the early 1970s were in as bad financial shape as they were at the beginning of "the golden age."

In 1971 Cheit, now dean of the business school at Berkeley, reported that "one-quarter of all private colleges and universities are now drawing on endowment to meet operating expenses." He added, "The present income squeeze is perverse."[14] Even in 1968–69, the nation's private colleges and universities were in debt for more than 26 percent of the book value of their physical plants, a total of nearly $3 billion. Nearly 20 percent of all private colleges with fewer than 500 students were running annual deficits of 8 percent or more of their current operating budgets, and 16 percent of those with 500 to 1,000 students were doing so.[15]

To many it suddenly seemed that colleges had little real management and were fiscally irresponsible. Howard Bowen's description seemed all too accurate: "The basic principle of college finance is very simple. Institutions raise as much money as they can get and spend it all. Cost per student is therefore determined primarily by the amount of money that can be raised. If more money is raised, costs will go up; if less is raised, costs will go down."[16]

In addition, the formation of the OPEC cartel in 1973, and the resulting higher prices for oil, suddenly caused fuel bills to triple or quadruple. Double-digit inflation in the late 1970s brought rapid increases in the costs of library books and periodicals, educational and scientific equipment, and labor. The possible financial collapse of the social security system mandated higher college contributions to its members in the system. As health care costs ran up, major medical insurance costs escalated. New expenses for the handicapped and for the implementation of affirmative action plans became necessary. As tenure tightened, the number of lawsuits against universities rose, and the size of university legal staffs often had to be tripled, at considerable expense. The computer revolution required costly purchases of new hardware. More detailed federal accounting procedures, the rise of state coordinating agencies and their voracious demands for data, and nervous state budget officials seeking greater accountability forced the expansion of white-collar institutional research, accounting, and reporting staffs. Finances came to dominate campus management.

On top of all these developments, the number of young people available for the freshman classes peaked, then began to decline in 1978. Between 1979 and 1994 there will be a one-fourth drop in the number of 18-year-olds in the United States. In 13 states of the Northeast and Midwest the decrease in high school graduates between 1979 and 1994 is expected to be especially severe:

Rhode Island	49%	Pennsylvania	39%	Iowa	34%
Connecticut	43%	Michigan	36%	Ohio	34%
Massachusetts	43%	Minnesota	35%	Wisconsin	34%
New York	43%	Illinois	34%	Indiana	30%
New Jersey	39%				

These 13 states are the home of 42 percent of all degree-granting institutions in the United States and 51 percent of all private four-year colleges and universities.[17]

The sharp decline in prospects for college enrollment is something totally novel in U.S. higher education. There were temporary drops in enrollment in 1917–18, in one year of the depression, 1933–34, in 1942–44, and in 1950–52. But these were extraordinary years. The number of young people coming to colleges and universities for an advanced education has increased steadily since the Civil War. Higher education has never before had to deal with a prolonged decline in potential students. Moreover, the 15 percent decline in the birth rate between 1961 and 1975 was the sharpest drop in births in U.S. history and a drop twice as severe as that of the 1930s depression decade.[18]

Thus, the situation that higher education confronts is a most serious one financially and demographically.

What makes the situation revolutionary, however, is the concurrent eruption of several other major forces and shifts which threaten to transform the structure of higher learning in America—so much so that the wry, gentle, candid Clark Kerr, who is, with David Riesman, the finest analyst of U.S. higher education, has said, "Change in new directions may come to mark the current period. . . . This is an era for educational planning."[19] At the same time that institutions have to deal with cutbacks and decline, they are being pounded by several assaults on their present structure and programs and by demands for overhaul and change. To cut back and to restructure: these are the two powerful pressures.

What are the major forces and shifts?

1. *The changing student clientele.* As we are learning, demography is to a considerable extent destiny. And American campuses face a demographic

change of life. Not only will there be one million fewer 18-year-olds in 1994 than there were in 1979, but the composition of the 18-year-old cohort will be quite different. There will be fewer white students and more blacks because white births have dropped far more sharply since 1960 than black births. There will be a new army of Hispanic students, one as large as that of the blacks. And there will be a much larger number of Asians. Our "nation of immigrants" was overwhelmingly a nation of European and African immigrants. Since the 1970s, a decade of immigration as active as any in U.S. history, we have become a nation of immigrants from Latin America and Asia as well. Here is a sample of the increase from the two continents, comparing legal immigration in the decade of the 1950s with that of the 1970s:[20]

	1950–59	1970–79
Cuba	79,000	251,000
Equador	10,000	44,000
Haiti	4,000	50,000
Korea	6,000	236,000
Vietnam	3,000	132,000
Philippines	19,000	312,000
India	2,000	143,000
China–Hong Kong	26,000	205,000

During the 1970s, 4.3 million legal immigrants and refugees and an estimated 7 million illegal aliens came to the United States. There were between 15 and 18 million Hispanic-Americans as of 1981; and, according to a recent study by the National Center for Health Statistics, the group has a birth rate 75 percent higher than the rest of the population and is the country's fastest-growing minority. In Detroit the lower schools now offer programs in Spanish and Arabic (Detroit's Arabic-speaking population is the largest of any city outside the Mideast).

The United States is becoming a radically different nation ethnically.

America's colleges and universities, among the finest in the world, have also become increasingly attractive to the better foreign students. The number of foreign young people studying on U.S. campuses has more than doubled in the past dozen years, from 145,000 in 1970 to 321,000 in 1982. American Council on Education officials guess that the number may almost double again in the decade of the 1980s. Already, at places like Texas Southern University, the University of Southern California, and Howard University, more than one in five full-time students is foreign.

Also, America's graduate and professional schools, easily the best on earth, are becoming a resource for bright young adults from all nations, most of which cannot afford to create their own high-quality postbacca-laureate and professional school programs. One in twelve graduate students at U.S. universities is now foreign. In 1980 foreign students received 16 percent of all U.S. doctoral degrees granted and one-third of all the doctorates in engineering.

In addition to the change in ethnic, racial, and national backgrounds of students, a second major change is in the age of those enrolled. Not too long ago, nearly all students in America's colleges and universities were between the ages of 17 and 24. In 1979, the National Center for Education Statistics estimated that 36 percent of the students were 25 years old or older. It is not unusual now to see corporate executives, engineers, military officers, and middle-aged women preparing for new careers on campus. Nor is it unusual to see professors and campus administrators enrolling at another university to study computer science, new techniques of surgery, or financial management. And more retirees are beginning to enroll for courses. At the University of Maryland's University College, the adult education unit, the number of students over 50 increased 51 percent in the 1970s. Also, the number of secondary school students in college is mounting, studying either part-time after school or in summer, or skipping their senior year to attend college early.

This change in the age group is one of the most significant shifts in higher education since the 1960s. Universities are being pushed and pulled out of their traditional role as teachers of postadolescent youth into a quite different role as educators of people of all ages after puberty. The implications for instruction, scheduling, admissions, and program content are enormous.

In an increasingly knowledge-based society, colleges and universities are becoming the central institutions in each community—for policemen, high school students good in science and mathematics, musicians, teachers, craftsmen hoping to start their own companies, families preparing to travel abroad.

Partly as a result of the great age change, and partly because of the escalating costs of higher education, a third shift is occurring. Fewer students now study four consecutive years at one college, and fewer study full-time. More students spend two years at a community college before entry into a four-year college or transfer from one college to another or drop out for a year or two of work and travel or do their graduate study at two or three institutions instead of one. And 40 percent of the 12 million individuals enrolled in higher education in 1980 attended part-time. The best universities especially continue to abhor part-time students, and some are almost cruel toward them. By 1990, however, more than half of all students will be learning part-time, including some of the most gifted.

Campuses will need to redesign their delivery of educational services, as some already are beginning to do, to adapt to these three major changes in the nature and attendance patterns of their clientele.

2. *The disintegrating college curriculum.* One of the more frequent laments in higher education during the past few decades has been over the downfall of the liberal arts curriculum. Several educational leaders still carry as their largest banner the return of some sort of integrated, large-core, four-year curriculum that will acquaint college students with the finest thought and art in the history of Western culture; the latest science, mathematics, and technology; the world of non-Western, nonwhite, non-Judeo-Christian peoples and their values and languages; and the various modes of thinking, belief, and research of our time. They want a common learning, a "whole" student.

It is a glorious aim and a whopping order. As a graduate of Columbia, whose scholars helped shape the modern liberal arts curriculum and which still maintains what may be the strongest general education program for undergraduates in the nation, I support this aim with all my nerve cells. Things do tend to come apart in our age, as Yeats said, and specialization without integration is dangerous.

But there are inescapable new facts, as Daniel Bell pointed out 16 years ago in his masterful study, *The Reforming of General Education.*[21] The United States has moved from elite to mass higher education, from having one-sixth to having one-third of all the young engaged in advanced learning. And that one-third has become far more varied in social class, ethnic background, and academic interests. Each year fewer students attend one four-year college full-time. The rise of community colleges means that each year more students stand the usual pattern of liberal education—to begin with general learning and history and move toward specialization and modernity—on its head. They begin as students of technology or horticulture, then move into science, history, and sociology or into botanical genetics, art history, and literature.

Also, with larger numbers of students going to graduate or professional school, and vast numbers of college alumni taking courses now throughout their lives, the urgency and the centrality of the four-year period of undergraduate life as the one opportunity for a liberal education have melted. Then too, there is the sheer growth of knowledge and the great increase in interest in cultures outside our own. And there is the peculiar fact that subjects like mathematics, theoretical physics, music, and dance are young people's games. (There has never been a major discovery in mathematics by anyone over the age of 35.) So students of some subjects need to be allowed to specialize early.

Above all, perhaps, the termination of America's dominance of the world economy from 1945 to 1974, when the United States achieved unprecedented wealth because industrial rivals like England, Japan, Germany, China, France, and the Soviet Union lay in World War II ruins and because energy from oil was incredibly abundant and cheap, has led more young people to educate themselves for work rather than leisure, to worry about productive careers as well as music, travel, and the quasi-literature of revolution. When a four-year college education costs $50,000 or more, as it now does in most of the best colleges and universities, a young person's thoughts are more likely to turn to economic returns than to "blissing out."

In addition, the jump in the number of adults on campus mandates that more courses be offered on weekends or evenings, or in short institutes. And more of the best students each year find meaning, breadth, and wholeness from new noncollegiate sources and on their own—from magazines, a very rich form of publication of our time; from travel to museums, New Mexico, or Greece; from retreats or specially designed experiences; from films, records, tapes, and the like.

Therefore, the idea of a return to the traditional liberal arts curriculums is as chimerical as the hope of a social return to tiny rural communities without alienation. The modern university has become a new kind of place with new populations dispensing vastly enlarged forms of knowledge. As Daniel Bell noted, "The rationale for general education (however much one sympathizes with its original civilizing intentions) has become enfeebled and the intellectual structure (despite the value of individual courses) has lost its coherence."[22]

The real need is for fresh emphasis on liberal *teaching* in specialized courses, as England's Eric Ashby has advocated, and for a greater emphasis on organizing concepts, even in courses on auto mechanics or Canadian history. William James once wrote, "The intellectual life of man consists almost wholly in his substitution of a conceptual order for the perceptual order in which his experience originally came."[23]

3. *The increase in competition within higher education.* Competition has not been absent from American higher education in the past century. The extraordinary number of colleges and universities guarantees that, as does the prevalence of athletics in higher education. But competition among colleges has begun to intensify and will increase significantly in the period ahead, requiring new campus modes of operation and new surveillance

procedures. It will be especially keen in four areas.

One is obviously the heightened competition for students. The total number of young persons will decline precipitously, and the number of academically very able young people has never been more than one-tenth of the cohort. (About 20 percent of all 17-year-olds score 450 or above—out of 800—in the College Board's Scholastic Aptitude Tests, or SAT's, for both verbal and mathematical skills, and only 3 percent score 600 or more in both sections).[24] Already there have been a few scandals where colleges have been caught paying fees to agents for the capture of freshmen, and some colleges have abandoned College Board admissions tests.

The selectivity of America's colleges and universities, except for approximately two dozen institutions out of 3,100, is returning to what it was before the Second World War, when even Harvard, Princeton, and Yale admitted 80 percent of their applicants. A third of all colleges currently admit more than 90 percent of their applicants; three-quarters admit more than 70 percent; and nine-tenths of the institutions admit over half of those who apply. Over 40 percent of all American students are attending the only college to which they applied. Of the 30 prestigious universities and colleges belonging to the Boston-based Consortium on Financing Higher Education (COFHE)—among them the Ivy League, the top women's colleges, Amherst, Duke, Williams, and Stanford—only eight institutions had four applicants for each freshman place.[25]

For those campuses hoping to raise the quality of their enterprise in the 1980s, inventive, competitive tactics will clearly be needed. Marketing, usually eschewed by universities and colleges, will be imperative for all but a handful. As Clark Kerr has put it, "The road to survival now leads through the marketplace. A new academic revolution is upon us." Higher education has entered a long period of consumer sovereignty, one which will require a great many adjustments in institutional behavior.[26]

A second area of growing competition will be for able black and Hispanic students and faculty. The moral commitment of most academic institutions is strong, and the legal pressures for affirmative action are persistent. But, unlike the past two decades, when the number of young blacks attending college increased sixfold and the number of black faculty in predominantly white institutions increased almost proportionately, the future will not permit further increases unless dramatic changes occur among America's 26 million blacks.

Black high school graduates now attend college in the same proportion as white high school graduates, even though black students score an average of 120 points lower than whites on the verbal SAT and an average of 135 points lower on the mathematical SAT, according to a December

1979 report by the College Entrance Examination Board to the U.S. Congress. Hence the likelihood for further large gains in black enrollment is slim. And since black family patterns continue to change—55 percent of all black children are now born out of wedlock—and female-headed households tend to be poorer and more conducive to school dropouts, there could be a slight decline in the percentage of academically talented black students in each succeeding 18-year-old age group.

The prospects for increasing the percentage of blacks on U.S. university faculties are only a little brighter. Blacks earned 447 Ph.D.'s in 1974 (out of 24,235 awarded) and 612 in 1979, a 37 percent increase. Though the numbers are still small, they are growing slowly. But, nearly one-half of these doctorates by blacks were in fields like education and social work, where faculties are retrenching. The number of black graduate students has been declining since 1980. And in some areas, like computer science, mathematics, physical science, agriculture, and engineering, black scholars account for less than one-half of one percent of the number of Ph.D.'s.[27]

What these figures suggest is that there will be more and more vigorous recruiting among a numerically stable or slightly diminishing pool of able minority students and scholars. We have less data on the Hispanic minority students and scholars, but indications are that large academic advances among the new Latin-American immigrants may not be likely, except among certain middle-class emigrés.

Third, the raiding among faculty will intensify. The proportion of highly creative, productive scholar-teachers has seldom exceeded one-tenth, and that talented tenth will become more valuable as the nation's dependence on research and new ideas increases. This will be especially so since the number of young professors admitted to the ranks will be small until the 1990s. With less new blood to choose among, closer scrutiny will be given to the best of the old blood.

The fourth area is the growing competition from noncollege and nonuniversity higher education. Museums now give courses in art and history. The military teaches foreign languages and electronics. Professional associations teach their members about periodontal surgery, graphic design, and tax law. Corporations like Arthur D. Little and Wang Laboratories now offer graduate programs in such fields as management and computer software engineering. Outside the traditional higher education institutions, an aggressive, service-oriented, nontraditional "third sector" of higher education is being born, especially designed to teach adults in a concentrated way in specific competencies. Harold Hodgkinson estimates that while 12 million people are currently studying in courses on regular campuses, almost 17 million may be studying in courses and programs outside colleges and universities.[28]

4. *The technological imperative.* The rapid growth of electronic technology in the past two decades presents universities with the first major transformation in the transmission and storage of ideas and information since the introduction of printing in fifteenth-century Italy and Germany. It is an absolutely shattering development, requiring rethinking for nearly every aspect of higher education.

New technology is altering the college library as we have known it for centuries. Teaching of certain limited kinds is now being carried out by computer-assisted instruction, or CAI, even in grade schools; and many college classes now include films or tapes. It is possible to put all of every college's lectures on tapes or video discs and receive a college education at home, assembling one's own curriculum and classes with the best-presented courses and lectures from all of America's institutions—one's own "college" with an all-American curriculum and classes. Electronics is changing our idea of the basic ingredients of a liberal education, as campuses such as Dartmouth College and Carnegie-Mellon University make computer literacy, like English composition, a requirement for all undergraduates. Nannerl Keohane, president of Wellesley College, recently said, "We cannot in good conscience claim to be educating persons today in the liberal arts, preparing them to be strong and critical and whole human beings able to make judgments about things that impinge most critically on their lives, unless we include the phenomena of technology."

Three of the many ramifications of the electronics explosion illustrate its tremendous impact on the structure of higher learning.

One is the incorporation of computers into higher education. Computers are now as essential as chalkboards, test tubes, and scholarly periodicals. In 1981 there were about 730,000 computer systems in operation in the United States, with an estimated 5 million computer terminals, according to an International Data Corporation study. By 1985 the number of systems is expected to double, the number of terminals to triple. Our entire economy is an increasingly information-based economy, in which nearly half of America's work force is engaged in processing information of some kind. Colleges and universities simply must have computer equipment, instruction, and research if they are not to be like Renaissance universities still teaching theology, Latin, and feudalism when the society is moving into astronomy, the classics, and international trade and exploration. Exactly how computers are to be inserted into everyday campus life, and how they are to be paid for, is a central intellectual and financial matter for college and university leaders for the immediate future, particularly since colleges must help train more persons who can handle the many new tasks imposed by computers.

A second issue is the renewal of links between industry and universities. The rapidly growing dependency of medical, scientific, and engineering research upon highly sophisticated electronic equipment forces the best universities to spend larger and larger sums for new technology. But the federal government, which had been generous with equipment allowances in health, science, and engineering research grants to university professors after the Second World War, has decided in recent years to trim equipment purchase amounts or disallow them altogether. So, as several major studies have noted, universities now face a new condition: the deterioration of their scientific equipment. More and more professors are being asked to make tomorrow's discoveries with yesterday's equipment. The largest corporations, however, do have funds for the latest technology and, of course, are in some cases the designers and manufacturers of the electronic technology. This has led directly to a sudden rash of new industry-university connections in the early 1980s.

This is not the first time colleges have been faced with this problem. As David Noble has written about the first decade of the 1900s: "The electrical-engineering training then offered in the colleges—with a few exceptions like MIT and Wisconsin—lagged seriously behind the industrial developments in the field; the expensive equipment necessary for 'state of the art' instruction was available at only a few of the larger schools, and this situation restricted most instruction to blackboard fundamentals. The industries, rather than the schools, were at the forefront of discovery in the field."[29] Then, as now again, industry and higher education formed intimate ties to their mutual benefit—so much so that it could be said that in the first quarter of the twentieth century scientific businesses significantly shaped the course of engineering and science programs and of research on American campuses.

Industry also contributed leaders to higher education and propagandists for research. The corporations, for instance, had to establish their own advanced technical schools and in 1913 formed the National Association of Corporation Schools (which 10 years later broadened into the American Management Association, or AMA). Out of the NACS, from New England Telephone, came Ernest Hopkins to the presidency of Dartmouth; Frank Aydelotte as president of Swarthmore in 1921 and creator there of the first "honors program," organizer of the Guggenheim Foundation in 1924, and the first director of the Institute for Advanced Study at Princeton in 1939; industrial psychologist Walter Dill Scott to the presidency of

Northwestern in 1920; and Herman Schneider to the presidency of the University of Cincinnati, where he gave birth to "cooperative education," whereby students work for part of their collegiate careers in industry, using the latest equipment, mixing campus knowledge with industrial experience.

And a few industrial scientists battled as hard as any university presidents for the indispensability of more research. Pulp and paper chemist Arthur D. Little, for example, formed his own consulting and contract research firm in Boston and became famous as a master salesman of research, constantly preaching to corporate executives and universities about "the handwriting on the wall," by which he meant the coming centrality of research to profits, to America's economic growth, and to intellectual advance.[30]

To enable students and faculty to have access to the latest electronic instruments and computer hardware in a time of growing financial hardship, colleges and universities have launched three new efforts. One is the expansion of cooperative education agreements with business firms, which also help students pay the escalating college bills. Another is the increase in instruction in engineering and science courses away from the campus, in the industrial and government laboratories and plants where the fine equipment is. And the third is a series of contracts with corporations, which seem increasingly ready to provide electronic equipment and research dollars in return for first options on the use of the research findings.

Here is a sample of the new agreements:

- The Celanese Corporation has given $1.1 million to Yale for enzyme research.
- The Monsanto Company has given $4 million to Rockefeller University for plant genetics, $23 million to Harvard for cancer research, and $25 million to Washington University of St. Louis for cellular research.
- Exxon has given $7 million to MIT for combustion research.
- E. I. duPont de Nemours will give $6 million to Harvard for a new department of molecular genetics and has given smaller gifts to California Institute of Technology and the University of Maryland, Baltimore County, in the same field.
- 17 microelectronics firms are contributing $12 million to Stanford for a new Center for Integrated Systems and advanced computer studies.
- Westinghouse Electric, Digital Equipment, and others give $5 million a year to Carnegie-Mellon University for its Robotics Institute.
- IBM and other corporations have given $4 million to establish the Center for Interactive Computer Graphics at Rensselaer Polytechnic

Institute. Control Data Corporation has similarly helped Purdue University.

- Hoechst A. G., a West German pharmaceuticals firm, has signed a 10-year, $70 million contract with Massachusetts General Hospital, a Harvard affiliate, for molecular biology research and development.

According to one Exxon official and former presidential science adviser, Edward David, industry now spends at least $200 million annually in direct support of academic research. This is only 4 percent of the federal expenditure, but it is climbing.[31] To get in on the trend, Cornell has hired Peat, Marwick Mitchell and Company to study ways that the university may better market its research know-how. And other universities are figuring how they too can overcome the problem of deteriorating scientific equipment.

A third major ramification of the electronics upheaval is in the area of university extension services. The famous old model, agricultural extension, where the latest scientific and agricultural research is brought to farmers and rural communities personally by university extension agents, may soon be substantially replaced by direct computer connections with the universities, supplemented by only occasional personal visits. Numerous medical schools and engineering schools are busy creating new medical and technology extension networks to physicians and business firms remote from major university centers. Perhaps most radical of all new extension activities is the National University Consortium, a small group of universities led by the University of Maryland's adult education branch, University College, which has begun beaming classroom instruction electronically via satellite into people's homes in communities not adjacent to a campus. Electronics is tugging colleges off their ivied estate grounds into elaborate, interactive communication networks with other institutions and the major users of knowledge.

New technology will do at least as much to higher education as television has done to newspapers.

5. *The faculty conundrum.* Nothing is so important to a college or university as the quality and vigor of its faculty. Yet several new developments threaten to eat like acid into faculty excellence in the future or require new faculty attitudes and practices.

College faculties are getting older, and by 1990 many faculties could be almost geriatric in makeup. Fewer new members are being hired as higher education cuts back, and even brilliant young scholars in some fields are having trouble finding suitable campus positions. At the same time, a new federal law has mandated that as of 1982 professors be allowed to work to age 70 instead of the traditional retirement age of 65. According to one estimate, the percentage of U.S. faculty members over 55 years of age could rise significantly in the future:[32]

1980	1990	2000
21%	35%	52%

This situation will bring new maturity, better judgment, and greater concern for the welfare of institutions by less transient scholars. But it will also mean more "dead wood," less attention to the new growth fields in academia, and increasing costs, since more older professors mean a more highly paid teaching staff. For any institution that wishes to increase its quality of instruction and research, the continuing rejuvenation of its faculty in the period ahead is supremely urgent.

Another issue is the rapidly changing compensation pattern for professors. While overall faculty salaries have been declining in purchasing power since 1975, the salaries of the talented tenth among professors and the salaries of scholars in certain fields where the competition from business is strong are rising appreciably. Higher education is racing toward a two-tier faculty salary scale.

More campuses, especially those that do not have faculty unions and those with a greater dedication to quality—and the two usually go together[33]—are moving swiftly away from across-the-board pay increases to raises based on merit. For example, the University of Tennessee, which had funds for a 9 percent faculty salary increase in 1982, for the first time gave no raises at all to some of its weaker instructors and increases up to 20 percent for its most creatively intellectual others, according to Vice Chancellor for Business and Finance Homer Fisher. Naturally this compels colleges to ask themselves exactly what they regard as "merit," given their organizational aims. Also, colleges and universities are being forced to pay differential salaries to obtain the most outstanding people in such academic fields as computer science and software, engineering, microbiology, several fields of business, and teacher education in math and science. Obversely, they are able to shave salaries in declining fields such as home economics, which many regard as an increasingly anachronistic nineteenth-century academic invention now that 52 percent of all women are in the work force, and certain parts of teacher education and social work.

A third shift in the faculty situation is the reassertion of institutional values and needs over the academic profession's own values and expectations. The switch to merit raises is part of this, as is the growth of part-time faculty. According to the National Center for Education Statistics, one-third of all teachers in higher education today work only part-time.

Though many of these part-time instructors are at the two-year colleges, there are more each year at the four-year institutions. Christopher Jencks and David Riesman, in their 1968 book *Academic Revolution*, wrote of the way that graduate schools, research scholars, and the academic profession itself had come to dominate higher education and faculty promotions and raises by the 1950s with their emphasis on research, publication, and national reputation. Indeed, the past 30 years have not been distinguished by great teaching or dedication to student growth. Courses proliferated as research-oriented members of faculties often taught the narrow topics they were interested in rather than the fields or subjects the students needed to know or wanted to know. But now market conditions are pressing colleges to design courses and programs that students, not teachers, find attractive and to reward those faculty members who enhance institutional survival and quality as well as their own professional reputation. Campus domination by exclusively research-oriented academics is being leached out.

The situation of those on the university faculties has been exceedingly tense in the past decades. As Neal Gross wrote in a very perceptive article in 1963, "Whereas other establishments have characteristically met similar situations with increased specialization and further division of labor, the university has primarily chosen the path of adding function after function to the tasks of the same personnel."[34] Faculty members have been expected to be great teachers and expert researchers; counselors to students; professionals ready to assist their community and nation or some city, state, or foreign government with its problems; and active participants in faculty self-government and university committees. Though earlier university presidents like Harper of Chicago and Gilman of Johns Hopkins tried to separate teaching and research, they met strong opposition from President Eliot of Harvard and most leading private and state universities. So professors have been in the awkward position of having to perform increasingly as versatile generalists for their institutions while receiving their status and financial rewards increasingly for specialized research, publications, and national attention as independent professionals.

These conflicting demands on faculty performance have not ceased. But the influence of the college organizations and their needs is rising again against the powerful pulls of the academic guilds and research faculty dominance.

6. *The tightening grip of outside controls.* In his 1972 Henry Lecture at the University of Illinois, the perspicacious Clark Kerr said that "full auton-

omy—to the extent it ever existed—is dead.... The greatest change in governance now going on is not the rise of student power or faculty power but the rise of public power. The governance of higher education is less and less by higher education. . . . The 'ivory tower' of yore is now becoming a regulated public utility."[35]

In the past decade Dr. Kerr's observation has been seconded by many of America's leading universities, presidents, deans, and faculty. To mention but two: President Steven Muller of Johns Hopkins in the Winter 1978 issue of *Daedalus,* "On the campus, yesterday's partner [the federal government] now appears increasingly as today's oppressor, indispensable but stingy, and ever more intrusive"; and President Harold Enarson of Ohio State in the October 1980 issue of *Change,* "The universities today are under siege. I do not exaggerate. The cumulative weight of federal and state encroachments is crippling the university, sapping morale, and destroying the very quality and accountability they were devised to foster."

Allowing for some hyperbole, the fact is that state budget officials, the courts, federal legislation and guidelines, new state commissioners of higher education, and newspaper editors have in recent years become much more active in trying to manage colleges and universities for them. Over 70 percent of all public institutions now cannot start a new academic program without elaborate application and approval procedures from their state coordinating boards, which can take three to four years. To some extent the new ropes of restraint are proper. Numerous campuses have been tardy in accepting full racial and sexual equality. Others have tolerated poor fiscal management or unrealistic and recklessly expensive academic ambitions. Some college faculty members have abused their privileges, and several admissions officers have cheated in the use of federal financial aid. But just as often the restraints derive from righteous or overzealous government officials for political reasons. They too have been overly ambitious and financially reckless.

Still, most colleges and universities have lacked adequate planning, strong internal management, and a transparent set of academic objectives. Higher education has drifted. And in a time of new austerity and growing importance of higher learning and research, drift needs to be replaced by thrift and purpose. If educational institutions are to reverse, or at least slow down, the trend toward outside interventions in their affairs, they must shape their own destinies in ways that are acceptable to the public and its elected leaders.

Thus, higher education in the United States has entered a revolutionary period, one in which not only the finances and the number of students are changing sharply but also the composition of the entire clientele, the kinds of courses and programs wanted and schedules for them, the degree of competitiveness among colleges, the technology needed on campus, the nature of the faculty, and the growing extent of external control and regulations.

Colleges and universities clearly need to plan for these—and other—upheavals and to construct a more active, change-oriented management style. The era of laissez-faire campus administration is over. The era of academic strategy has begun.

The Great Leadership Crisis

The American college or university is a prototypic organized anarchy. It does not know what it is doing. Its goals are either vague or in dispute. Its technology is familiar but not understood. Its major participants wander in and out of the organization. These factors do not make a university a bad organization or a disorganized one; but they do make it a problem to describe, understand, and lead.
MICHAEL COHEN and JAMES MARCH

Much innovation goes on at any first-rate university. But it is almost never conscious innovation in the structure or practices of the university itself. University people love to innovate away from home.
JOHN GARDNER

Even if you're on the right track, you'll get run over if you just sit there.
WILL ROGERS

AMERICAN HIGHER EDUCATION has entered a new era that requires better planning, strategic decision-making, and more directed change. To accomplish this, colleges and universities need new procedures, structures, and attitudes. What is especially important is a more sharply defined sense of how U.S. academic institutions should be governed, managed, and led. Yet, one of the most significant developments in postwar academic life has been the progressive breakdown of governance and leadership.

There is now a stalemate in the exercise of power on the American campus. University management is in shackles. While the balance of power in our Madisonian federal government has been tilting since the 1930s toward the executive branch, presidential power in U.S. higher education has gradually diminished before the buildup of strong faculty power and, since the 1960s, the rising power of students and outside agencies. At the very time that the need for strong leadership in higher education has reached new levels of urgency, academic management is in chains. Indeed, the whole subject of administration in higher education is befuddled and bound by rusty myths and hoary notions about authority, management, and leadership.

Analysts like James March have documented in detail the managerial inertia and chaos in education, referring to organizational choice in academic organizations as a "garbage can model" which in some ways is close to "pathological."[1] The crisis was noticed 20 years ago by one of the finest sociologists of the time, Columbia's Paul Lazarsfeld:

> We are confronted nowadays, in our universities, with a very serious problem which may be called an "academic power vacuum." When graduate education in this country began 60 years ago, no one doubted that the university president was a very important figure. Gilman at Johns Hopkins and White at Cornell were intellectual as well as administrative leaders. Stanley Hall at Clark was impressive as a president as well as a psychologist. Inversely, individual professors were deeply involved in organizational pursuits. Burgess forced the creation of a graduate faculty on the Columbia trustees; in his autobiography he describes movingly what it meant to him as a teacher and scholar. Silliman sacrificed his personal fortune to establish a physical laboratory in his home and finally convinced the trustees at Yale that natural sciences were not a spiritual threat to young Americans.
>
> Today, however, we witness a dangerous divergence. Academic freedom is more and more interpreted in such a way as to keep the administration out of any truly academic affairs; the faculty, in turn has come to consider administration beneath its dignity.
>
> But educational innovations are by definition intellectual as well as administrative tasks. And so, they have fallen into a no-man's-land. The president and his staff wait for the faculty to take the initiative; the professors, on their side, consider that such matters would take time away from their truly scholarly pursuits. As a result, many of our universities have a dangerously low level of organizational development.[2]

In his famous 1963 Godkin lectures at Harvard, Clark Kerr described the same predicament:

> The university has become the multiversity and the nature of the presidency has followed this change. . . . There is a "kind of lawlessness" in any large university with separate sources of initiative and power; and the task is to keep this lawlessness within bounds. . . .
>
> There are several "nations" of students, of faculty, of alumni, of trustees, of public groups. Each has its territory, its jurisdiction, its form of government. Each can declare war on the others; some have the power of veto. . . . It is a pluralistic society with multiple cultures. Coexistence is more likely than unity. . . .
>
> [The president] is mostly a mediator. . . . He has no new and bold "vision of the end." He is driven more by necessity than by voices in the air.[3]

The main standoff is between the faculty and the president (and his staff). Trustees have become quiescent and docile at most institutions. Alumni strength is formidable only at a few dozen of the older private colleges and universities and several of the flagship state university campuses. And the assertion of student power, so strong in Latin-American and Middle Eastern universities, has seldom been sustained or deeply interested in helping to run the institution, although it is now clearly a constituency to be consulted. The extremely large number and variety of American colleges and universities allows students to transfer in order to satisfy their special wants; they are not stuck in a handful of state-run universities as in other countries, forced to play a shaping role in those universities because they have no others to which to flee. As Lazarsfeld observed, academia's institutional paralysis derives chiefly from the neatly balanced powers of the campus executives and the professional scholars.

Part of this day-after-day struggle is inevitable because the academic profession is unique among America's learned professions. It is the only profession that works almost exclusively inside institutions and the only one whose practices and standards are controlled by local lay boards. Physicians, lawyers, and architects usually work in small offices or for themselves, not in sizable organizations; and their standards and behavior are controlled by national or statewide review boards of their peers. Engineers fall in between, with a majority in organizations.[4] The academic profession is not a self-policing profession. The American Association of University Professors has, since its founding in 1915, been principally a narrow protective league that guards faculty rights such as academic freedom and tenure rather than an encompassing professional association that insures professional standards, behavior, and obligations and censures or expels culpable members for fraud, abuses of intellectual freedom, incompetency, and gross violations of ethics.

In essence, then, academic scholars constitute an institutionalized quasi-profession, ultimately regulated by their institutional boards of lay trustees and the boards' chief executive officers, the presidents. Professors thus should always look out for their institutions, which afford them a place to work. But they must at the same time guard the privileges and standards of their profession from institutional and lay board encroachment, and work for their personal professional advancement. Tension is unavoidable.

Presidents too carry within them an inevitable tension. They are in most cases former professors and often former leaders—department chairmen, deans, or provosts—of faculty professionals. Yet they are also the executive arm of the lay governing board and the most important persons concerned with the quality, direction, and future of the entire institution. They are presidents of organizations, yet nonpracticing members of their guilds. Therefore, some of the balance of power is inevitable, even perennially necessary.

But a large part of the standoff between faculty and presidents is a historical peculiarity. The participants stand on a soft sandstone block permeated with myths, outmoded positions, biases and naivete about organizational necessities, surprising ignorance about political and institutional authority, and neglect of the current realities of the academic profession.

First, the myths. Actually there is only one myth with three deep roots. The basic myth is that each college or university is close to an Athenian democracy of professional scholars who know each other and share a bundle of values and aspirations, which they practice in their institutional lives. This college of learned men and women decides in an orderly and mostly rational way on all matters pertaining to the academic life of their institution, constantly updating the curriculum, departmental structure, and priorities for academic investment to accord with the latest scientific, intellectual, and artistic advances. It also polices and renounces its own weakest sectors. It is, and forever should be, a free society, one unburdened by political interference, business practices, or worries about market conditions, finances, and competitive forces, so that the scholarly collective can point the way to ever higher levels of reasonableness and civilized life for all of us.

There is the story of the Oxford don who was reproached by a wounded RAF pilot home on leave in 1942 for continuing his academic work as if London were not being bombed, people were not getting killed, the Nazis were not threatening European civilization, and the don's own nation were not in danger of being invaded. "Why aren't you doing something, anything, in these terrible hours to help defend civilized society?" asked the wounded officer. The don, his arms full of books, replied, "I, sir, am the civilized society people like you are defending!"

This snug little republic of scholars is self-governing for the most part but believes it requires a few caretaker-administrators to keep track of the students, provide the material necessities, and protect academic freedom, peace, and stability. But these presidents, deans, and bureaucrats must be watched vigilantly for intrusions, especially in such areas as academic priorities, personnel choices by the scholars, and subtle pressures toward more businesslike, socially urgent, or politically sensitive behavior. On matters less academic, from admissions and athletics to residential arrangements and sexual rules, there is said to be shared governance between the collegial body and the administration. However, the view holds that in the ideal academic commune there is no need for any administrative authority. As Paul Goodman, a popular figure in the 1960s, wrote in a widely read book, "I am proposing simply...for the students and teachers to associate in the traditional way and according to their existing interest, but entirely dispensing with the external control, administration, bureaucratic machinery, and other excrescences that have swamped our communities of scholars."[5]

This view, held by many professional scholars at a majority of America's colleges and universities, derives much of its legitimacy from three historical beliefs.

The first is that there was once an Edenic time in U.S. history when a condition of faculty control and Athenian self-government did exist on most campuses. Before the rise of bureaucracy, business, accounting, and efficiency experts, and power-hankering presidents, there was a happier, collegial age—one to which campuses should return. English professor Hazard Adams reports, "The myth persists of this Golden Age."[6]

Except in a few rare instances, no such time ever existed. In fact, the reverse is true. Throughout most of the history of American higher education, clergymen, politicians, merchants, pedagogical entrepreneurs, and autocratic presidents have run the colleges, often with a stern grip. As a report by the Carnegie Foundation for the Advancement of Teaching observed in 1908, "The powers of the American college president resemble those of the president of a railroad."[7] It is the ascension of professors to a position of equal power with campus presidents that is recent, beginning in the 1920s and achieving parity in most leading institutions by the 1950s. The earlier age was not golden but cast iron. The present time is aureate by comparison.

The second belief is Anglophilic—that England's venerable universities have enjoyed, and still enjoy, faculty self-government, and that American university faculties should emulate their British counterparts. At least at Oxford and Cambridge this was true roughly between 1700 and 1880, and in some ways even until the 1960s. But as W. H. Cowley, the former president of Hamilton College and professor of higher education at Stanford, wrote before he died in 1978, the faculties at Oxford and Cambridge prior to the twentieth century were so weak and complacent that people like Adam Smith, Edward Gibbon, and Matthew Arnold complained openly of their "scandalous torpor." Oxford and Cambridge were so self-righteous and insular that they were compelled to submit in the 1870s to reforms suggested by a royal commission and enforced by parliamentary decrees. Both universities ignored the rise of technology, and Oxford for the most part even ignored the rise of modern science. Both universities, for example, dismissed Max Planck's quantum theory and Einstein's work on relativity in the early 1900s as absurd. And, as Cowley has noted, "Every English university established during the past two centuries has followed a governance pattern different from that of Oxford and Cambridge."[8] The wish to pattern American university administration after the pre-twentieth-century government of two medieval universities in England seems a bizarre desire.

Third is the belief that German universities between 1850 and 1915 were controlled and run by their professors, who had complete freedom to teach and research what they wished, or *Lehrfreiheit.* This was an extraordinary period of academic productivity and research in Germany, and it is said Americans should emulate the Germans of that era. After the opening of the University of Berlin in 1810, and especially after the Revolution of 1848, German universities did pioneer in research techniques, library collections, and meticulous fact-finding, usually under conditions of considerable freedom. Between 1850 and 1915 about 10,000 American students studied in German universities, especially at Berlin, Leipzig, Heidelberg, Halle, Bonn, Munich, and Göttingen; and many, like Andrew White, the founder of Cornell, and Daniel Coit Gilman, founder of Johns Hopkins, came back deeply enamored with the German devotion to intensive research and German faculty *Lehrfreiheit.*

But two facts are often overlooked. Of the 10,000 U.S. students, more than one-half studied philosophy, and most of the rest studied theology, philology, ancient history, Oriental and European languages, medicine, and chemistry. These are not subjects conducive to controversy, although German Biblical criticism could be considered an exception.[9] Also, while German universities appeared to be academically free, they were actually run by the education ministers of each state. The professors were considered civil servants, and academic freedom was gained only by avoiding political and social issues and matters sensitive to the Prussian and local leaders.[10] A "Curator" ran each German university, except the curriculum, for the state. John Stuart Mill once wrote about nineteenth-century universities in a letter, "The characteristic of Germany is knowledge without thought; of France, thought without knowledge; of England neither knowledge nor thought."[11]

German *Lehrfreiheit,* therefore, was a tightly bounded and fragile system of academic freedom and faculty self-determination—and a system idealized by Americans. Indeed, all three of the alleged historical roots of faculty control in American higher education turn out to be, on examination, rather shriveled roots.

Next, the outmoded positions of the protagonists in the presidential-faculty standoff. Two in particular are worth mention.

When Arthur Lovejoy of Johns Hopkins and John Dewey and E.R.A. Seligman of Columbia started the American Association of University Professors in 1915 to gain a measure of autonomy from the autocratic presidents and trustees, the largest university in the United States was the University of Chicago with 4,400 students and a 350-member faculty. The average American four-year college and university had 510 students, and the average faculty was smaller than the membership of a modern fraternity or sorority house. Academic departments still did not exist at smaller colleges, and research was minimal. So the idea of a little Athenian democracy among the scholars on each campus was entirely possible. Faculty members knew one another, and a certain unity of work habits existed.

Over the decades, however, the average enrollment of the institutions grew enormously, according to federal statistics.

	4-year	2-year
1920	597	154
1930	923	217
1940	1,073	329
1950	1,767	503
1960	2,278	776
1970	3,793	2,492
1980	4,070	3,604

But averages disguise the fact that more than half of all college and university students, and nearly half of all professors, are now in the 10 percent of institutions that enroll more than 10,000 students. Colleges with fewer than 1,000 students, which were 98 percent of the total in 1915, are still 39 percent of the U.S. total. Today, though, they enroll less than 5 percent of all students and employ less than 6 percent of all teachers. Thus, the overwhelming majority of American professors are part of fairly large faculties, and one-fourth belong to faculties of 800 or more, often split into separate faculties of arts and science, engineering, law, business, medicine, agriculture, and the like.

As two analysts have said, the faculty meeting is "as cumbersome a vehicle of governance as the town meeting in New England has become."[12] Size alone inhibits the regular exercise of faculty control over their institutions. As one student of university governance and planning has put it, "Faculty senates, for the most part, are gradually withering away, leaving only an empty forum for the speeches of academic politicians. The real effectiveness of senates seems to be at an all-time low."[13]

The other outmoded position is that described by Columbia's Walter Metzger, the leading historian of the U.S. academic profession. In 1915, the primary threats to academic freedom came from imperious presidents, trustees, and state governors. When the University of Pennsylvania dismissed the radical economist Scott Nearing in 1915, Chancellor Day said, "That is what would happen to an editorial writer of *The Tribune* if he were to disregard the things for which the paper stands"; and trustee George Wharton Pepper added, "If I am dissatisfied with my secretary, I suppose I would be within my rights in terminating his employment." Also, individual faculty members were the targets. As Metzger says, a chief attribute of the college of the time was its "localness."

Today, the threats come not so much from presidents and trustees as from state and federal government leaders, commissioners of higher education, federal agency officials, unruly students, the courts, and budget officials. The autonomy of whole institutions and whole faculties is now a prime target, demanding joint presidential-faculty-trustee action rather than old-time adversarial attitudes. As Metzger writes, "The theory of academic freedom as it has been articulated in this country has become, in critical respects, outmoded. . . . American universities have been remodeled while the ideas once consonant with them have not."[14]

Another contributing factor to the current leadership crisis in higher education is the persistence of biases and naivete about organizational necessities. Americans live in a capitalist industrial society and for the most part work in medium-sized and large organizations run with the help of bureaucracies. Yet many professors, like Chinese mandarins, have a bias against business and commercial activities. They abhor organizational needs, and they detest bureaucracies. Like blacksmiths, cowboys, and bookstore proprietors, university scholars tend to be in modern society but not really part of it.

This makes planning, organizational behavior, good financial practices, and modern management difficult in higher education. Many colleges and nearly all universities are fairly complex organizations, but one-half of the ruling group behaves as if they were not. And the other half—the presidents and their staffs—often refuse to introduce the operating styles and procedures from the best organization theory and practice, management, and planning, partly out of fear of faculty criticism but partly because they usually share the biases and naivete of the faculties, despite the need to make their complex enterprises function better.

Twenty years ago, one scholar wrote that large organizations now "provide the environment in which most of us spend our lives."[15] The modern college or university is among these organizations, requiring new attitudes, practices, and management styles. But many in higher education are Luddites, clinging to preorganizational values even though they live in urban Berkeley, Boston, or New York, fly jet-engine aircraft to meetings, use computers regularly, deal frequently with huge corporations or government agencies, and are members of multimillion-dollar education enterprises.

Then there is the authority problem. One does not have to be a political theorist to realize that dual leadership does not work or that little gets done when the king and the barons of the realm have equal power and different views of where to go or how to proceed. Yet many colleges and universities make little apparent effort to break out of their dual authority and stalemates. Some professors even question the need for any authority, management, or central leadership, adopting the Bakunin-Kropotkin-Marx-Lenin anarchist position that organizations and societies can be run like a "postal system,"[16] as Lenin put it. (When the New School of Social Research was established in New York City by a group of liberal and idealistic professors in 1919, they decided against a president and tried to run the college by professorial committees. It lasted two years.)

The fact is that every society and every major organization within a society must have a single authority, someone or some body of people authorized to initiate, plan, decide, manage, monitor, and punish its members. Leadership is imperative. "Name a great American college or university and you will find in its history a commanding leader or leaders who held its presidency," said W. H. Cowley.[17]

Walter Metzger, a fierce and eloquent defender of faculty prerogatives and one with a characteristic antibusiness bias—he once wrote that "the worst of all strong possibilities is that academic institutions . . . will adopt the strategies used by commercial businesses"[18]—recently acknowledged the need for a stronger authority on campus and better management.

> I would part with the notion that curbs on administrative power answer all of academic freedom's needs. They answer only part of its needs; the other and equally essential instrument is effective academic government.
>
> It was well understood by the makers of our Constitution that freedom could be jeopardized by the weakness, as well as the tyranny, of officials. Even so strong a supporter of checks and balances as James Madison saw the need for a powerful president to protect the interests of the nation, especially in its relations with foreign states. The modern university, in no less precarious contact with its environment, should make use of this political wisdom.
>
> What this means is not that professors should be less secure—the tenure of the federal judiciary was not thought to bear adversely on the energy of the national Chief Executive—but that administrators should be better served. They should have a higher density of competent assistance (it is a shibboleth that administrations are overstaffed—they are undersupplied with ministerial talent, though they may be very well stocked with scribes).

> They should have powers commensurate with the task of protecting the interests of the university. . . . But they should not be left to work alone.[19]

There is an acute need to restore clear authority in some fresh form to American higher education. The situation described by Rourke and Brooks in their book *The Managerial Revolution in Higher Education* is stifling thoughtful action just when institutions most need to act decisively and strategically: "Faculties have put themselves in the indefensible position of being willing neither to assume the burden of guiding a university's academic development nor to concede to others the right to do so."[20] This is at best masochism, at worst suicide.

Last, there is the reluctance to face current realities. Nearly all the conditions that gave the AAUP faculty position of the 1920s value and realism have changed. The ideology appears stuck in a historical freezer while the university has become larger and more complex; faculty working arrangements have changed; the respect for experts, intellectuals, and artists has grown; and social science has flashed new light on the behavior of organizations and the paths to organizational change.

As I mentioned earlier, the scale of collegiate life has changed. No university in the Middle Ages or Renaissance exceeded 800 students,[21] and few academic institutions in the United States did so until 1910 or so. Today the tight little band of scholars is more likely to be a large, busy federation of intellectuals who scarcely know each other, even at many of the better small colleges. Sociologist Burton Clark described the new reality a decade ago in a perceptive article:

> A faculty member does not interact with most members of the faculty. In larger places, he may know less than a fifth, less than a tenth. Paths do not cross. The faculty lounge is no more, but is replaced with coffee pots in dozens of locations. The professor retains a few interests in common with others, such as higher salaries, but he has an increasing number of interests that diverge. . . . The decision-making power and influence of the faculty is now more segmented—by sub-college, by division, and particularly by department. . . .
>
> The campus is a holding company for professional groups rather than a single association of professionals . . . more like the United Nations and less like a small town.[22]

One-third of today's teachers are part-time professors whose main allegiance is often to another organization, profession, or style of work. One-fifth of all campuses have faculty unions and one-fourth of all who serve on U.S. faculties are now trade unionists, paying dues and being represented by lawyers, negotiators, and outside union leaders, and fighting for better pay and working conditions rather than for professional standards and the strength and vitality of their habitats.[23] A faculty union movement that began with two community colleges in Michigan in 1965 and spread to four-year institutions in the late 1960s may soon enlist one in three teaching faculty in higher education. As Walter Metzger says, "The academic profession in recent years has grown considerably less profession-like."[24]

There is also the reality that some kinds of colleges—most two-year community colleges and predominantly black institutions, many church-affiliated colleges, and a large portion of the former teachers colleges that are now state colleges—have seldom practiced faculty governance and still do not. While the ideology of faculty control pertains to all U.S. professors, the reality is that perhaps only one-third of all faculty members exercise control of the academic sector.[25] (Most of the highest-quality campuses, though, are in the shared governance category.)

Also, since the Second World War the power of *individual* faculty members has increased on campus while the power of the *collective* faculty has waned or crumbled. Research grants, media attention, lucrative consulting practices, academic prizes from their professional associations, and student glorification have given some scholars enormous influence in their institutions. A department chairman whose colleagues have plentiful outside funding or who can attract great numbers of students is a real force, as is a dean of agriculture or business with strong outside connections. At the same time, faculty senates have become increasingly ineffective, even empty; many campuses now have trouble raising a quorum in their senate meetings.

Also, as Clark Kerr, among others, has observed, "There has been remarkably little faculty discussion of educational policy."[26] Another scholar says, "Faculty members tend to be focused predominantly on their own individualized and specialized activities rather than on departmental problems and problems of university-wide significance. The new result... has been the neglect of many organizational problems and a no-man's land of decision making in the universities."[27] And Burton Clark finds that "the role of faculty authority is shifting from protecting the rights of the entire guild, the rights of the collective faculty, to protecting the autonomy of separate disciplines and the autonomy of the individual faculty member."[28]

Hence, although the ideology of the professoriate posits a collective and continuing concern for their institutional homes and workplaces, the reality is that collectivity is increasingly rare and faculty and staff concerns are seldom for the well-being of the entire college or university or for the integrity of academic affairs of their universities, their schools, or even their departments.

Nor is the reality about college and university presidents one of widespread courage, purpose, or leadership, as presidential rhetoric occasionally claims. The feared autocrats who held college presidencies in the early twentieth century have mostly been replaced with mediators, fundraisers, and genial survivors. Their acquaintance with planning, management, financial forecasting and controls, and organizational behavior is often minimal. It is hard not to agree with Nobel laureate Herbert Simon: "Comparing colleges with other organizations in our society, one sees that their most striking peculiarity is not their product, but the extent to which they are operated by amateurs. They are institutions run by amateurs to train professionals."[29]

Amateur is not a dirty word; its root is "to love." Most presidents love their institutions and the scholarly life. Many work extremely hard, with a dogged hope of raising quality. But their recognition that they are executives of sizable organizations that need active management, strategic choices, and frequent change to stay abreast or ahead is often minimal. And a growing minority of college presidents are cordial hangers-on and fretting pessimists. A recent survey found that 10.5 percent of all presidents and vice-presidents said they expected their institutions to be closed, merged, or taken over soon.[30] As W. H. Cowley wrote, "Too few of the college presidents of today seem to be leaders. Too many are headmen."[31]

The net effect of these myths, biases and naivete, curious notions about authority, and avoidances of realities is that the contemporary college and university is without the power, inclination, and organizational expertise to lead itself in a positive way as an integral enterprise. It tends to posture when it should be planning and deciding priorities. It is faced with the specter of decline and substantial change, yet it finds it difficult to pull itself together and fashion new procedures and seize the best tools of management to protect the institution as a whole.

American colleges and universities have been superbly adaptive, particularly to new sources of funding, but also to new markets, changing values in society, and the emerging academic frontiers. But institutional adaptation assumes a climate of stable finances and enrollment, gradual change, and moderate growth in the economy. The present climate is one of tightening finances, declining enrollments, rapid change, and a steady state economy. So slow, piecemeal adaptation needs to be replaced by strategic planning and a new management style in higher education. Colleges and universities cannot afford to continue to live by what Charles Levine calls "the Tooth Fairy Syndrome,"[32] the belief that if they muddle along as they have in the past some benefactors or new conditions will somehow miraculously appear from under a pillow to keep them going or restore their happy days.

Retrenchment, constricting finances, new competition, marketing, and rapid changes in the academic and demographic areas all spell the end of the traditional, unobtrusive style of organizational leadership on campuses. In the new era, says policy analyst Robert Behn, "The manager's style of leadership must be active and intrusive."[33] American higher education needs to transcend the current faculty-administration stalemate, to take its own management more seriously, and to create new forms of institutional decision making if it is to cope with and help shape the new environment in which it finds itself.

Fortunately, the process has begun.

CHAPTER THREE

New Management Wine in Old Academic Bottles

Mankind are more disposed to suffer, while evils are sufferable, than to right themselves by abolishing the forms to which they are accustomed.
THOMAS JEFFERSON

The major test of a modern American university is how wisely and how quickly it adjusts to important new possibilities.
CLARK KERR

The great need for anyone in authority is courage.
ALISTAIR COOKE

MAN DOES NOT LIVE by bread alone. He needs communities, governments, and organizations too. And associations need someone or some small group to run them.

For dozens of centuries, the tribe, city-state, and small nation were the dominant associations, and the authority, rule, behavior, and sources of legitimacy of chieftains and kings were a central concern, as the social and political literature from the Old Testament and Confucius to the Renaissance and Calvin reveals. The most brilliant work of this era was Aristotle's *Politics,* which combined political theory, leadership analysis, organizational behavior, social psychology, and moral purpose.

From Machiavelli and Hobbes to Hegel and T. H. Green, the national state assumed prominence. The role of the state and the prerogatives and duties of the person or persons exercising the sovereign power versus individuals and their rights were the major issues. But during the past century in industrial nations, the business corporation has become prominent, also conducting affairs on a national or international scale, also exercising great public influence and control, also becoming a source of people's allegiance and welfare. It too has had powerful men at the apex: American innovators like J. Edgar Thomson, James B. Duke, Theodore Vail, Alfred P. Sloan, and David Sarnoff.

The rise of large organizations within and alongside the national government had two results. One was forcing a new tack on social and political analysts, who had to give attention to economic as well as political institutions. Persons as varied as Karl Marx, John Dewey, Georges Sorel, G.D.H. Cole, Herbert Hoover, Benito Mussolini, Karl Mannheim, and Reinhold Niebuhr began to talk about a capitalist society, a corporate state, or as John Galbraith calls it, "the new industrial state"—the nation-state with other large organizations inside and often in competition with government. The other result was the birth of two new scholarly fields to study the new economic communities. The field of organization management is one. The other is organization theory, practice, psychology, and politics.[1]

Management is the study—and actual direction—of organizations other than the comprehensively political, i.e., organizations outside those with the monopoly use of coercive power. Management is to organizations other than the state what statecraft is to the state.

Management is usually associated in people's minds with business and commerce. Originally this was the case. Management and organization studies arose specifically to provide greater coordination and efficiency for corporations with intricate mining and manufacturing operations, as in the work of Henri Fayol, Frederick Taylor, and Elton Mayo. Or for extensive, complex transportation and communication enterprises like the railroads and the telephone companies, as in the historic 1938 book by Chester Barnard, *The Functions of the Executive* (which 20 years later had been reprinted 18 times and was selling better than it had in the late 1930s).[2]

Barnard, a quiet, reserved Harvard dropout who became president of New Jersey Bell Telephone Company and later president of the Rockefeller Foundation, was the father of organization theory, proposing that the modern corporation was an economic and social organism like the feudal manors of the medieval period.[3] Corporate organizations, to him, were both profit-making enterprises with corporate goals and human fulfillment enterprises, where people satisfied their individual needs for ambition, status, friendship ties, and respect, and other urges. Barnard neglected the matters of leadership and competitive solvency; but he tempered the push of the rational management and production efficiency experts. And he sired the birth of organization science through scholars like James March, Richard Cyert, and psychologist Herbert Simon (who won a Nobel Prize in economics for his work) and of "the human relations school" of organization analysis: Chris Argyris, Douglas McGregor, Keith Davis, William F. Whyte, Abraham Zalesnik, and Frederick Herzberg, with Abraham Maslow as the psychological guru. According to Herzberg, "Industry, the child prodigy of rationality and science, has increasingly assumed the leadership role in the search for solutions to the problems of man's psychological needs. . . . In contemporary society business is the dominant institution."[4]

But in the United States the recent move has been away from mining, manufacturing, agriculture, and the production of goods to service companies, government agencies, nonprofit corporations, and the production of services. Daniel Bell has predicted: "It is likely that, by the year 2000, only 10 percent of the labor force will be industrial workers. If this seems low, the fact is that today only 17 percent of the labor force is engaged in factory work. . . . If 10 percent seems low, who might have predicted, 50 years ago, that only 4 percent of the U.S. labor force today would be in agriculture?"[5] We have become what Bell has labeled a postindustrial society, or, as others have called it, a knowledge society, service society, or information society.

One in six professionals in America is now employed by nonprofit organizations, of which there are now an estimated 6 million. Not only are nonprofit organizations, which include colleges and universities, a major portion of the U.S. economy at present, but they are the fastest-growing sector.[6] The Educational Testing Service, for example, with huge modern headquarters in Princeton, New Jersey, is a growth industry among nonprofits as IBM is among profit-making organizations. So are the University of Houston and Miami-Dade Community College. We no longer live in an industrial or business society. We live in a multiinstitutional society.

This means that management is no longer *business* management but is now a core concern for all contemporary organizations, especially the rapid-growth nonprofit sector, which includes colleges and universities. As Peter Drucker has written:

> Increasingly the dominant institutions to be managed and organized, even in the business field, are not manufacturing companies, not single-product companies operating in one country or one market alone, not companies employing primarily manual labor. They are businesses in the service industries—banking or retail businesses, and nonbusinesses such as hospitals and universities. They are multiproduct, multitechnology, multimarket businesses. They are multinational businesses.
>
> And increasingly, the central human resources are not manual workers—skilled or unskilled—but knowledge workers: company presidents but also computer programmers; engineers, medical technologists, hospital administrators, salesmen and cost accountants; teachers, and the entire employed educated middle class which has become the center of population gravity in every developed country.
>
> In other words, the model of yesterday is becoming less and less pertinent. But we do not, so far, have a new model.[7]

Since the best colleges and many of the 160 universities in the United States are the main hothouses for research and new ideas, which increasingly drive the U.S. economy and culture in new directions, and since they are the powerful gatekeepers for individuals who will be the professionals, leaders, and political and economic chieftains of tomorrow, they will no longer be allowed to remain "organized anarchies." And if they are to cope effectively with demographic changes, financial crises, and the need for structural and academic shifts, higher education institutions must learn to manage themselves.

In the past several years, this is exactly what has begun to happen. Management is coming to higher education slowly, begrudgingly, but coming. Again, Peter Drucker:

> An increasing number of students in advanced management courses are not business executives but executives from hospitals, from the armed services, from city and state governments, and from school administrations. The Harvard Business School even runs an increasingly popular advanced management course for university presidents.
>
> The management of the non-business institutions will indeed be a growing concern from now on. Their management may well become the central management problem—simply because the lack of management of the public-service institution is such a glaring weakness, whether municipal water department or graduate university.[8]

One of the most rewarding scholars to read in this new domain of the management of service, high-technology, government, nonprofit, and higher education organizations is Douglas McGregor, who was a professor of psychology and management at MIT from 1937 until his death 13 October 1964, except for a six-year stint (1948–54) as president of Antioch College. When he went to Antioch, he believed that good organizations are made largely by improving human relations, trusting people more, and challenging people to rise to their potential. He brought this optimistic belief, along with his companion professorial belief that the faculty should run a college or university, to the college presidency. But when he left to return to teaching in the spring of 1954, he delivered an unusual confession to the Antioch College faculty and alumni:

> I believed, for example, that a leader could operate successfully as a kind of adviser to his organization. I thought I could avoid being a "boss." Unconsciously, I suspect, I hoped to duck the unpleasant necessity of making difficult decisions, of taking the responsibility for one course of action among many uncertain alternatives, of making mistakes and taking the consequences. I thought that maybe I could operate so that everyone would like me—that "good human relations" would eliminate all discord and disagreement.

> I couldn't have been more wrong. It took a couple of years but I finally began to realize that a leader cannot avoid the exercise of authority any more than he can avoid responsibility for what happens to his organization.[9]

Back at MIT, McGregor revised his notions. Though he remained too optimistic about human nature, he toughened his views on management and added some keen analysis, to arrive at a fresh view of the leadership needed in the emerging new organizational economy.

For McGregor the old "hard" management, with rigid hierarchies and bureaucracies, was acceptable, even necessary, for the early industrial age, with large factories and unmechanized farms, with a huge unskilled blue-collar class, with low levels of education among the population, and with widespread poverty and scarcity conditions. But with the rise of the welfare state and an abundant society, the "carrot and stick theory" no longer works well. Also, people are more educated and industry is moving in new directions: scientific, specialized, service-oriented, and professional. He noted that 60 percent of all employees are now white collar, and "in a few years the single largest and most influential class of employees in most organizations will be professional managers and specialists of many kinds." And professionals, skilled craftsmen, and specialists have something that auto workers and copper miners do not: a career, field, or expertise that links them with their national colleagues in competence as much as it does with their corporations. To McGregor this made the old industrial engineering increasingly irrelevant. Industrial and commercial enterprises were becoming more like universities.

But, as he learned at Antioch and saw at MIT, colleges and universities—going in the other direction—needed more managerial control, and "authority is the central indispensable means of managerial control." Universities are becoming more like service, high-tech, or professional corporations. The authority needed is not the old kind of giving orders but one that decides on realistic objectives, devises shrewd strategies, and defines long-term goals toward which the members of the firm can agree to work. This requires a radically new kind of "soft" management, a management by objectives.[10] In McGregor's estimation, "Management has not yet considered in any depth what is involved in managing an organization heavily populated with people whose prime contribution consists of creative intellectual effort." He added, "I believe we are going to see a basic, almost revolutionary change in managerial strategy during the next two or three decades."[11]

It is this "almost revolutionary" new managerial strategy that is being introduced into American higher education. Most professors, when they hear the words *management* or *planning*, bristle. Images of insurance companies or bureaucratic federal agencies spring to mind. But the kind of management being forged is neither the alien one of business management[12] nor old-time "hard" management. It is something new.[13] And it is one that faculties will have a hand in shaping.

The new management for higher education is being hammered out blow by blow under the duress of financial deficits, cutbacks, enrollment declines, and the demands of the paying clients. It is also being assembled in the less fiery area of new courses, programs, and workshops for academic executives, coaxing them into new habits, introducing them to financial and strategic planning, performance controls, and collaborative decision making.

First, the sledgehammer of necessity, illustrated by a tale of two cities in Connecticut: Middletown and Hartford.

Middletown is the location of prestigious, little Wesleyan University, founded in 1831. In the early 1960s Wesleyan sold its American Educational Publications, which included the famous *My Weekly Reader,* to Xerox for 400,000 shares of Xerox stock. Xerox stock multiplied in value in the 1960s and Wesleyan became more richly endowed per student than any other college in the nation. Wesleyan's leadership responded accordingly. Though Wesleyan enrolled only 1,400 students, it installed graduate programs, even five Ph.D. programs. The campus built a handsome new center for the arts and a sizable science center. The faculty asked for and received the most generous sabbatical policy in the United States: one semester off after every three years, at full pay, and one year off after every six years, at full pay. The college also enjoyed one of the highest faculty salary scales and one of the lowest student-faculty ratios. By 1970 Wesleyan was widely known as the country club of the American professoriate.

Though one of the richest of all colleges, however, by 1970–71 Wesleyan was in deep financial trouble. In that year it was forced to take $14 million from its endowment, including $10 million from the principal. A projection indicated that the university's then $170 million endowment would be completely gone by 1981 and Wesleyan would be insolvent. When President Etherington resigned to pursue political interests, Colin Campbell, a cheerful, scholarly, round-faced lawyer from the American Stock Exchange, was named to succeed him.

When President Campbell assumed office, the student-faculty ratio had dropped to 6.5 to 1, and the swollen faculty was teaching 900 courses, with nearly one-half the classes having 10 or fewer students. The square-feet-per-student facilities were among the highest in the nation. The administrative and counseling costs were also among the highest per student. Operating revenues funded a mere 46 percent of the operating expenditures, and fund raising was weak. The stock market had dived, and Wesleyan's endowments, 85 percent in common stocks, had plummeted too. Prudent management at Wesleyan was absent, and the campus, one of the finest in the land academically, was rushing toward the waterfall of bankruptcy.

President Colin Campbell knew that he would have to wage a long campaign of persuasion to convince the Wesleyan faculty to live within its means and that to do so he would have to shape a rational plan for heading off bankruptcy while maintaining the college's excellence. He applied for a planning grant from the Exxon Foundation and received it. And he hired two executives who knew accounting, financial forecasting, and computers from Peat, Marwick Mitchell and Company—Richard Greene and Burton Sonenstein—as vice-president for administration and finance and as treasurer. With the academic vice-president, Campbell, Greene, and Sonenstein adapted Peat Marwick's computerized SEARCH model of financial forecasting to Wesleyan's needs and gradually pinpointed the causes of the crisis.

A major decision has to be made at this juncture by any academic administrator, and it is a critical one. To alert the faculty, staff, and students to the unpleasant realities, to enlist their help in restoring financial stability, and to begin corrective action, an open airing of the alarming facts and their causes seems imperative. Yet a full, honest revelation of the mess is embarrassing to those who helped create it, damaging if it is broadcast in the newspapers and/or television, and potentially destructive to admissions recruiting, fund raising, faculty morale, and the reputation and stature of the college. To the horror of his colleagues and many alumni who were alarmed at the display of dirty laundry, President Campbell opted for nearly full openness, though he tried to keep the disclosures inside the Wesleyan campus community.

The bleak scenario he unveiled led to a priorities study, rating all parts of Wesleyan's life in order of their centrality. Quickly, the Master of Arts in Teaching program was cut, administration costs were lowered, and the number of students was raised from 1,400 to 2,200 to increase income. Then, after considerable haggling with the recalcitrant faculty and amid vitriolic charges that a new Wall Street–business administration was wrecking Wesleyan's traditions, academic quality, and Lilliputian charm and threatening precious academic prerogatives, a five-year Plan for Action was adopted by the Board of Trustees, now activated to its fiduciary obligations, in October 1975.

The plan was a conservative one, leaving the bloated academic programs as they were in order to concentrate first on the urgent financial issues. Simply, the plan sought to reduce expenditures while raising income, so that withdrawals from the endowment could be reduced by one-third, from $9.2 million in 1975 to $6.6 million by 1980. To reduce expenditures, Wesleyan's management cut expenses for administration and maintenance. It also tried to lift the astonishing 6.5 to 1 student-faculty ratio to 12 to 1, still a notch below the 13 to 1 ratio of peers like Amherst, Williams, and Dartmouth, and increase enrollment to 2,450. To raise income, President Campbell planned to double the annual alumni fund, obtain $11 million in gifts between 1975 and 1980, increase tuition, adopt a new investment policy for the endowment with a more diversified approach ranging from venture capital risks and real estate fliers to blue-ribbon bonds—with six separate managers—and return 25 percent of the overhead dollars from faculty research grants to the departments to stimulate more outside grants.

By spring 1979 the annual erosion of the endowment had been arrested. But because the student-faculty ratio stubbornly did not rise above 10 to 1, Wesleyan's tuition was forced to soar to Ivy League levels, above Wesleyan's peers and among the highest in the nation. So President Campbell, Burton Sonenstein, and the five others who now made up the president's cabinet—Greene assumed a position elsewhere in 1980—embarked on a second-stage five-year plan.

This plan addressed the hub issues of the curriculum, faculty leaves, and academic structure, which were frozen in a rich 1960s mode during a time of rapid technological change and terrible financial squeezes. Among the recommendations: recruit a more national student body to counter the decline in Northeast prospects; do not use endowment funds beyond 5 percent of their market value annually; raise the student-faculty ratio to 13 to 1; increase student enrollment to 2,600; establish new summer programs; initiate a capital fund campaign, especially to renovate the stately but shabby main library, provide adequate athletic facilities for women, and bring computer literacy to the campus; institute regular department reviews to insure planning and quality; overhaul the academic program, with its more than 1,000 courses, several tiny colleges, and some graduate programs with almost no students; consider eliminating one or more varsity sports; increase class size, since 40 percent of all courses had 10 or fewer students and 20 percent had five or fewer students; and review Wesleyan's philanthropic policy of faculty leaves, which cost Wesleyan more than $1 million a year, with a tenth of its faculty away at all times. Also, the subsidized faculty mortgages should be raised from 5 percent to 9 percent, and the trustees should be encouraged to become more active in fund raising. In effect, Wesleyan's first plan balanced the budgets by passing the costs to the students and their families via high tuition and big federal loans. The second plan tried to come to grips with the internal reforms which had been postponed for a decade.

President Campbell unveiled the plan for the 1980s in September 1979 in diplomatic language but blunt, raw detail—moving further into his policy of complete openness with the faculty, students, and staff. In a speech to the campus community, he said, "Obsolescence is not confined to automobiles and other products of technology. Academic programs . . . grow old too." He pointed out that, "Wesleyan is quite vulnerable. It remains exposed because it is overextended financially, and its academic organization may not have kept pace with institutional needs and student interests." Campbell quoted "a distinguished social scientist" who wrote that "the American university is like a tribe rife with internal dissent at the very time when external enemies threaten." He paused, looked up, and added, "That is a remark worth pondering." The president reminded the faculty and students that "the American university [has] passed from its Golden Age to its Age of Survival," and said, "If we care about Wesleyan, the one choice we do not have is to ignore the danger."

President Campbell spent the 1979–80 academic year soliciting and patiently listening to criticisms, improvements, and additions to his plan. He met with alumni and faculty, trustees and students. No major flaws were found in his plan, but there was little readiness by the faculty to accept it. Indeed, when Wesleyan professors seemed negative, and some continued to attack the "businesslike" Wesleyan management, the 1980 plan was not even submitted to the faculty for a vote of approval. As Vice-President Sonenstein said to me, "Naturally we regretted not having faculty endorsement. But the situation is very serious, and we must move ahead. Anyway, ours by necessity is not a bottom-up planning process. It is a top-down process."

In 1981–82 the percentage of alumni giving reached its highest percentage in Wesleyan's history—54 percent—making it the 10th highest among colleges in the country. The students were among the brightest ever. The president had obtained over $1 million in special funds from various foundations, alumni, and friends for innovations at the college. With alert financial management and computer modeling, Sonenstein had helped Wesleyan to become the first institution to respond to President Reagan's cuts in student aid and loans. Word spread that Wesleyan had replaced reckless profligacy with solid, farsighted planning and management. And so, after a decade of abuse for his gentle, cheerful, but courageous and firm management, pulling Wesleyan back from the brink of bankruptcy,

President Campbell—and Treasurer Sonenstein—to their surprise, received sustained applause from the faculty when they presented the 1981–82 annual report. As one instructor said, "We still don't like what's happening. But it's good to know we have decent leadership. He's kicking our fannies, and saving our fannies. And the clever bastard is finding new resources for the innovations we really should be making here for the next decade."

Further upstate, in the Connecticut state capital, is the University of Hartford. In 1977 the small university, located on 200 acres in West Hartford (the affluent end of the city), was just 20 years old. Like a pickup softball team, the university was a motley collection of older schools around Hartford—an art school, a school of music, a small two-year school of electronics, and colleges of arts and sciences, business, education, and engineering—united in the late 1950s to form a new private university. In 1977 the faculty was poorly paid, and many members were part-time or had second jobs. Faculty morale, like the tuition, was low. The students were local, mostly commuters. Management was mainly of the manual, back-of-the-envelope variety. The trustees did their duty in a perfunctory way. The university had $16 million of long-term debt. Physical facilities, especially for engineering and student housing, were barely adequate. Enrollment was beginning to decline. The endowment was less than $4 million.

When the new president, Stephen Joel Trachtenberg, with degrees from Columbia, Yale Law School, and Harvard and experience as an assistant at the Department of Education in Washington and as vice-president of Boston University, arrived in 1977, his highest priority was to improve the young university academically. He told me, "I began with the academic side because that's what I know best. I became my own provost. Now we are tackling the financial side."

He concentrated on people. President Trachtenberg raised the salaries of the best faculty members, arranged graceful departures for others, and bought out the contracts of several with tenure. He gradually replaced seven of the eight deans, even the basketball coach and dean of admissions, so that each unit would have more vigorous, skilled leadership. Nearly 45 percent of the present full-time faculty of 305 have been hired since 1977. As he says, "I used everything from tears and rosary beads to Attila the Hun tactics. But you can't attract students or produce much intellectually without a superior faculty and administrators, and that means good people."

But good people need equipment, facilities, and encouragement. President Trachtenberg found funds for a new computer center through a daring, innovative lease-back arrangement, and lured one of Harvard's top computer experts to head it. He won a $250,000 National Science Foundation grant to fund new equipment and curriculum development for 2,000 students in 31 courses. He increased the library budget. He received a $300,000 challenge grant from the National Endowment for the Humanities, which will not only force the university to raise a matching $900,000 by 1984 but also improve humanistic studies. He started construction on a new building for the engineering school "without a dime in my pocket for it," and it is now totally paid for with funds he raised. He bought an apartment building to house the increased number of out-of-state students his admissions office was recruiting.

The president opened an Office of Contracts and Grants to encourage and help the faculty submit grant applications, which doubled in number between 1977 and 1981, bringing in $1.6 million in the latter year. More faculty members were granted sabbaticals for research and travel; in 1980 an annual outstanding teacher award ($1,000) was initiated; and the university-sponsored research grant fund for the faculty quintupled between 1977 and 1981. The faculty senate was given an office in the administration building and a secretary, and top administrators attended all meetings for the first time.

President Trachtenberg sends every faculty member a card on his or her birthday and sends flowers if anyone's family goes to a hospital. Those newly hired find a bottle of red wine and a note from the president on their desks when they arrive. Any professor who invites students home for Thanksgiving dinner receives a giant turkey from the university. Faculty members are invited to the the president's home for dinner and conversation to build collegiality and discuss new ideas. (At one recent dinner, an alumnus pledged $750,000 for the university's first faculty chair.)

In 1979 a planner from Yale was brought in to help construct the five-year plan published the following year. The academic year 1981–82 was designated the "year of the curriculum," and every school was requested to do a searching analysis of its programs. An honors program was started for the brightest students. And President Trachtenberg, who believes that each college or university must have a distinctive character, has started integrating the University of Hartford into a school focused on technology, business, and the arts. When he came, the university had three part-time instructors teaching insurance, despite the fact that Hartford was one of the greatest insurance centers in the Western world. Now there are four full-time scholars in the field and a new actuarial program. "We ought to have the best insurance program in the United States," Trachtenberg believes.

In July 1980 the president selected Dr. Carol Guardo, a strong-willed, planning-oriented scholar, as his provost, and he moved into the areas of finance and administration for repairs. Like Wesleyan, the University of Hartford had raised tuition 20 percent a year for the first four years to finance its takeoff and provide decent faculty salaries. But then the president had to find new monies from internal reorganizations and modernization. On 1 January 1982 a new vice-president of finance came aboard, and Trachtenberg has been hoping to bring the whole management structure up to good medium-sized business standards, including computer-model financial planning. President Trachtenberg has also tried to avoid using one penny from his meager endowment. Unusually frank and humorous, he says that when he told his mother in Brooklyn about his presidency in 1977 she asked him about the endowment. Hearing it was only $4 million, she said, "That's not an endowment. That's a petty cash fund!" So he has annually ploughed back all the interest, dividends, and capital gains, and with only a few gift additions has doubled the endowment in four years to $8 million.

Aware of the University of Hartford's comparative youth and weak reputation, President Trachtenberg has expanded advertising and public relations efforts, with attractive graphic design, so that the greater Hartford area and indeed extensive parts of the East Coast know about his scrambling young university. He says this is vital because he hopes to attract more students from other states and abroad and increase his 4,500 full-time students from one-half in residence to three-quarters, while holding on to the university's 4,500 part-time undergraduate and graduate students. He believes Hartford is a pleasant middle-sized city with a vigorous political, business, and cultural life, and the university's students can benefit from and contribute to its vibrancy. So far, enrollment has not dropped.

As for the faculty, many members are said to be skeptical but astonished that so much has happened to their campus so fast. For the first time, a minority believe the University of Hartford might just become a truly fine and distinctive little university of technology, business, and the arts in the next decade or two.

One president is battling to trim the luxurious and overly abundant academic offerings left over from the fat 1960s for the sleeker, more pointed requisites of the 1980s against a vociferous faculty of extraordinary pride and quality. The other is struggling to bring a modicum of quality, academic coherence, and pride to an adolescent campus with a gossamer administration from earlier days. Both university presidents though, like dozens of others, are crafting as they go a fresh management style on their campuses—still deferential to professorial customs and alert to faculty needs but newly forceful and purposeful, despite epithets and ostrich behavior about finances. But more about the new leadership style later.

In addition to on-the-go reshaping by a new breed of presidents, a few universities have begun to put in place programs to train presidents, provosts, deans, and department chairmen in the methods of financial planning, strategic decision making, quality controls, marketing, communications, data collection and management, computer modeling, and environmental scanning. Not only to provide new skills, these programs are also conducive to consciousness-raising among academic leaders, many of whom have considerable trouble accepting the idea that leaders are supposed to lead, decide, set priorities, plan, and monitor.

Harvard, for example, has established a summer program in academic management that is run chiefly by its graduate business school faculty and stresses data-based, active management and financial planning and controls. Pittsburgh's Carnegie-Mellon University has a similar summer program that emphasizes strategic planning, competitive analysis, and computer modeling. Several institutions have created executive development programs in-house for their administrators. Wichita State University, an urban, state-supported campus in Kansas with six colleges and 15,000 students, in 1976 started (with a Kellogg Foundation grant) a multi-pronged, continuing program to develop leadership abilities and techniques in order to manage steady state or slightly declining conditions. Wichita State uses outside lecturers, workshops, retreats, and intensive seminars to upgrade the proficiency of deans, senior faculty members, vice-presidents, and department chairmen in planning, decision making, alternative futures modeling, and the like.[14]

Perhaps the largest in-house management training program is at the University of Texas, where the Institute of Higher Education Management runs two-, three-, and five-day workshops for deans, department chairmen, vice-presidents, and presidents of the 14 campuses of the University of Texas system. The subjects: financial forecasting; budgeting and allocations; faculty evaluation and development; academic planning; assessment of programs, schools, and institutions; and shared management and decision making. According to Director Donald Lelong, an academic planner who was recruited from the University of Michigan in 1978 to establish and run the Austin-based institute, "We concentrate on academic management, not business management such as administrative vice-presidents handle." Dr. Lelong and his assistant use scholars and professionals from Texas and other states on the faculty.

The institute was one of the recommendations of a blue-ribbon commission set up by the Texas state legislature to investigate Texas higher education and was established by Chancellor Don Walker of the University of Texas system. Lelong charges fees to the campuses, whose presidents strongly urge but do not compel their aides and faculty leaders to attend. University administrators from elsewhere—"from Massachusetts to Hawaii," claims Lelong—have started coming to the workshops, which are limited for but not closed to academic leaders outside Texas. And the institute this year has received additional funds from the governor's office to expand the service to all public colleges and universities in Texas. Lelong says, "The institute was created mainly for defensive reasons: to counter charges that Texas universities are not well managed. But now the institute is beginning to seem like a necessary aid to each institution's offensive strategies to cut costs, raise quality, and provide direction. We still have complaints that we are too school-like and textbook-oriented in our approach, and that our instructors tend to forget they are teaching experienced adult executives not young students. But we are the first institute of our kind in the nation, so we are making corrections and improvements after every workshop."

The University of Pennsylvania has a young, self-sustaining Higher Education Finance Research Institute, directed by a short, stocky, cocky, one-time colonial historian, Robert Zemsky, and aided by a youthful wizard in computerized educational assessments, Michael Tierney. The institute has developed a small portfolio of software packages to help colleges, hospitals, and other nonprofit institutions project their financial situations, play with trade-offs to balance their budgets, and assist in financial planning. The institute often works with the Washington-based Academy of Academic Development. In Zemsky's view, universities face several conditions:

1. "Higher education faces a liquidity crisis of major proportions." To him, "the next five years will prove critical."

2. Yet, financial planning and management on most campuses is still primitive; "we actually know precious little about how institutions of higher education finance themselves"; and academic programs and finances are curiously uncoupled ("The job of the treasurer or controller is to save, while that of the provost is to spend").

3. But he believes the highly developed financial practices of business firms are not really applicable to colleges and universities. Experts from corporations and places like the Wharton School can help, but only in limited ways .

4. So, universities need to create—quickly—a new kind of financial manage-

ment that is refined, based on comparative research about the operations of universities, that links academic planning and finances in an intimate way, and that is appropriate to the peculiar kind of institutions that colleges are.[15]

This is what the Finance Research Institute in Philadelphia is trying to do. And it pays for much of its creative work by counseling, training, and consulting with other campuses on their financial difficulties and plans.

To assist with the introduction of computers in higher education, a group of colleges and universities banded together in 1964 to pool information on the latest technology and its software, and the cleverest uses on campus—for instruction, research, libraries, and management information systems. The combine is called EDUCOM and is headquartered in Princeton, New Jersey. EDUCOM now has 360 fee-paying members in all parts of the country and abroad.

In late 1975 word had begun to spread that Stanford was having some good results with a new computer modeling system that assisted with financial forecasts and educational policy trade-offs. William Massy, Stanford's vice-president for business and finance and one of the model's three parents, and Joe B. Wyatt, then administrative vice-president at Harvard, were both on the board of trustees of EDUCOM, and they obtained a grant from the Lilly Endowment to see if the Stanford computer scheme could be adapted by EDUCOM to other institutions. EDUCOM officers experimented at Lehigh, the State University of New York at Albany, and the University of Pennsylvania. After favorable indications, they hired a tall, lean, talented redhead who grew up with computers, Daniel Updegrove, to further refine their efforts and create a simple, nonprescriptive interactive computer modeling system to help any president, vice-president, or dean do financial and enrollment planning, cash-flow analysis, and faculty tenure planning.

Called the EDUCOM Financial Planning Model, or EFPM, Updegrove's new model plugged into the IBM 370/168 computer at Cornell, was tested in 1978 at Carnegie-Mellon, Yale, and Cornell universities, and then offered to any college or university in the nation for a relatively modest fee. Today it is the most widely used model in higher education, helping theological seminaries, universities, and community colleges as well as more than 130 hospitals, to plan for everything from athletic programs and buildings and grounds operations to improved medical school programs and financial aid schemes.[16] (It was on his EFPM computer system that Burton Sonenstein calculated that federal cuts in student aid would force Wesleyan to end its policy of giving financial help to all its students who needed aid.)

There are other organizations that are rushing to fill the new demand for better management skills in the academic world. The American Council on Education, for instance, through its Center for Leadership Development and Academic Administration, headed by Joan McCall, runs a series of two-day colloquies for presidents, academic vice-presidents, and deans on subjects like academic quality assessment and control, financial planning, legal issues, and personnel selection and development and has a new department chairman training program for the estimated 50,000 academic department leaders in the nation. ACE's neighbor in the "educational Vatican" at One Dupont Circle in Washington, D.C., the American Association of State Colleges and Universities, now has a Resource Center for Planned Change which stresses better recognition of social, economic, legal, and technological trends and internal planning to respond to, get a jump on, or defend against these changes.[17] And a Boulder, Colorado, organization, The National Center for Higher Education Management Systems, or NCHEMS, has been moving away from its stiff, highly quantitative, and analytical management science activities into more decision-oriented workshops, planning, and consulting. (President Trachtenberg employed NCHEMS consultants in April 1981 to examine the academic plans and management reforms he had in mind.)

Thus, some of America's academic leadership is sculpting a new management style by trial and error on the job and by going to seminars and classes as they did when they were students to learn how complex organizations work, how computers can assist them, and what contemporary management and planning are all about.

The outlines of the new academic management style are slowly becoming less fuzzy. To some, the new management style is not so much different as it is a subtle change in tone and manner. In times of trouble or external danger, families, communities, organizations, and societies tend to look toward a center, to be more tolerant of strong leadership, to expect more unity and direction. Many faculty members I have spoken with in the past two or three years, while still loyal to their profession and jealous of their controls over academic programs and academic personnel, now openly wonder if their administration is vigorous, courageous, and decisive enough, if their executives have some priorities, plans, and strategies to deal with the novel difficulties, and if their leaders have the right values to get more businesslike while keeping educational and intellectual values uppermost. There appears to be less self-assurance and fierce independence among the professoriate. There is also a new vigilance over the academic leaders, who are suddenly expected to be something more than beneficent caretakers and unobtrusive providers. More scholars grant that the first moves to halt the erosion are up to the president and his top aides, not up to themselves or the department chairmen, although they preserve full rights to thorough and penetrating criticism, even dissent.

For their part presidents and chancellors seem Hamlet-like. Their instincts tell them to become even more cautious and unassertive. Strong actions might alienate a governor, a rich alumnus, an interest group. Cutback management is far less pleasant than growth management, and injured parties can be vocal, even vicious. Gingerly, proceed gingerly. Indeed many campus executives have quietly adopted an academic camouflage. In the past year I have asked a number of educated persons, including academics, to name the presidents of any five of what they would regard as the top 25 colleges or universities in the land, other than their own. A surprising number had difficulty recalling the names of five. This is not a time of assertive academic leaders, of renowned presidents addressing the big issues.

Yet presidents and vice-presidents sense the need to act, to shape a plan for their institutions. They almost feel the breath of newspaper editors, political officials, budget officers, alumni and faculty leaders on their necks. Above all, they know they should make tough decisions. They want to find new ways to make those decisions with real faculty involvement but without a faculty circus. And they know that they are expected to pull a hat trick—to trim and find more economical ways of operating while actually raising quality further in the 1980s, to become better by being leaner.

People like George Weathersby and Aaron Wildavsky claim it can, and should, be done. Weathersby, the innovative commissioner of higher education in Indiana, says:

> Unavoidable choices create new opportunities. . . . Visibly limited real resources provide each institution and each state with a special opportunity to clarify priorities; simplify missions of programs and institutions; eliminate less productive units; restructure debt; reconsider pricing policies, especially in the public sector where higher educational services have been historically underpriced, to their own and others' detriment; review and restructure academic programs to be more efficient or more attractive to students and outside funders; or reconsider admissions policies to focus on high priority missions or programs.[18]

And Wildavsky, the blunt, eminent, unpredictable policy scientist from Berkeley, in a speech to the Association for the Study of Higher Education in March 1982, told his listeners that the next 10 years are a golden time for making all those changes professors and presidents frequently said they wanted to make if only—if only their colleagues weren't so smug and comfortable, if only there weren't so many vested interests, if only people could somehow be pressed to respond to new needs. "While the time is right, while stringency is severe, we ought to act so as to change the programs we would have liked to abandon or scale down long ago."

Wildavsky puckishly recalled that Mary Douglas once said there are four decisive arguments in organizational change: there is no time; it is unnatural; God prohibits it; and there is no money. He added, "The last one of these is available today for those who wish to be decisive with a purpose."[19] For Wildavsky, overdue reforms and bold new initiatives in higher education come chiefly from massive outside enticements of money or from real internal stringency and a struggle for institutional preservation and individual livelihoods.

But higher education's new management style is more than just a slight shift in tone and manner, at least at some colleges and universities. It is a belated recognition that universities too are organizations and that management is no longer a tool exclusively for large profit-making corporations but a body of knowledge and techniques indispensable for any complex organization. More and more, academic leaders are beginning to sense that unless their campuses have some solid, active, rational management they may not make it through the next decade, or may not pass through the period without wounds and distentions. The old stalemate must be broken. New patterns are imperative.

Harvard professor Theodore Levitt recently wrote:

> The crucial importance of management has been eclipsed by the historians' almost obsessive childlike fascination with the technological artifacts of 19th century industry and the flamboyant entrepreneurs of that era. . . .
>
> Management consists of the rational assessment of a situation and the systematic selection of goals and purposes (what is to be done?); the systematic development of strategies to achieve those goals; the marshalling of the required resources; the rational design, organization, direction, and control of the activities required to attain the selected purposes; and, finally the motivating and rewarding of people to do the work. . . .
>
> It is one of the great modern mysteries that, although so much is owed by our times to the organizing and productive genius of management, the world must constantly be reminded of this fact, which it seems so obstinately reluctant to learn and believe. And, curiously, it is precisely in the world's intellectual enclaves—in the universities, and among writers and journalists—that this obstinacy reaches its apex. Somehow, results are presumed to happen as if by immaculate conception.[20]

At least in some colleges and universities the obstinacy is melting. Pounded by the possibilities of decline and bankruptcy, more presidents are beginning to manage their institutions.

But what kind of management? This is the dilemma. College presidents can't return to the turn-of-the-century leadership styles of Harper, Eliot, Butler, and Gilman. Neither can they transfer corporate leadership styles to their campuses, especially since more corporations are altering their styles to adjust to the growing number of knowledge workers and the declining number of manufacturing hands in their midst. When the academic executives of the University of Maryland attended a weekend workshop at the Xerox Corporation's "school" in Virginia, they heard about how Xerox trained its salesmen, middle managers, and executives to the Xerox strategies, goals, and manner. The question was asked whether their research laboratory people in California were included in Xerox's training programs. The answer was "No, we treat them as a special entity, with their own needs and behavior for creative work." Modern corporations recognize that their own universitylike components require a different management. The American Telephone and Telegraph Company's Bell Laboratories, with their engineers, astrophysicists, biochemists, psychologists, applied mathematicians, metallurgists, and "computer jocks," have always been managed, but not like A.T.&T. Clearly, the 19 Bell Laboratories in nine states, with a yearly budget of $2 billion and with 22,000 employees, need to be managed. But the Bell Labs would not have produced seven Nobel Prize winners since 1927 and would not continue to produce 500 patents a year if the researchers were managed like a tool and die company.

The kind of management higher education needs does not exist yet. But it is being created chink by chink by the new breed of deans, provosts, and presidents, drawing upon the most usable elements from corporate management, the newer management of service industries, and the latest findings of organization studies, psychology, management research, and similar fields. The management of highly educated people in nonprofit service organizations is one of the major new areas of research and development. And the management of colleges and universities, which constitute one piece of the burgeoning nonprofit sector of American society and a vital part of our new knowledge-based economy, is a subject that will command a great deal of creative attention in the immediate future.

Some of the ingredients of education's new management style are coming into focus, however.

Administrators are replacing their passive role with a more active one. The characteristic presidential style of the past few decades has been a passive one.[21] The faculty often led the way during this period of growth, with the president mainly riding herd to keep the stampeding growth a relatively balanced one. But professors have no stomach for leading the way during contraction and little desire for selecting academic priorities among their own efforts. In one study in the late 1960s, where senior faculty members and academic administrators were asked to rate the importance to their institution of 47 different goals, they rated all 47 nearly equal in importance.[22] So in the 1980s the initiative has shifted to the institution's management. It is the president, provost, and financial vice-president, along with the deans, who are now expected to point the way, choose the priorities, devise a plan, and construct an academic strategy. The faculty-administration stalemate of the postwar period is yielding with reluctant speed to a clearer authority for the executive and more active leadership from the management. As Francis Rourke and Glenn Brooks found in *The Managerial Revolution in Higher Education:* "Periods of growth and affluence appear more likely to leave decision-making power in the hands of academic officials and to invite widespread decentralization of expenditure. Periods of serious scarcity . . . tend to give more power to financial officials and to push a university toward centralized decision making."[23]

At the University of California system headquarters, a 3 percent cut in real dollars in the 1982–83 budget has prompted President David Saxon and his decisive, good-humored, frank vice-president for academic affairs, William Frazer, a physicist from the San Diego campus, to end the practice of across-the-board cuts for all campuses and institute selective cuts based on academic priorities, manpower needs, quality, and similar criteria. At Dartmouth, new president David McLaughlin, a former corporation president, said to me, "We have several faculty committees, and they are very helpful. But they sometimes have difficulty seeing the needs of the whole institution, comprehending financial implications, and taking the long view. The chief executives in these times must decide. We are the ones responsible for our institutions, not the committees." On campus after campus, the administrators appear to sense they are expected to become far more active, interventionist, and decisive than in the past. Most are uneasy. A few are a bit frightened about the new mantle of leadership on their shoulders.

But the days of merely applying a watering can to stimulate faculty initiatives are gone. Passive laissez-faire management is over. The period of active presidential leadership is here.

Finance is assuming a new prominence. In higher education the business officers have usually occupied a back seat quietly. They merely made suggestions and seldom dared to discuss academic matters. Today, new vice-presidents of finance plan and decide alongside the president and academic vice-president. In fact, much of the planning is now often driven by financial concerns for the near future. Stanford financial executives, worried about heading off the university's constant shortfalls of dollars, developed one of the most sophisticated financial forecasting models in the nation.[24] The University of Pennsylvania moved from centralized management to decentralized school and unit management in a partially successful attempt to improve its financial picture.[25]

Financial officials are now among the busiest innovators. At the University of Southern California you can pay all four years of tuition when you register, exempting you from all future tuition raises. At Washington University in St. Louis and at Cleveland's Case Western Reserve University, you can pay the four years of tuition in monthly installments like a mortgage, taking up to eight years.

Financial vice-presidents are also teaming up with their presidents to devise strategies to keep their enterprises afloat. At Brown University, in Providence, Rhode Island, Vice-President Richard Ramsden, formerly the director of the Consortium on Financing Higher Education, has helped President Howard Swearer pull Brown out of serious financial difficulties. Ramsden computerized the meal-planning system, computerized the heating-and-cooling system, computerized the alumni records, helped reposition the investment portfolio into higher-return items, and assisted with the $155 million capital fund drive, begun in 1978. The results: lower costs, higher income.

At Rockefeller University in New York City, David Lyons, vice-president for business, claims he is the first person in his position to bring in a business perspective. "They always had someone with an academic or science background here in the past," he says. "But in the past there were no money problems. Now we look in every unit for savings." It appears that the new prominence of college and university financial executives is having an effect. The following figures in constant 1967 dollars indicate that annual costs per student nationally have dropped some and may have stabilized.[26]

1960	1965	1970	1975	1979
$2,097	$2,882	$2,869	$2,487	$2,507

Perhaps most significant of all, finances and academics are coming together. Increasingly, departments and schools are no longer designing their academic futures without studying the financial implications carefully. And financial planners are not making decisions without consulting the faculty, deans, and provosts about the educational and program implications. Finances and academics, long separated, are now being linked. The old habit of starting programs or adding staff without concern for long-term costs is over. This does not necessarily mean the end of Greek or music classes with three students, or of expensive medical programs like kidney dialysis. It does mean the beginning of conscious decisions, based on trade-offs, to keep a few known "losers" if they are regarded as indispensable or to add a very high-cost program if it is deemed essential.

One fact that is often overlooked is that a major portion of the operations on most campuses is nonacademic, lending itself to the finest business practices. Universities include housing, dining halls and cafeterias, security forces, athletics, buses and other vehicles, counseling and medical help, placement offices, student entertainment, travel, record keeping for students and alumni, purchasing, endowment management, heating and cooling systems, scientific equipment, printing and publications, bookstores and art supply stores, maintenance, cleaning, construction, and financial bill-paying itself. To preserve money for the intellectual heart of their colleges, these areas are getting financial attention as never before, in some cases with surprising economies.

Campus governance is taking new forms. As education leaders become more active and need to decide more swiftly, and as finances and academics are being joined, the old, looping Ping-Pong game between the administration and the faculty is no longer adequate, especially since faculty senates are slowly collapsing or becoming dormant. A new kind of cabinet government is taking shape. The campus president must move more quickly and vigorously but continue to have faculty advice and guidance—and have someone with whom to share the blame for mistakes. The professors, especially the senior ones, want to help decide their own and their institution's futures—but not too openly and without full responsibility for their decisions. Enter a new body: the Joint Big Decisions Committee.

This new kind of committee is usually composed of selected senior faculty members and key administrators, with some junior faculty, students, or trustee members sitting in at some institutions. The president is usually not a member. It is generally chaired by the chief academic officer. It has instantly become the center of power in most cases.

The committee's work and membership are well known, but its deliberations are kept secret. It advises the president on what to do. These new bodies are springing up like mushrooms in higher education. They will almost certainly be a major force in campus governance and management in the years ahead, as well as a new spawning ground for academic executives. (Economist Harold Shapiro, new president of the University of

Michigan at Ann Arbor, is the former chairman of his campus's Budget and Priorities Committee.)

At Princeton it is called the Priorities Committee. It has 16 persons on it: six from the faculty, six students (four undergraduate, two graduate), and four administrators. The provost chairs the meetings, which occur twice a week from October to January, then monthly till May. The main task of the Priorities Committee is to decide on the annual budget. According to Associate Provost Richard Spies, President William Bowen takes "98 percent of the committee's suggestions." Some observers say, however, that the committee's annual focus provides Princeton with little in the way of longer-range planning and that the strictly budgetary nature of the committee's concerns makes Princeton one of the best run major campuses financially but one that lacks academic foresight and educational initiatives. Princeton has no faculty senate.

At Northwestern University, the faculty-administration Committee on Budget and Resources has been more insistent on planning and academic program-cutting than the provost and president are prepared to be. At Temple University, however, the Resources and Priorities Committee has been more timid than the administrators. At Ohio University, President Charles Ping, Provost Neil Bucklew, and Vice-Provost for Planning James Bruning had to slash their institution's budget considerably. So they formed the University Planning Advisory Council, with nine faculty members, six administrators (including three deans), and three students, all appointed by the provost after consultation. UPAC meets about 20 times a year. All discussions are secret. Nearly all of its priorities are accepted. In 1981 the council voted to take one percentage point off faculty salary raises for projects that would benefit the whole university. Business school professor John Stinson, a member of UPAC, said, "I can't have a very good management department if the university is sick."

Martin Trow, director of the University of California at Berkeley's Center for Studies in Higher Education and chairman of Berkeley's Academic Senate for the past two years, explained his views on the new governance patterns to me this way. "In the 1980s the faculty and administrators are going to have to create a new working relationship. Faculty must give the academic management more executive power, and more authority for overall planning and priority-setting. But administrators must give faculty the opportunity to examine the plans and priorities with the full strength of their critical and analytical expertise. Faculty will have to understand confidentiality and executive leadership better than they do now. Administrators will have to understand the value of candor and honesty and of professional scrutiny and criticism."

The communications process is becoming more open. Fifteen years ago Francis Rourke and Glenn Brooks observed that "traditionally many academic administrators were as secretive about the details of university affairs as a branch of the armed forces might well be about its most cherished secrets. . . . Subterfuge thus became a characteristic style of university administration." But in their 1966 study they noted, "In recent years however there has been a persistent trend toward a more 'open' style of university administration. This has been true with respect to both the disclosure of information to the outside world and the modification or elimination of some of the traditional 'information screens' . . . within the academic community."[27] This was happening, they said, because of new pressures from external agencies like the federal government, state officials, and the press for accountability.

In the past few years, the movement toward openness has taken a second leap forward, especially toward internal groups. Presidents have found that change is facilitated and debates are better rooted in reality if they provide the shock of recognition about the seriousness of internal affairs. And more administrators each year believe that openness about new directions is more conducive to rallying faculty, student, and alumni support behind initiatives as well as productive of better academic plans because of criticisms and improvements from others. One president said to me, "Management can never be a let-it-all-hang-out process. But a university has a special obligation to make the process as truthful and open as possible."

At Ohio University and Wesleyan University, the presidents now discuss their proposed cuts, new ventures, personnel changes, and financial priorities openly with their faculties. At the State University of New York at Albany, President Vincent O'Leary, a man with an extraordinary grasp of the details of every department and unit of his campus, talks openly and regularly about his intentions not only with his Long-Range Senate Planning Committee but with all department chairmen, deans, and any interested faculty members and students. J. Fredericks Volkwein, assistant to President O'Leary, says, "Our general budget is now an open book."

In his pathbreaking book *The Human Side of Planning,* David Ewing contends that "few errors damage the human side of planning more than errors in communication."[28] He strongly recommends that in a modern organization, which is no longer pyramidal but now composed of many action centers, forceful and rational persuasion becomes vital for change. To persuade effectively, he says, a manager must "communicate generously." The new breed of academic presidents is taking this admittedly risky path.

People are becoming more important. It seems trite to say, but higher education is a people business. Two-thirds or more of any college's budget goes for academic, staff, and executive salaries. A college and university is usually judged by the quality of people it has. Yet many campuses have strangely paid relatively little attention to the quality and productivity of their people. Until recently a majority of institutions granted tenure to their instructors almost automatically, and in traveling around the United States it is not hard to find campuses with 80 percent or more of the faculty on tenure, where numerous administrators are merely credentialed bureaucrats, serving time. Search committees at many institutions do a routine job, leaning more each year on advertisements in the *Chronicle of Higher Education* and a few other periodicals for obtaining new people.

Now, however, without new monies and additional students, a university's chief hope for increased productivity, higher levels of academic quality, and better management is to improve the performance of the people already at the college and make every new appointment count. Luckily, never before has there been such a large talented pool of young scholars and experienced middle-management executives to draw from. The average university may have a 40 percent turnover in its faculty and staff in the next decade. By carefully selecting the right faculty and staff, and by buying out the contracts of the weakest tenured professors, an institution can effect a transformation even if it makes few other changes.

In one interesting study it was found that the two key variables for innovation toward educational excellence were external stimulation and the quality of the internal teaching staff. Better resources and more free time for teachers were not nearly so important. The authors maintained that "innovation does not require free resources so much as it requires people to push innovation."[29] Energetic professionals, especially ones well attuned to the latest and finest national and international developments in their fields (since much so-called innovation is actually judicious borrowing), are the primary ingredients of organizational vitality. The famous auto executive Alfred P. Sloan made a point of sitting in on all key personnel decisions during the formative years of General Motors.[30] And one business leader, George Olmsted, Jr., chairman of the S. D. Warren (Paper) Company, wrote with a dash uncharacteristic for an annual report:

> Investors, security analysts, financial people, and others from time to time ask about the Warren Company. What's our productive capacity? How many tons will we ship? How do we figure depreciation? What profit will we make three years from next Michaelmas? And so on . . .
>
> But rarely, if ever, do they ask the one real "gutsy" $64 question—what have you got for an organization? What sort of people are they? How do you

recruit and train them? Who is going to run this business—and do the thinking for it—five years from now, ten years, 20 years?

This is the business. The rest is spinach.[31]

This more intensive focus on the quality of the people on campus has become a major component of the new management style. Presidents and provosts are sending back tenure recommendations of acceptable but not superior scholars to deans and departments. Search committees are being more carefully assembled and are being given more specific mandates than finding a "replacement." Universities like Harvard and Stanford have long given the most careful attention to appointments; but now lesser institutions, aspiring to greater excellence, are doing so too.

As they concentrate on the quality of people, not merely credentials, colleges are finding that the best persons are not always professors, or people who have long experience in higher education. Stanford University selected a corporate executive to lead its graduate business school to the highest ranks, and he succeeded. Columbia University has hired the former director of operations for New York City as its first director of internal management. To help improve its ragged financial operations, introduce financial planning, and stave off fiscal crises, the University of Chicago chose the former director of welfare in Massachusetts as its new vice-president for financial affairs. Vanderbilt University appointed Chester Finn, Jr., a very able aide to Senator Daniel Patrick Moynihan, as a professor of educational policy, and Finn promptly emerged as a leading figure in the field.

More and more, ability, character, and performance count as well as degrees and academic ladder-climbing. But this trend is viewed with concern in some quarters. The veteran sociologist of higher education, David Riesman, observed to me that

> just as we had a run of Quakers as presidents in the 1960s and 1970s, like Clark Kerr, James Perkins, and Ernest Boyer, now we have a run of lawyers: at Harvard, Columbia, Wesleyan, Berkeley and until recently Yale, Chicago, and Michigan. I worry about this vogue. The escape from civic courage and judgment, where presidents avoid the big issues and tough decisions affecting the long-term integrity and quality of their institutions, is a terrible problem now. Here lawyers can help. But as a person who is a lawyer myself, I worry about the lack of planning sense and executive traits in lawyers. I also worry because most lawyers are not scholars. They may not have the ability to lead their institutions academically into the intellectual, scientific, and artistic areas of the future.

And Richard Alfred, of the University of Michigan's Center for the Study of Higher Education, a community college watcher, notes that the change from growth at colleges to reallocation and cutbacks, the growing size and complexity of community colleges, the spread of trade unionism among the two-year college faculty, and the new demands for financial, planning, and executive skills have created a serious problem for community college leadership. "Where are the new academic administrators of community colleges to come from?" he worries, noting that more community colleges each year are choosing executives from industry as presidents.

Technology is becoming a more integral tool for management. In 1956 only four universities had computers. By 1964 the number had jumped to 500.[32] Now it is rare to find a college or university without a computer. Offices of institutional research, which began keeping data on internal operations, sprang up alongside the growth of computer capacity. (Computers tend to be omnivorous devourers of data and solution-providers stalking for problems to solve.) But as universities have entered a period of stress, the computer has also become an indispensable tool for dealing with forecasting, reallocations, financial planning, and retrenchment. In her study of five different universities, one researcher found an enormous expansion of the information base at each of them:

> This was caused in part by the increased requests for information from outside agencies, including the federal government and the state control board. But the expansion of information capacity also stemmed from internal needs to cope with retrenchment, such as better projections of enrollment by department, better record keeping of expenditures and fund balances, and more data on credit hour production by departments. Administrators indicated that they needed more information during retrenchment for two reasons: they could not afford to make mistakes and they needed to justify their retrenchment decisions.[33]

The new breed of executives is computer literate, or at least capable of using computer calculations. Their offices often have terminals. At the State University of New York's College at Geneseo, for example, Academic Vice-President Thomas Colahan, a historian unfamiliar with computer languages himself, keeps hurling "what if" problems at his computer literate staff. What if we had to cut back somewhere in the sciences? How much would we save if . . . ?

But not many campus executives feel comfortable yet with computers and similar technology. Harvard's leaders have been stubbornly averse to using computer modeling and all quantitative management tools.[34] So have most institutions run by ex-professors from the humanities or from history and political science. Former Harvard vice-president Joe B. Wyatt believes "there will be nervousness among academic executives about the new technological tools of management for another decade or so. But eventually they will be comfortable with computers, as some already are."

The new conditions mandate that presidents and deans move toward a more rational resource-allocation mode. That mode requires the rapid manipulation of quantities, which requires computers. As Anatole France once said, "People who can't count, won't count." This is certainly true for higher education. Earl Cheit wrote: "A new style is emerging on campus. Unlike the old one, which sought improved quality mainly by adding income, the new one relies mainly on control, planning, evaluation, and reallocation to provide institutional strength with fiscal constraints. This new style means converting loose collections of professionals into managed institutions, using more formal approaches to decision making, relying more on systems."[35]

The future is becoming as important as the present and the past, and administration is yielding to management. You can still hear the old saw on many campuses, "We don't do things that way," implying that the present policies and procedures are rooted in the past and its leaden traditions, and that this is how it should forever be. But with the revolution going on in higher education, the future is assuming a new importance in the administration of the best-managed campuses.

College presidents who do not look ahead, who do not plan, become prisoners of external forces and surprises, most of them unpleasant. In the new style of academic management, the campus leaders are constantly looking ahead to see where the college or university will be in the next three, five, or ten years. They are deciding now what to do about the likely tomorrow. As David Ewing says, "A higher order of management intelligence, once a luxury, is now becoming a condition of survival."[36]

To look toward the long-term viability of institutions, it has been necessary for educational leaders to do less worrying about day-to-day operations and more thinking and deciding about the future. It is no use running a good railroad if you don't see that people are more and more using automobiles, trucks, buses, and airplanes. Administration, the efficient arrangement of everyday activities, is decreasing as a nearly full-time activity in higher education. Management, the shrewd shaping of the mix and nature of the organization's activities, is becoming equally important.

Campus presidents, vice-presidents, and deans who are always too busy and who make many little decisions are now increasingly ineffective leaders, too lazy or myopic to see what is vital, strategic, and essential. As Peter Drucker says, "Effective executives do not make a great many decisions. They concentrate on the important ones."[37] And the important decisions revolve around the long-range stability, public support, and quality of the institution.

The new future-oriented academic leaders have had to discipline themselves to delegate more, to engage in new kinds of activities, to behave differently. Management, unlike administration, demands leadership and the motivation of others, using information, ideas, and well-conceived purposes. The whole organization needs to be stimulated to look ahead, think of long-term consequences, be alert for new opportunities. As Albert Hirschman has said, "Development depends not so much on finding optimal combinations for given resources and factors of production as on calling forth and enlisting for development purposes resources and abilities that are hidden, scattered, or badly utilized."[38] President Lawrence Cremin, of Columbia University's Teachers College, for example, through a series of brilliant little books, articles, and lectures of his own, as well as through forums with experts of all kinds, position papers, and personal persuasion, has prompted his faculty—and other educational school faculties—to move away from their preoccupation with schooling to the radically new needs for schools of education in our technology-saturated time.

The behavior of education leaders dedicated to good management is different from the behavior of those who are traditional administrators. Administrators prefer people, individual projects, specific routines; managers prefer ideas, linked initiatives, new ventures. Administrators tend to be cool, amiably neutral, businesslike; managers tend to be spirited, committed, entrepreneurial. Administrators are usually cautious, passive, and conservative; managers are often risk-takers, active, and adventurous. Administrators love details and efficiency; managers love large objectives and effectiveness. Administrators are often clever and manipulative; managers are often gutsy and outspoken.[39] Thus, the change to a greater future orientation and sharper management in education requires a willed shift of the psyche, a new courage to be, to do.

The external environment and the market are receiving more attention. At one university I know, the officials until two years ago were setting enrollment targets based entirely on their wishes and the wishes of their faculty. They did not know, nor seek to know, birth statistics, high school graduation rates, migration patterns, or any other demographic data about their state or region. (Over 85 percent of the students in America attend college within 200 miles of their homes.) Some colleges to this day base their plans almost exclusively on each department's or school's desires. This is why many states have overbuilt higher education facilities, house too many academic programs, or wear strange fits between their universities and their economies and cultures. In Michigan, for example, there are 44 state campuses, 25 mediocre nursing programs, 14 teachers colleges and schools of education (six of which are among the largest 15 in the country and none of which turns out more than a handful of urgently needed mathematics and science teachers), and not one first-rate school of engineering in the highly industrial state.

If there has been any major transformation in outlook in higher education in the past few years, it has been in the acute new awareness of the economic, political, and cultural environment surrounding the campuses and of the market for educational services. The market has caused business, engineering, biology, computer science, and veterinary medicine programs to bulge while schools of home economics, social work, and education and departments like English, sociology, French, and art history are half-empty. It has brought millions of adults onto campuses that have never figured out quite what to do with experienced grown-ups as students. The market has exploded with demands for short, concentrated courses while campuses have long, leisurely courses. While many colleges and universities still teach as if a majority of their students are going to be scholars themselves, the market for would-be professors has shrunk.

As for higher education's environment, it has turned from solicitous and supportive to censorious and cold-blooded. Regulations are being imposed, appropriations are being slashed. Consumers by the hundreds of thousands now question whether their costly investment in college will really prove worthwhile. Colleges and universities are being shaken from their self-regarding world of internally generated wish-lists and abundance. They have entered a new world of consumer markets and scarcity. Based on market research, for instance, Carleton College has two different sets of admissions literature, one for Minnesota students and one for all others.

At Baltimore's all-women Goucher College, the faculty fought to continue training ladies politely in the liberal arts for the better graduate schools and for a life of cultured leisure, when more young women each year were not going to graduate schools and wanted professional and business careers. Applications dropped. Finances became precarious. After Rhoda Dorsey became president in 1974, a few tenured faculty were let go, classics and foreign languages were trimmed, Goucher II was opened for women who had not finished college, corporate internships were instituted, and work with computers, management, and economics was strengthened. President Dorsey and her dean are now discussing Goucher's "market niche" with trustees—how Goucher can position itself a notch below, say, Bryn Mawr and Smith but above the litter of small women's colleges. Goucher's management was compelled to come to grips with the new demographic, coeducational, and economic environment and to study what kind of education the bright young women of today were seeking. Goucher does not want to lose its liberal arts soul. But neither does it want to descend into cashmere decadence.

In the emerging style of academic management the outside world looms much larger. The preferences and ambitions of individual faculty, while still highly regarded by most academic leaders, plays a diminished role. The model of mechanical generation is being replaced with the model of biological congruence.

Planning is becoming essential. I once watched a gray-haired executive vice-president spend several hours preparing his university's budget. He cut dollars here, added a bit there, shifted funds from one field to another, and placed his very few free dollars in what he regarded as a coming area. The same person a few days later told me that he did not believe in planning. He said planners were dreamers and usually unrealistic and arrogant. Yet here he was, year after year, autocratically allocating huge sums of money according to priorities and a plan locked in his head of where his institution should go.

What academic leaders using the management style are doing is turning these private plans, based on personal aims and prejudices, into ones that are public and based on data, explicit objectives, and rational strategies. Planning makes the implicit, inarticulate, and private explicit, articulate, and public. It brings decision making out of the closet. It replaces muddling through with purpose. As David Ewing said, "Planning makes it possible for organizations to make the great leap from an animal-like form of existence to a higher, more purposeful manner of operation."[40] For an organization like a university, dependent on knowledge workers who cannot be ordered about by management but must be persuaded to work roughly in unison toward some goals to which they can subscribe, the creation of a widely known plan of action becomes vital. Also, cutback management forces the private decision making of yesterday to explain itself, defend itself—especially to those being retrenched.

As I will explain later, the new planning in academia is not the highly quantitative, detailed planning of two decades ago. It is more like the planning that General George Marshall did so well, not an imposed blueprint but an agreed-upon strategy. And it is outside-in planning, attuned to the external conditions as well as internal strengths and traditions.[41] More institutions are devoting more time and money to strategic analysis and planning. The new academic executives realize the folly of spending large sums of money to compete in the present, but pennies to come out strong and ahead of others in the future.

CHAPTER FOUR

Slouching Toward Strategy

In human affairs the logical future, determined by past and present conditions, is less important than the willed future, which is largely brought about by deliberate choices.
RENÉ DUBOS

Alice: *Would you please tell me which way I ought to go from here?*
Cheshire Cat: *That depends on where you want to get to.*
LEWIS CARROLL

My center is giving way. My right is falling back. The situation is excellent. I attack.
MARSHAL FERDINAND FOCH

I N HIS POEM "Little Gidding," in *Four Quartets,* T. S. Eliot wrote:

We shall not cease from exploration
And the end of all our exploring
Will be to arrive where we started
And know the place for the first time.

Hundreds of colleges and universities in the United States are learning to know their places for the first time. As with individuals in desperate straits who are forced to ask themselves who they really are and what they value most, campuses across the land are being pressed to inquire What business are we really in? and What is most central to us? and How shall we proceed?"

Imagine three institutions.

St. Swithin's College was a fine Roman Catholic college for young women, long noted for its strong emphasis on liberal arts education and ladylike manners. Numerous of its alumnae are married to conservative and affluent businessmen and professional men. Its full-time enrollment, however, has declined in the past seven years from 900 to 600. To prevent faculty cuts and to balance its books, the college became nondenominational to qualify for some public dollars. Then it went coeducational and began an evening program for adults. Two years ago it started programs in office technology, business administration, and computer programming. It also rents the lovely college each summer to the owner of a small string of adult tennis-and-fun camps. Now the students want coed dorms and liquor on campus, since liquor is sold to anyone 18 years old or over in the state. The male students want better athletic facilities. The provost is eyeing cuts for such underenrolled programs as Latin, music, religion, French, and philosophy. The professors are upset. A growing number of loyal and prominent alumnae are furious about the drift of the school, which has moved away from the kind of college they have loved.

What business is St. Swithin's in? What is central? What should it do?

David University is a noted campus of 9,000 students, sometimes called "the Harvard of the Southeast." It has a strong sports program, which has helped its student integration efforts, and a famous tradition as a liberal, faculty-dominated institution with nationally ranked programs in English, physics, and chemistry. Secular, nonconformist, rigorous, David University is viewed as an intellectual and scientific oasis that has turned out good writers, physicians, science and math teachers, and business leaders. The undergraduate and graduate business programs are packed, but the education school's enrollment has dropped by one-half in the past five years, graduate students have declined from 3,000 to 2,100, and many humanities and science courses are undersubscribed. The university would like to invest in several promising fields: strengthen its mediocre biology and computer science departments, expand international studies, and perhaps start a small, specialized engineering school. But David University has serious financial problems with its strong, high-cost faculty, its expensive science and athletic programs, its liberal scholarship grants to the able poor and minority students, and its "best in the South" library. To trim expenses, the university has fallen behind in scientific equipment, cut its library acquisitions, let go one-half the maintenance staff—the buildings' white columns have not been painted in five years—and reduced the administration and the untenured young portion of the faculty by one-third. Tuition is now so high that the admissions office reports a serious decline in applicants and a major drop in average SAT scores of entering freshmen. The university has as its highest priorities not to let go any tenured members of the faculty and to keep their salaries high. It has also supported the sports program as much as ever, which is popular with alumni. But the university is now seen as a slightly shabby place that is plummeting academically without superior junior faculty, and one badly positioned for the academic frontiers of the next decades.

What business is David University in? What is central? Where is it headed?

Athens State University is a former state teachers college that is now a bustling arts and sciences university with 24,000 students. Located at the edge of the state's largest city, it offers courses in nearly every subject except agriculture, astronomy, and medicine. Its buildings and professors are undistinguished. The entrepreneurial president, a childhood friend of the governor, was president of the city's Chamber of Commerce last year and is committed to growth and public service. Athens State University runs seven days a week, day and night. It has a weekend college and evening college. It admits anyone who has finished high school. Six years ago it started its own special two-year "opportunity college," including courses in cosmetology and auto repairs, to head off the creation of a community college across town. The university advertises on billboards, buses, and television, and it has four storefront branch locations. It has few graduate students, except in its business and law programs. Its faculty do little research. The professors formed a faculty union a few years ago, hoping to raise their exceedingly low salaries, reduce the number of part-time teachers, raise academic quality, and win a faculty senate. The reputable old state university upstate in Sparta, with mounting support from the legislature and State Board of Higher Education, complains about the "empire building," lack of planning and standards, and money-consuming propensities of Athens State in a time of tight budgets. (The schools of law, business, social work, and engineering at ASU are not accredited, and the governor last month approved a $10 million building request for a new school of mass communications there: radio, TV, tele-communications, and public relations.) The president counters that he is "meeting the real needs of the people, at a much lower cost per student to taxpayers than the elitist campus upstate."

What business is Athens State University in? What is most central to its operation? What is its strategy?

Actually, if you dig you will find a strategy of sorts buried in the activities of each of these campuses. St. Swithin's is trying to survive and cling to a set of values in a changing culture. David University is hoping to keep its distinguished senior faculty pleased, its nonconformist liberalism intact, and its sports program strong. Athens State is seeking to offer people from all walks of life the higher education they say they want, with economy. But the strategies are not coherent. Neither are they conscious, agreed upon, and openly arrived at by the faculty, administrators, and trustees. It may be that four-fifths of all American colleges and universities are more or less like these three fictional campuses.

The word *strategy* derives from the Greek verb *stratego*, meaning to plan the defeat of one's enemies through the effective use of resources. The

Greek word for general is *strategos*.[1] For many centuries the word strategy was used chiefly by the military. But in recent centuries it has been used increasingly by governments, as in a strategy to defeat the opposition party in the next election, to reduce inflation and provide more jobs, or to improve the arts in the nation. And since the Second World War, strategy has become a term used extensively in business.

In the past decade, though, any organization with competitors, with aspirations to greatness, or with threats of decline has come to feel the need for a strategy, a plan to overcome. The March of Dimes organization to conquer polio was in trouble after Jonas Salk introduced his vaccine; its strategy was to switch out of polio into birth defects. The Cleveland Symphony Orchestra, faced with a changing population in Cleveland, strategically introduced an "ethnic night."[2] The cotton producers have assembled a strategy to defend themselves against the invasion of synthetic fibers. Stanford University's leaders had a strategy to move the school from its 1950s position as a moderately good private university for California's affluent families to its 1980s position as one of America's six or seven finest universities for a national and even international body of superior students.

To have a strategy is to put your own intelligence, foresight, and will in charge instead of outside forces and disordered concerns. The priorities are always there. The question is who selects them. When the pressures are in charge the present gets attention not the future; fighting brush fires and improvisation take precedence, not planning; defense is the game, not offense; and political and psychological infighting rules, not meeting the outside needs, threats, and opportunities.[3] Strategy means agreeing on some aims and having a plan to defeat one's enemies—or to arrive at a destination—through the effective use of resources.[4]

The beginning point is self-consciousness for the organization. It is knowing the place for the first time, understanding what business you are in, or want to be in, and deciding what is central for the health, growth, and quality of the organization.

The phenomenon of knowing a college or university as if for the first time is akin to the experience people have if they stare concentratedly at a Necker cube.

At first it seems to most people that the square face on the lower right is the one closest to your eyes and that you are looking down on the cube from its left. If you stare awhile, a strange shift in perception occurs. The facet on the upper left suddenly seems nearest, and you feel underneath the cube and to the right. Eventually, you may even see the cube, as the Cubist painters did in the 1920s, as only 12 straight line-segments on a flat surface and not really a cube at all.

A concentrated institutional analysis of a college can also bring a new perception of the old place. A person becomes conscious of the organization and what it is doing as he or she never was before. It becomes possible to examine freshly what business the college is in and how it is going about it. The hidden or unspoken priorities become apparent. Suddenly, it is evident that the business of the college is in reality whatever the community says it is, or to find adequate work for a tenured group of remarkable faculty, or to deliver a classical education to anyone who cares about such a thing. Its business may even be revealed as the establishment of a truly great technical college of 1,500 students by the 1990s.

This process of rediscovery and reevaluation of ends is being forced on colleges and universities. If a campus has to chop a few million dollars from its annual budget, as the University of Washington and the University of Minnesota had to do in 1982, it quickly fixes attention and compels an evaluation as never before of what is central and what needs to be done. Defining what business a college is in and then allocating resources to come out ahead in that business is tough, intricate, dirty work. "Planning strategy is like performing surgery without an anesthetic," says David Ahlers, of Cornell's Graduate School of Business and Public Administration, who used to do strategic planning at a major bank. But it has been routine—and necessary—at many of the best-managed large corporations since the 1960s. It is now coming to American higher education too.

At the Columbia Broadcasting System, or CBS, for example, there were debates after World War II about what business the company was in. A pioneer in radio and television, was CBS a technology firm? Was it a news and communications outfit? At first, the executives decided it was a technology firm and that the market for consumer electronics items was about to explode. So they started producing and trying to sell CBS radios, television sets, and other electronic items. CBS lost hundreds of millions. The firm discovered, belatedly, that it had little expertise in efficient manufacturing and even less in marketing and consumer sales. Then CBS, observing the rapid growth of television, sports, and leisure activities in the late 1950s and early 1960s, decided it was really an "entertainment company." It invested in a Broadway musical called *My Fair Lady* and made a bundle. In the early 1960s CBS bought the New York Yankees. With innovative entertainment programming like "Beverly Hillbillies," the company rose to dominance in the television network ratings. Its profits were phenomenal. But some of CBS's "faculty" were unhappy. The best producers, directors, and newsmen thought that CBS ought to be doing high-quality communications, especially news—real public service and democratically educational stuff. Several key executives and newsmen quit, and one news vice-president resigned in disgust when the television network bosses decided to show an eighth rerun of an "I Love Lucy" show rather than the first Senate hearing on the Vietnam war.

Many persons assume that strategic planning in business is superior to government strategies and far more successful than the strategic planning in nonprofit organizations and universities. This is not so. The recent history of American business is filled with strategic miscalculations and fiascos as well as successes. And government planning has had its share of successes, from the Tennessee Valley Authority to Medicare, as well as costly blunders. Moreover, in the past few years, some colleges and universities are beginning to show signs that they can act strategically with the best of organizations if they put their minds to it.

There is good strategy making and bad strategy making—by cities, military units, political parties, government agencies, religious groups, reform movements, corporations, and colleges. Books like Peter Hall's *Great Planning Disasters* are instructive; and Robert Miles's *Coffin Nails and Corporate Strategies*, a slightly disorganized but fascinating account of how the major U.S. tobacco companies responded strategically to the mounting evidence about the medical effects of smoking, reveals how within each industry as well as each company there are victories and catastrophies. What matters is the quality, daring, and sagacity of the strategy formulation, not who does it.

This is illustrated by examining the approaches to strategy making at some institutions of higher education—specifically three colleges, two universities, and a famous graduate professional school.

HOOD COLLEGE, FREDERICK, MARYLAND. Founded in 1893, Hood has been a small college for women, in a charming town 45 miles northwest of Washington and west of Baltimore. Principally white, Protestant, and middle class, students in the past have often been the less academically able daughters of families in the Middle Atlantic states. Hood was founded by pastors of the Reformed Church, and it is still affiliated with the United Church of Christ.

The college's mission for its first 80 years was to prepare young women principally for well-run homes, cultured living, and genteel careers. The main programs were home economics, teaching, and liberal arts. The board of trustees was fiscally conservative, the budgets were always balanced; the endowment was small. The faculty, about half women, was paid like that of a high school. With 600 or so students, Hood has had a friendly, extended family atmosphere. There is no student center and no sororities.

During the cultural revolution of the 1960s and the takeoff of the women's liberation movement, the college tried to remain an oasis of traditional values and virtues. By the early 1970s enrollment had dropped slightly to 570 women, and the students went to the board of trustees to demand some changes. The president resigned and a new president was selected. He promptly commissioned some market research to help decide how to stimulate admissions applications. A lost-applicants study helped to suggest that the college could remain all-female if it stressed education for careers and continuing education. Handsome new recruiting publications were printed, the admissions office worked harder, new career programs were started, and enrollment rose again. But the new president, who drained the college's financial reserves to pay for his quick-fix marketing changes, moved on after only three years.

Martha Church arrived as the new president in 1975. She was appalled by the state of the finances and the inequity of faculty salaries, and she was concerned about the lack of direction for the college. Within months, she selected a long-range planning task force, which she chaired after a trustee launched the effort. Dr. Church, a geographer with a Ph.D. from the University of Chicago, also took on the general direction of finances herself, realigning scholarship aid and cutting back on plant maintenance to help increase faculty salaries, and stimulating an effort to increase annual donations. (Annual giving has gone from $60,000 in 1975 to $685,000 in 1982.) In 1978 she started an $8.8 million capital campaign, for which $9 million has been collected. She also opened the college's budget for all of the faculty to see. The budget has been in the black for the past four years.

But the central question was What should be the direction of Hood College?

President Church and the task force took note of the college's tradition of home economics, teaching, and liberal arts. But both also took note of the new role of women and blacks in society, the shrinking job market for teachers, and the increasingly technological nature of daily work. And President Church studied her college's environment. Frederick was a lovely town that was slowly becoming a commuter village for moderately affluent and arty Washingtonians. Maryland's public university and college system had no campuses in the vicinity. There was a specialized army base, Fort Dietrich, nearby, with a collection of experts in chemical, biological, and cancer research. And along Route 270, between Washington and Frederick, high-technology firms were building new plants, as they had along Route 128 around Boston; more families with science and technology interests were moving into Montgomery County to the southwest and Frederick County. Also, women's colleges were returning to acceptability again, and more people were beginning to worry that, as one study noted, "the special and distinctive educational environments that characterize the special purpose college are rapidly disappearing."[5]

By 1976 Martha Church and the task force had arrived at a direction and a strategy. They decided to maintain the college's tradition of preparing women for home and career. A well-groomed person of integrity herself, President Church kept the honor system, the strong student self-government, and an atmosphere of decorum. She encouraged the faculty to strengthen the liberal arts underpinnings and redefined career training as preparation for careers of the future: biotechnology, computer studies, management and economics, applied art, Hispanic-American studies, and early childhood development and elementary schooling (which accords with the new upsurge in births in the United States and with intelligent motherhood at any time).[6]

For the minority of very able young women there would be honors work, a 3–2 engineering program (three years at Hood, two at an engineering school), individualized majors, and a strengthened premedical and prelaw program. The college has capitalized on the army's biological researchers nearby as part-time faculty and in 1982 hired a first-rate woman molecular biologist away from Fort Dietrich for full-time teaching. One in eight undergraduates at Hood now majors in biology, biomedical technology, or premedical studies. The high-tech firms have also helped with funds for new equipment in computer studies and with adjunct faculty in management.

Faculty reaction has been cautious but supportive. In 1981 the faculty introduced a stronger core curriculum in liberal arts to balance the work on careers. President Church says she is trying to make haste slowly. She works hard at explanation and persuasion, and faculty committees are busier than ever before. The board of trustees has become more active, especially during the capital campaign. In the spring of 1981 the board conducted a self-study and later brought in financial consultants to help restructure the endowment portfolio.

Hood's enrollment strategy appears to be four-pronged. Recognizing that Hood College will appeal mainly to young women of average and above-average abilities, the college is ranging more broadly geographically for resident students. Because of the new population in the college's backyard, it is enlarging its commuter population, including more part-time adults. Hood is stressing a greater variety of backgrounds among students, religiously and racially (10 percent are now minority students). And it is keeping the undergraduate program one especially designed for women, but enlarging the graduate programs at the master's degree level and making them fully coeducational. In addition to the 1,100 undergraduates now at Hood, there are 700 graduate students, mostly part-time.

President Church told me that while finances are still wobbly and the college's records are only now being put on computers, she has appointed a director of planning and institutional research and refined the three-year financial forecasts. Freshmen applications for fall 1982 were up 40 percent. "It's been rocky, but the faculty and administration have now agreed on a new direction and a strategy, and we have a master plan in a loose-leaf binder in which every department has spelled out its goals and strategies for reaching them—with dollar amounts attached."

RENSSELAER POLYTECHNIC INSTITUTE, TROY, NEW YORK. RPI, as it is known, is America's oldest private engineering school. Troy, located near the entrance to the old Erie Canal, was one of the cradles of early American industry. But most industry has left and it is now a quiet, dingy, blue-collar town, across the Hudson River from Albany, the state capital. The college, once a pioneer in engineering education, had fallen behind by the 1960s. Academic leadership and fund raising were weak. Many of the buildings and laboratories had kept their pre–World War II charm and grime.

Then in the early 1970s a forceful, combative dean of the School of Engineering, George Ansell, decided to renovate the 2,500-student engineering school, one of the nation's largest. With approval from the board of trustees in 1974, Ansell spent $15 million, much of it borrowed from New York State, to modernize 30 laboratories and rebuild most of his school's buildings. He eased out some tired faculty and brought in about 40 new whiz kids and a few senior stars (some on "soft" money from research grants). He tripled the amount of research, and doubled the number of graduate students. Convinced that engineering education had become too dryly academic and analytical rather than usefully inventive and design-oriented, Dean Ansell enlisted 36 corporations to put up $25,000 a year to operate a new computer graphics center that would be among the best in higher education—in return for first looks at new computer graphics findings. He claims, "Our CAD-CAM facilities are possibly the best of any campus now." The other RPI schools—the medium-sized school of science, and the small schools of management, humanities and social science, and architecture—moved less quickly.

In 1976 an RPI alumnus and trustee, an aeronautical engineer who had been in charge of NASA's Apollo spacecraft project to put a man on the moon and later became the deputy administrator of NASA, was selected as RPI's president. His name was George Low, and he was famous as a demanding workaholic, a fierce competitor, and a tense, meticulous administrator. "Attention to detail is the only way to run any organization," he says. Low hit RPI like a proud, tough Marine drill instructor meeting slouching, soft, long-haired recruits.

Several things came together promptly to erupt into a new strategy for RPI. There was Troy's, and RPI's, distinguished past. There was the institute's great academic strength in materials science and polymer chemistry. There were Dean Ansell's moves into more research, graduate work, and computer-assisted design. There were dozens of untapped RPI alumni who were corporate leaders. There was the competition: MIT, Cornell, Georgia Tech, Purdue, Carnegie-Mellon, Illinois, Cal Tech. There was the overlooked fact that RPI sat between two of the greatest scientific research labs in the world: General Electric's in nearby Schenectady and IBM's downriver at Yorktown Heights. ("We have a great set of bookends: GE on one side, IBM on the other," quipped one RPI executive.) There was New York State's neglect of high-technology industry despite its corporate headquarters prominence. There was Japan's new challenge to U.S. technology. And there was the character of President George Low.

Impatient, intolerant of poor quality, Low is by nature a planner, designer, and builder. "What I learned at NASA," he says, "was to bring things into being. It conditioned me to believe that technological improvement leads to economic growth." He is also worried about the country. "In recent years America has lost its competitive edge. 'Made in Japan' has replaced 'Made in USA' as a recognized standard of high quality. Productivity, the source of all economic value, is lacking."

He wrote in his 1980 annual report: "We need people who are of the highest caliber technologically and who can apply social consciousness to the problem-solving, decision-making process. It is not enough to know only what can be done. We must know too what ought to be done. And then we must do it as well as we know how." In the same report, he wrote of RPI, "We want to be one of the small number of first-rank, distinguished technological universities in America."

RPI and President Low decided to go for broke. The college borrowed more than $40 million and dipped into its $90 million endowment for another $6 million to reestablish itself among the top technology institutions. President Low announced a $38 million, three-year capital funds drive in 1978. By 1981, he had collected $52 million, much of it himself. RPI bought an unused, old chapel on the edge of the campus from the Roman Catholic Church and turned it into an architecturally stunning computer center with 300 remote terminals around campus; then Low found a donor to pay for one-half of the $7 million conversion. He built a new library and laboratory. President Low began to raise the salaries of the best professors to the level of a combined "market basket" of the top 25 technological institutions and pressed the recruiting of eminent scientists and scholars. In 1980, with an alumnus gift, he began the Darrin Scholars Program, to give 21 of the finest young scholars each year their personal computer, a faculty mentor, and a large scholarship—to lure the best young scientists away from competitors. Low explains, "We had to get equipped first with good buildings and people, and the money for these."

The college decided unabashedly to become a full partner with industry, and made four moves to link its own push for distinction and eminence with the continued growth of high-tech industry nationally and in New York State. One was the Center for Manufacturing Productivity, built with gifts from General Electric, General Motors, Boeing, Norton Company, United Technologies, Eastman Kodak—and robots donated by Cincinnati Milacron. A second was RPI's Center for Integrated Electronics, with a building donated by the Norton Company and a $4 million gift from IBM of an EL-2 electron beam lithography system. This center concentrates on VLSI work (very large-scale integration) to develop the next generation of semiconductors that will squeeze 100,000 or more transistors onto a dime-sized chip of silicon. According to director Andrew Steckl, the center emulates the industry-university-government coalition Japan has mobilized to get ahead of the United States, and he claims that RPI is a natural because "more chips are made in the Hudson Valley than in Silicon Valley."

Third, President Low started an "incubator" program, renting the institute's unused space in its older buildings to infant high-tech firms. The new companies—there are now nine—pay low rent and use RPI's library, computer graphics center, and faculty researchers. Sometimes they pay the rent with stock in the firm. Last, RPI is building a research park. This is old hat by now, with everyone from the University of Utah to Princeton creating research parks. But President Low, who got the idea from a visit to Stanford, believes RPI's will be unusually attractive and successful, especially if he can get corporate help to build up the 12,000 acres RPI owns at the Hudson River's edge. Naturally, the leaders and citizens of Troy and the neighboring towns have been galvanized by RPI's bold initiatives. They talk of a "second industrial revolution" for the Troy area and speak with new affection for the old elite college on the hill.

In July 1982, to add to the momentum, the governor announced that, because of the institute's strategic commitment to industrial renewal and technological research, New York State would help finance a $30 million building on the campus of independent RPI, to be called the New York State Center for Industrial Innovation. Low and his faculty will move their three existing centers of manufacturing productivity, computer graphics, and integrated electronics research into the new structure, increase research in all three areas, and furnish help for the state's manufacturing and high-tech industries when called upon. RPI will pay off the bond over 40 years, but New York will pick up all the interest.

RPI has had to put aside improvement in student life, and one faculty member told me that he felt the new management was "a bunch of rough riders with spurs." Dorothy Reynolds, assistant to the president, admits that many of the initiatives and strategy have come from the top, but she adds that President Low keeps checking his ideas with the students and the faculty in frequent meetings.

Next there will be a newly renovated building for the humanities and social science people because Low believes that scientific and technological expertise combined with management skills and rooted in the humanistic tradition is the way for RPI to go. There is now America's first Ph.D. program in technical and science writing at RPI. And there is a new dean of the management school, Robert Allio, to lead it into new spheres. His specialty: strategic planning for technology companies. (He is editor of *Planning Review*.)

BARAT COLLEGE, LAKE FOREST, ILLINOIS. The nuns of the Religious Order of the Sacred Heart have been teaching young women at Barat for more than a century. Located in a wealthy suburb 30 miles north of Chicago, the college once thought of itself as "the Manhattanville College of the Midwest," training about 800 well-bred Roman Catholic women a year as Manhattanville trained the Catholic female elite in the East. In the late 1960s, Barat, never an enterprising school financially, ran short of funds, became an independent college with a lay board of trustees and more lay members of the faculty, and began relaxing the rules for student life. Now one-fourth of the students are Protestant, one-tenth are blacks, and there is a sprinkling of Jewish and Oriental women. Two-thirds are commuters. Since Sister Judith Cagney became president in 1974, however, enrollments have continued to drop, to 400 full-time students and 300 part-timers. Finances have continued to be very tight.

Despite the size of the school, it has 18 academic departments, mimicking the research university structure, although there are only two or three faculty members in most departments. In 1975 the college began planning, employing the then widely tried NACUBO (National Association of College and University Business Officers) model. But, according to former vice-president for administration Theodore Marchese, the NACUBO planning scheme was time-consuming, demanded lots of faculty paperwork, and generated too many separate plans since each of Barat's 30 or so units had to file one. Also, it neglected the external environment and was not strategic. So in 1977 Marchese and Sister Judith Cagney merged budgeting and academic planning in their own scheme, with initiatives expected from the faculty and staff. Little change came forth though, and by 1979 the college began to worry about its survival, especially since fund raising was soft. Barat needed a strategy to turn the corner, to enable it to persevere.

Vice-President Marchese then tried a third tack. He had been reading in business publications about corporate strategic planning, and he began sending copies of the best articles on strategy to his fellow college managers and some faculty. After the 1980 Christmas vacation, the president was prompted to form a Strategic Planning Team, composed of 10 of the college's best people, selected by the president. The problem: What business should Barat be in and how can it get there? The SPT, as it was dubbed, met all spring, then went on retreats in June 1981. They came to know their college for the first time. Also for the first time, they assessed externalities such as women's education, their competition, patterns of college-going, new technologies, and the continuing education boom. And they squarely faced the possibility of further retrenchment and even closing the college doors.

Barat's Strategic Planning Team decided that Barat was structured awkwardly both for their own students and for the larger potential market of students. The college needed to stop imitating the large, high-powered colleges and stress what it could do best for the students it had, two-thirds of whom had SAT verbal scores below 500. Thus, the SPT radically recommended that the departmental structure be scrapped, and five or six interdisciplinary centers be created, such as the arts, mathematics and computers, social studies, science, business, and humanities. Such majors as mathematics and biology would be dropped. Each student would be trained in a core set of useful "competencies"—speaking, writing, and interviewing, say, or computing, bookkeeping, and management—which are appropriate for work in the emerging people-plus-technology service society. (Many Barat graduates, the SPT found, got jobs mainly in offices, stores, or firms requiring social and basic computational skills.) The team labeled the new curriculum "holistic." It also recommended a major new effort in adult education, with many classes at night, and new cooperative programs with commercial and industrial organizations in the greater Chicago area. In the spring of 1982, the Board of Trustees approved the new strategy and went one step further. They decided Barat should be coed.

In June 1982, Sister Judith Cagney retired as president and Dr. Marchese left for a new position in Washington. A retired, energetic vice-president of Abbott Laboratories has become acting president and seems to approve of the suggested faculty-administration-trustee strategy to turn Barat College into a coeducational college emphasizing training in the basic academic and social competencies for work in service-oriented or bureaucratic organizational life.

UNIVERSITY OF MINNESOTA, MINNEAPOLIS–ST. PAUL, MINNESOTA. One of America's largest (50,000 students) universities, this state institution is often also listed as among the best public universities in quality, despite its relatively open access. But the state's youth population is declining; Minnesota has become a more industrial state; and some people are beginning to question the institution's expensive sprawl. The president, C. Peter Magrath (pronounced Magraw), came from a presidency at the State University of New York at Binghamton in 1975. At Binghamton Dr. Magrath had produced, with the help of English professor Sheldon Grebstein (now president of SUNY's College at Purchase), a brilliant planning report from a special Committee on Academic Priorities that analyzed the campus situation with succinct clarity, reviewed the strengths and weaknesses of each department with unprecedented candor, and set priorities and parameters for future movement.[7]

A strong proponent of strategic planning—he has written, "Planning will be one of the magic words of the 1980s. . . . If educators do not plan, then somebody else will surely do it for them"[8]—President Magrath wrote a mission statement and created a Planning Council to develop a comprehensive planning process in his first year at Minnesota. Composed of vice-presidents, provosts, deans, faculty, and two students, the Council members argued for three years about how the university should plan. They did, however, invite leading academic and financial strategists from other campuses, such as Raymond Bacchetti of Stanford, Ronald Brady of the University of Illinois (now at the University of California), Raymond Haas, then at West Virginia University, and Richard Van Horn of Carnegie-Mellon University, to meet with them in all-day seminars. This raised their consciousness about planning and opened their minds to new possibilities. By spring 1978 they had reached some conclusions, the core of which was that the university should have 40 major planning units (academic and service), and each unit should plan its own strategy for the future. Planning at Minnesota began in 1979.

Meanwhile, Dr. Magrath, who reads widely, inquires broadly among faculty and deans and political and business leaders, and prefers to be his own executive vice-president, created a new office of vice-president of administration and planning and named an estate planning professor in the law school, Robert Stein, as the officer. Stein, who believes that "it is absolutely essential for universities to address their environment, their programs, and their future in a more systematic way if they are to grow in quality and move into the academic fields of tomorrow in a time of constraint," says he quickly learned several things. Professors have trouble looking ahead. Universities love to explore process and methodology but hate to make decisions. Faculty governance in a large university has almost become nongovernance. Decisions in a university often get made randomly—by deans, legislators, a financial officer, the president.[9] And planning is not a line position but a presidential staff position that requires expert coaxing, persuading, and negotiating.

Dr. Stein also found a young professor of management on the Planning Council, Carl Adams, who had worked on the PPB (planning, programming, and budget) system under U.S. Secretary of Defense Robert McNamara. Stein made him a special assistant. Together they shaped Minnesota's strategic decision-making process and started it going. Adams says, "A major problem in university planning is the large number of people who say you can't start until you know more. It is vital not to succumb to the many perfectionists, pessimists, and postponers. Educational planning is new. It needs to find its way as it goes along." After launching the planning process, Stein became dean of the law school. A scholar of Scandinavian literature, Nils Hasselmo, succeeded him as vice-president.

During the first planning round in 1979–81, the deans and directors of the 40 units submitted their plans, mostly optimistic, a few grandiose. The president studied them all and made comments and suggested corrections on each. Then budgets were drawn up, linked to the plans.

But just when the University of Minnesota units had completed their plans to 1985, the legislature in late 1980 asked the state university to take a $14 million cut in appropriations the next year. So the second cycle of biennial plans, in 1981–83, had to include specific retrenchments rather than vague plans for continued moderate growth. President Magrath asked each unit to plan this time on steady state financing and submit plus-and-minus 5 percent alternative plans, and he required each unit to list its priorities. At the same time the planning office obtained data from the American Association of Universities on costs at other schools of law, agriculture, business, arts and sciences, dentistry, and the like. This provided the president with a sense of which Minnesota schools were high or low in funding compared with their national peers.

When the state legislature, pressed by a deepening recession, proposed another $60 million in cuts for the University of Minnesota in fall 1981 along with cuts for all state agencies, the university's planning process suddenly took a pronounced shift. Bottom-up planning by units assumes two things: no change in the total structure of the units themselves and the superiority of many little plans rather than an overall university strategy. But now the fiscal emergency compelled greater all-university decision making. What business was the entire University of Minnesota really in?

For example, the university has long had a two-year "general college" in its midst to handle the less prepared students. But there were six new community colleges in the greater Twin Cities area, and the University of Minnesota itself had opened two new two-year technical colleges in other parts of the state. Wasn't the general college a vestigial unit from the 1940s?

Overall university priorities rapidly became as important as individual unit priorities at Minnesota. Top-down planning and a total university strategy began to replace bottom-up and dozens of piecemeal strategies. For the first time, the University of Minnesota was forced to examine itself freshly as a totality in the light of all the new state colleges and community colleges that had sprung up around it in recent decades. The anarchic confederation was required to become a federal union. What could the university do best? What should it be doing? What should it peel off? What should it invest in for continued intellectual growth?

Central management and decision making blossomed, and all-university thinking increased. A new four-person Budget Executive was created, consisting of the vice-presidents of academic affairs, finance and operations, administration and planning, and health sciences. It recommends resource acquisition and allocation options and decisions, coordinates the 40 plans, and evaluates unit quality and progress for President Magrath. Each unit was urged to free up 10 percent of its budget to cover sudden retrenchments and to provide venture capital for promising new programs and projects. Consultation with the faculty has been speeded up. Patricia Swan, chairperson of the Senate Finance Committee, says her committee met weekly in 1981–82 and with the president monthly. Some divisions are unexpectedly taking long looks at their future. At the College of Biological Sciences, for instance, Dean Richard Caldecott told me his school is doing more "lateral planning"—cooperation with other schools— and that his advisory committee, in deciding on how to handle a 5 percent cut in appropriations, opted for more phased and early retirements and buy-outs (with two years' pay) for older professors in order to keep the brilliant young scholars. "They agreed," said Caldecott, "that the future of our college and of biology was with the best young people not the old-timers. It was extraordinary."

With the shift to all-university concerns and with President Mágrath insisting that academic strategy drive financial and resource decisions, power has coagulated in the academic vice-president's office. As colleges and universities race toward the formulation of academic strategies, either the president must emerge as a strong academic planner and leader or the academic vice-president, or provost, must move into the center of decision making for the institution's future. Decision making *among* units becomes as important as decision making *within* units.

At Minnesota, which has dismissed the idea of across-the-board cuts, Vice-President Kenneth Keller, a former engineering professor and a strong, imaginative executive, sees the provost's new role clearly: "In the 1980s, universities must either make tough choices or stagnate. And there is no way to make tough choices except centrally. But there is no way to learn about the intellectual growth fields of tomorrow or to evaluate quality except through the best faculty and their units. So I have more painful decisions to make but I go to a lot more meetings with deans and faculty." Dr. Keller believes that at large universities deans will also rise up as much more central figures in academic management in the years ahead. Law school dean Robert Stein agrees: "Deans will increasingly be expected to deliver. If they don't, university presidents should replace them."

Harland Cleveland, director of the University of Minnesota's Hubert Humphrey Institute of Public Affairs, said to me that his major concern was a reformation in the way people think about policy matters.

> The real enemy to progress now is excessive specialization. It has increased productivity but has gone so far that specialization is dysfunctional. In politics we have one issue fanatics. In education we have territorial fighters. We have more experts in small areas but more fragmentation and anarchic bickering. The trick is to move educated people toward more integrative

thinking, to see more connections and consequences, to realize the ties between present decisions and future quality, between their little area of work and the whole organization of which they are part.

Integrated, strategic thinking will also help us move ahead despite fewer resources. The hallmark of specialized experts is their sense of doubt and gloom. The mark of integrated thinkers is their sense of new possibilities and action. At Minnesota, outside pressures and good management have combined to make us gradually think more wholly and farsightedly.

Because the University of Minnesota is so huge and many-divisioned, President Magrath and his aides have had to be patient, to creep toward a content-laden academic strategy for the institution through an obstacle course of awareness sessions, new processes, and financial setbacks. For large, varied organizations, this may be an almost obligatory way. James March has come to believe that "it is not possible to lead an organization in any arbitrary direction . . . but it is possible to influence the course of events by managing the process of change. . . . Such a view of managing organizations assumes that the effectiveness of leadership often depends on being able to time small interventions so that the force of natural organizational processes amplifies the interventions."[10] And Raymond Haas argues that academic strategies should "unfold," bend the established forms slowly, and use existing officers as much as possible. He feels there is an "overwhelming inertia against planning as a process and against formal analysis as a basis for decision making." So refining the process through many foot-dragging practice sessions is vital. He notes, "Among airline pilots, sports stars, and administrators it is well known that long hours of practice in a controlled process is the sole approach to sound performance when an urgent situation arises."[11]

When the University of Minnesota had to trim its lard and slack and slice into a few academic programs to fund its best and most important ones, it had developed a crude, democratic process for doing so. A strategy popped out of the process.

CARNEGIE-MELLON UNIVERSITY, PITTSBURGH, PENNSYLVANIA. This 80-year-old university occupies a 90-acre campus four miles from downtown Pittsburgh. Once the Carnegie Institute of Technology, or Carnegie Tech, it merged in 1967 with the nearby Mellon Institute, an industrial research facility. When Richard Cyert was named president in 1972, the university was running deficits annually and its enrollment was declining. The campus was mainly an engineering college with a college of fine arts attached, and a relatively new (1949) graduate school in industrial administration and an even newer (1968) tiny graduate school of urban affairs.

During the boom years of 1950 to 1965, the institution was led by a former Indiana farmboy who had become a noted chemist, John "Jake" Warner. He left two legacies. He fervently believed that Carnegie Tech should never enroll more than 3,000 students, and he established the first computer science department in America in 1956 (ahead of Stanford and MIT). President Cyert thus took over a mediocre, academically polyglot campus that was one of the smallest universities in the land but one that had a running start in the growth field of computer studies. A scholar of organization psychology, Cyert wrote a letter to all deans and the entire faculty two months before he began his presidency, "This university needs an explicit statement of goals as well as a strategy for achieving them." He advocated a new policy committee which "should decide the priority of the plans and with it some indication of the directions in which we should allocate our funds. . . . We should determine what we want to do in political science and so on." Even before he took office, Dr. Cyert was determined to find a potent strategy for Carnegie-Mellon.

"In the early 1970s, we were drifting," Cyert told me. "We taught a little of this and some of that. Our engineering faculty aspired to being the best in Pennsylvania. We had to learn how to think nationally and competitively with the best." There was no question that the president wanted to reshape the whole institution. His old friend, psychologist and Nobel laureate Herbert Simon, confided to me, "Dick was very determined to make this a nationally important place. He was almost autocratic at times in the early years. But he gradually learned to be more persuasive and democratic with the faculty. Now he meets with people constantly and delegates more." Another executive says, from behind his word processor, "Carnegie-Mellon is different. Leadership here is strong, aggressive. Most universities react. We are proactive." Again, Herbert Simon: "We were small and behind the pack so we had to take gambles. And we were flexible enough, and gutsy, ambitious, and strong-willed enough so we could take gambles. We had to be smarter, more competitive to move up. Cyert is remarkably good at that." Richard Cyert, in a speech to an American Council on Education workshop in 1981, said, "Planning works best when it has been shaped to a great extent by the faculty. However, there will be no planning at all without discipline being imposed upon the organization from a central source. Nobody likes to plan. Faculty members . . . are not great risk takers. Many moved into academic life because they want certainty and security. Thus, the planning process must be initiated from the president's office."

In Cyert's first year, each dean and department head—"We purposefully call them heads not chairpersons here," said one faculty member—

submitted strategic plans to a Faculty Policy Committee that the president
had assembled from the finest, most forward-looking professors. Then
there were inspections of each department, and in 1974 a Long-Range
Planning Committee was created, consisting of six deans, two provosts,
and the vice-president for business. Cyert chaired the committee. It was to
"think the unthinkable," and it led to substantial changes.

Because President Cyert is a scholar in the field of organization theory
and strategic planning, Carnegie-Mellon's academic strategy is probably
the most methodically conceived in American higher education.

Without solid financial operations, Cyert believes, excellence is impossible. He moved quickly in 1972 to erase the red ink and has operated in
the black every year since. Doug Van Houveling, vice-provost for computing and planning, says: "We are really sharp financially. Every department
adheres to its budget. We installed the Interactive Financial Planning
System of EXECUCOM in Austin, Texas." Student financial aid was
restructured. In 1972 a faculty of 450 taught 3,900 students; in 1981 a
faculty of 425 taught 5,400 students. Sponsored research has gone from
$12.6 million in 1972 to $36.7 million in 1981. In 1976 Carnegie-Mellon
started a $100 million capital fund drive ("My vice-president made me do
it," says Cyert frankly), and it was successful. The school's endowment
has gone from $95 million 10 years ago to $135 million today.

The physical plant is not attractive, and there is a shortage of student
housing. "I have six roofs that leak," Cyert laughs. But Provost Richard
Van Horn says, "We had to concentrate on people and programs. That
was critical. Now we are beginning to fix our facilities." Weak department
heads and deans were removed and strong new ones installed. Every
academic program was renovated. In mathematics, for example, a diffuse
department was transformed into an applied mathematics department
that now ranks behind the top four (MIT, Cal Tech, NYU, and Brown).
Cyert recruited a brilliant applied mathematician from Michigan to lead
the change. In psychology, the management decided to stress cognitive
psychology and social psychology, aiding the work in computers, learning
theory, and organizations. A small group of social scientists, with special
strength in economics, public policy, and the sociology of organizations,
was added in the late 1970s, "from scratch," claims Cyert. The program
in education was dropped, foreign languages trimmed. The president ran
Saturday morning seminars with his department heads on strategic em-
phases, identification of outstanding scholars they might try to recruit, and
faculty-recruiting tactics.

According to Herbert Simon, "Comparative advantage is very big at
Carnegie-Mellon." Cyert believes that since his university is small it must

carefully choose a few important intellectual areas to work in and then try to do them as well as anyone in the nation. To him, the location in Pittsburgh, the engineering and industrial management and research tradition, the ethnic backgrounds and practical bent of many applicants, and the head start in computer science almost mandated the distinctive cast that Carnegie-Mellon should strive for. "We have remade ourselves into a *professional* university," Provost Van Horn says. "We do art, drama, and music but we teach them in connection with professional theater. We now have one of the best musical theater programs in the nation. We don't just appreciate and study, we try to do and to act. We brought in a new dean for our College of Humanities and Social Sciences to create a novel kind of professional liberal education. Despite some strong faculty objections, we bent English toward rhetoric, foreign languages toward translation and speech. In history we concentrate on social history and have an unusual Ph.D. program in applied history."

Carnegie-Mellon now has one of the most innovative and rigorous programs in computer science in the nation. Soon every Carnegie student will be expected to have his or her personal computer terminal. Using its expertise in computers, engineering, physics, and industrial management, the university established a Robotics Institute to help industry design "the factory of the future" and help operations in environments dangerous or inaccessible to humans.

The question at Carnegie-Mellon always is: what advantages do we have and how can we best exploit them for the good of the region, the nation, and our own organization? Cyert contends, "The aim of strategic planning is to place a campus in a distinctive position. We must face the fact that colleges and universities are in a competitive market."

Another way to get a competitive edge and achieve distinction, Cyert believes, is to move early into the intellectual frontiers of tomorrow, as Carnegie Tech did with computers. "After I became president," says Cyert, "I started a series of meetings and dinners with industrial and scientific leaders to find out what they thought would be the hot fields a decade or two from now." Two fields mentioned were statistics and pure and applied biology. Cyert and his deans were able to gather a superb little cluster of statistics professors for Carnegie-Mellon, but they have twice tried unsuccessfully to transform the biology department. The university, however, has just lured a noted cell biologist from Harvard and will try again to win eminence in molecular biology and genetic engineering.

One striking thing about Carnegie-Mellon is that despite all the forceful, decisive, strategic activity, there are few detailed plans on paper. "The key element in strategic planning is to get everyone in the organization to think that way," says Dr. Cyert, who doesn't believe in four-color booklets with detailed projects. Carnegie-Mellon's plans are largely an attitude, a shared widespread leaning toward technical, mathematics-based, professional, useful education, always hunting for a niche or upcoming field in which to establish national eminence and undisputed quality. The president, who likes to combine rational probes with entrepreneurial daring, says, "We try to stay nimble and be quick."

Richard Cyert has also learned the politics of strategy making. He listens more and now meets tirelessly with people. A short, broad-nosed, slightly rumpled man, the president says, "I used to want to solve all our problems and create a coherent, forward-looking academic program overnight. I needed to learn to work with people so they would become planners themselves, and would think strategically. I'm still seen by a few faculty as a bit of a martinet. But I'm getting better at the human side."

President Cyert and his wife pledged $100,000 in the last fund drive—all their life's savings and some of his future earnings. "Margaret and I believe Carnegie-Mellon is the kind of organization that is critical for our society."

TEACHERS COLLEGE, COLUMBIA UNIVERSITY, NEW YORK CITY. Though it has lost 1,000 students in the past eight years because of the declining demand for teachers, Teachers College is the largest comprehensive graduate school of education in the world, as well as the most famous and in many ways the most eminent. Its 4,500 students come from nearly every state and 85 foreign countries. Its library houses the finest collection of educational materials on earth. Teachers College, especially when John Dewey was on its faculty, has strongly influenced the curriculum and quality of America's schools. Its president, Lawrence Cremin, an alumnus who took office in 1974, is the leading historian of American education and perhaps the most innovative mind and outspoken voice in the field of American schooling.

But these are tumultuous days for colleges of education. Schools are closing. Teachers have unions like truckdrivers. Several surveys have found that education schools now get the students with the lowest academic ability of all professional schools in higher education. And technology has radically altered the delivery of ideas and information: records, television, computers, films, tapes, and calculators. No one is more aware of this than President Cremin. In his inaugural address in September 1974 he said, "We have been living through a revolution that may well be as profound as the original invention of the school." He proposed that the Teachers College faculty end its almost exclusive focus on schooling of the young and also prepare professionals for the new spectrum of education at day-care centers, museums, television stations, libraries, publishers, corporate training programs—and for learning across the entire life span. To spell out his vision, and the reasons for it, in 1976 he published the book *Public Education*, a succinct and arresting statement.

But how could anyone transform a famous teachers college in a time of retrenchment? (In 1974 Teachers College had 182 full-time professors; in 1981 it had a faculty of 137.) This was a special problem because, like most schools of education, a portion of the faculty was not especially innovative or research-oriented and numerous departments behaved as quasi-independent satrapies.

Dr. Cremin says, "I took the deanship myself for the first two years. I handled budget allocations. I rewrote the booklets on promotion and tenure. I insisted that every faculty opening belongs to the whole college, not the department, and shifted resources. And I opened our financial books for all the faculty to see. Unveiling the budget was an eye-opener. It gave people a sense of our grim reality and helped build a consensus for change." New professorships appeared in such areas as telecommunications, the family as educator, and educators-in-industry. TC's Institute for Urban and Minority Education became one of the nation's largest centers for research and counsel on the problems of the disadvantaged. A new Microcomputer Resource Center studied and taught the application of computer technology to education. Internships were arranged for practice teaching not just in schools but in other educational agencies such as TV stations, family service centers, bank training centers, and museums.

In Cremin's first two years, Teachers College somehow ran in the black. But the next six years were red-ink years, mainly because the president believed he had to improve the student dormitories, build a modern library, and buy new equipment. Finances are a nagging problem for President Cremin. Not only does TC lack a tradition of serious fund raising, but its graduates are nearly all in teaching or educational supervision posts.

So that the faculty would become more future-oriented and market-oriented, Cremin, along with his provost and his dean, forged a series of planning and innovation mind-stretchers to increase a sense of financial reality, expedite educational change, and reveal the rapidly changing environment outside the college. He chaired a College Policy Council of faculty members, students, and administrators to deliberate on the college's affairs. It asked for a statement of priorities from every dean and director. Cremin commissioned one professor to write "The Decade Ahead: A Review of Demographic and Socio-Economic Projections Relevant to Future Enrollment at Teachers College."

After a lively meeting of the faculty in December 1978, the president appointed a Task Force on the Program of the College the next month. One year later the task force reached a startling conclusion: TC needed a "comprehensive reconceptualization." As the report said, "The future of the College can be assured only if we respond institutionally to the alterations in our external environment. . . . Even if we improve the efficiency of the existing program units, the College may be in an even more precarious position in five to ten years than it is now. . . . The institutional design itself needs to be considered."

Very much an intellectual leader who revels in educational policy discussions, President Cremin responded to the report in an 18-page, mostly supportive point-by-point paper. He was stirred by the faculty's surprising boldness, but with uncharacteristic skittishness he wrote, "My own committment has always been to minimalism and incrementalism with respect to institutional change. . . . My sense is that the need for collaboration across units may be greater than the need for general reorganization." Yet, in the same reply he wrote: "We need to focus insistently, not so much on the internal arrangements of Teachers College in their own right, but rather on the relations between Teachers College and the external world. That external world is partly a world of 'markets,' in the form of potential clients and opportunities for the support of research, development, and service. It is also a world of rapid change in the nature and character of education and in the tools and concepts with which we approach education." The president seemed to be playing down internal changes, yet suggesting that external conditions may be calling up the "comprehensive reconceptualization" the faculty task force recommended.

Then, at a Board of Trustees meeting on 22 October 1981, a trustee asked President Cremin two questions: What vision did he have for Teachers College 10 years hence? and How did he plan to achieve that vision? The queries rocked the unflappable Cremin and turned his usual effervescence into introspection.

He examined his school and discovered that there had been over the past years, almost unwittingly, an expansion in both size and excellence in applied psychology work and work in the health sciences (nutrition, teaching to prevent illness, etc.). He called it a "large 'sea change' in the character of the College." He asked the professors in charge of the divisions of psychology and health education to dash off memoranda on what might be the central thrusts of work in their fields in the next decade. Psychologist Harvey Hornstein replied that postindustrial society was rapidly changing interpersonal relations because of new service industries, larger and more organizations, and more international contacts. As Daniel Bell has observed, "The postindustrial society is essentially a game between persons."[12] There would be a greater need to educate people to deal with other people. Health scientist Barbara Stevens answered that since contemporary disease is increasingly self-inflicted (alcoholism, obesity, tobacco smoking, drug abuse, stress, accidents, neuroses), there would be a greater need to educate people in the attitudes and behaviors to prevent illness and maintain physical and mental well-being.

One month later President Cremin composed a memo to the trustees called "A Vision of Teachers College in the 1980s and How We Might Achieve It." The faculty task force suggestion for a "reconceptualization," new conditions in the external world, a recognition of the quiet changes in the college's own faculty and programs, and a flashing sense of the larger needs for education in the future came together inside Cremin's skull, as in Arthur Koestler's "Eureka" moments of creativity.

With gushing prose—Cremin is normally one of the finest prose writers in the education field—he wrote:

> Education, person-to-person relationships within organizations, and health maintenance and promotion—the three constitute marvelously interrelated and complementary thrusts for Teachers College during the foreseeable future. They all involve kindred processes of teaching and learning, and each is intellectually and academically supportive of the others. . . .
>
> I believe we need an even more inclusive conception of our mission.... The context in which Teachers College will be working . . . will be one of a great national effort to "reindustrialize" or "recapitalize" the United States, and through the United States, the free world. In that effort, it is clear that we shall have to devote as much attention to investment in "human capital" as to investment in new material technologies.
>
> Given that need, and given the three central thrusts of the College's program, it seems to me we might best describe the Teachers College we should like to achieve during the 1980s as "the preeminent international human resource development institution." . . . No other graduate school, and certainly no other college of education, is as well positioned as we are to become "the preeminent international human resource development institution." If we realize the vision, we shall be unique.

The trustees were impressed, especially since 1987 will be the hundredth anniversary of the founding of Teachers College and they hope to mount a Centennial Resources Program. The College Policy Council debated the new vision, then hesitatingly passed a resolution approving its broad outlines on 5 May 1982. Eight days later the Board of Trustees also endorsed the new mission. At TC a new academic strategy was born.

According to Lawrence Cremin, "We shall have to mount a doctoral-training program and a postgraduate continuing education program of unsurpassed quality." He foresees hundreds of professionals of many kinds in mid-careers coming annually to Teachers College, as the Klingenstein Fellows now come from independent schools for an upgrading year at TC. He expects difficulty. "None of the professions we serve has created a systematic program of this sort," he says. Also, the change is "fiscally hazardous" because doctoral education is the most expensive training of all, and Teachers College is financially independent of Columbia University and has no undergraduate base. TC's $25 million endowment is barely adequate. Yet, there is hope that improving America's "human capital" in a variety of educational ways could bring Teachers College resources that training just teachers, principals, and superintendents does not.

Each of these institutions is groping toward an academic strategy—a clearer sense of its educational goals and objectives and better means of allocating resources in order to get there. Small institutions grope differently from large ones. Public colleges and universities move differently from private ones. Specialized colleges move differently from comprehensive ones. But many now feel the urgency of getting their acts together and of being shrewder, more farsighted, more externally aware, and more competitive. An old aphorism maintains, "When it gets dark enough, you can see the stars." The period ahead for higher education is a dark one.

The journey toward academic strategy is thick with nasty dilemmas. There is, for instance, the famous "planner's dilemma." The greater the threats and more rapid the change, the greater the need for planning. Yet the greater the uncertainty about tomorrow, the larger the chance that today's plans will be inadequate or insufficient.[13]

There is also "Hirschman's dilemma." Every organization and institution is "permanently and randomly subject to decline and decay, that is to a gradual loss of rationality, efficiency, and surplus-producing energy, no matter how well the institutional framework within which they function is designed." Yet development, renewal, and growth come mainly from uncovering, stimulating, or enticing people within the organization to bring new fervor and imagination to their tasks.[14] Or "Kaufman's dilemma," which holds that "it is only by a steady accumulation of changes over longer periods that truly extensive transformation will take place." Yet when the environment changes rapidly, slow organizational change usually leads to demise and disaster.[15]

Clearly, the simplistic, highly rational plans and the lethargic, highly political incrementalism of the past are not appropriate for higher education today. Planning has changed dramatically in recent years. The more alert colleges and universities have taken note of the change and have begun flailing delicately to embrace the new form of strategic decision making.

CHAPTER FIVE

Planning: The Turbulent State of the Art

If you do not think about the future, you cannot have one.
JOHN GALSWORTHY

The proper study of mankind has been said to be man. But . . . in large part the proper study of mankind is the science of design.
HERBERT SIMON

Plans are nothing. Planning is everything.
DWIGHT EISENHOWER

WHEN I TOLD A FRIEND in Berkeley, California, that I was conducting a study of management and planning in American higher education, she was incredulous. "Really? I thought that universities didn't believe in management. As for planning in education, is there any?"

As I have suggested, the past few years have brought to higher education a sudden rush of activity in the areas of management and strategic decision making. But her incredulity was proper. Only a few years ago, in the mid-1970s, Michigan's Michael Cohen and Stanford's James March made a curious discovery: "In our interviews, we never heard an administrator deny the importance and virtue of planning within the college. . . . Moreover, it was generally accepted that the plan should be comprehensive. . . . Despite this unanimous acceptance of the importance of planning, we saw little evidence of planning in American colleges and universities." The two scholars did note that "most schools had a physical capital plan of some sort." And they found that "some schools have academic plans," but that "few administrators thought the academic plans useful in decision making." The reason? "They rejected the idea of scarcity. At best they were lists of what the various departments wished Santa Claus would bring them. At worst, they were fantasies."[1] Lewis Mayhew, another higher education analyst, confirmed the fact. "As recently as the

1970s, large universities could be found with no other plans than next year's budget and architectural models of a possible future physical plant."[2]

The absence of strategies for future action has deep roots, of course, in factors endemic in college and university life. But in part university executives have shied away from applying their analytical intellects and powers of persuasion to the design of their institutions' futures because the field of planning itself has been in disarray for at least a dozen years now. The old idea of planning, which is the one most people in academia still carry in their brains, has been largely discredited. The new form of strategic planning is still in its infancy, still struggling to walk steadily and speak clearly.[3] According to management professor Carl Adams, "Planning is at the crossroads. The theory is in a state of disorder, and the practice is rediscovering old insights, refining present constructs, and trying out new twists."

Planning is as old as civilization. The Greeks planned cities; Plato's *Republic* is a plan. The Romans planned, and so did the Chinese in the Han dynasty and the Incas of Peru. Sir Thomas More, John Knox, Diderot, Rousseau, and Jeremy Bentham drew up plans. The *Federalist Papers* are to a considerable extent a planning document. Alexander Hamilton's 1791 "Report on the Subject of Manufactures" to the U.S. Congress was a plan to make the new republic less dependent on foreign countries for manufactured goods; it has recently been called "the most memorable plan for national economic planning that our early history affords."[4] Thomas Jefferson had a strategic plan for the United States when he negotiated the Louisiana Purchase in 1803, and he devised an educational plan for Virginia and later one for the University of Virginia. A good number of these pre-twentieth-century planners were utopians; but as Frank and Fritzie Manuel have reminded us: "Paradoxically, the great utopians have been great realists. They have an extraordinary comprehension of the time and place in which they are writing. . . . They have discovered truths that other men have only vaguely sensed or have refused to recognize. The utopian often emerges as a man with a deeper understanding of the drift of his society than the hard-headed problem-solvers with their noses to the grindstone of the present, blind to potentiality."[5]

National economic planning, which has become popular in the past half-century and was an international rage for the two decades after World War II, is actually quite new. There is not a word about it in all the writings of Marx and Engels. It started chiefly with Lenin's New Economic Plan of 1921, the first Soviet Five-Year Plan in 1928, and the German democratic socialists in the 1920s.[6] National economic planning became a major activity in the United States during the prewar New Deal,[7] although in some ways the most extraordinary planning document of the period was commissioned by Herbert Hoover: the 1933 two-volume federal study *Recent Social Trends in the United States.* In recent decades, Swedish, Cuban, and Communist Chinese planning have captured the attention of socialists and radicals. French "indicative planning," whereby the state leaders developed strategies to transform the sclerotic, provincial French industries into growth-oriented, internationally competitive ones through education, jawboning, inducements, and coercion,[8] has been especially watched. As recently as 1975 the *New York Times* proclaimed the time had come to set up a comprehensive national economic plan for the United States.[9]

Actually the discipline of economics itself, as it has evolved since Adam Smith, assumes that *everyone* is a strategic planner, scanning the environment, possessing internal values and goals, weighing the costs and benefits of numerous alternatives, making choices among various options, and deciding through investments and purchases on a course of action. As Herbert Simon says, "Economics in fact draws a romantic, almost a heroic picture of the human mind. Classical economics depicts mankind, individually and collectively, as solving immensely complex problems of optimizing the allocation of resources."[10]

Most of the young graduates of American university programs in planning between 1950 and 1970, however, did not become economic planners. They went primarily into three areas: city planning, transportation planning, and planning for various state and federal government agencies. And Robert McNamara and the Rand Corporation bred a generation of strategic military planners out of young economists and political scientists. The most famous product of the new strategic defense studies was the planning, programming, and budget (PPB) system, created by Charles Hitch, established in the Department of Defense in 1961, and decreed by President Lyndon Johnson in 1965 to be used by the federal government's civilian agencies as well.[11] Though never fully implemented and often criticized, the linkage of long-range objectives, specific programs, and budgets for them was a brilliant addition to the strategist's arsenal, and one that is suddenly being rediscovered in the 1980s for use in higher education.

PPB actually helped change the course of American planning because it was a crippling blow to the two dominant forms of planning that had been popular in the postwar decades: management science and incrementalism. Management science, useful in other quarters of society and championed by a school of university rationalists, has never been widely embraced by colleges and universities except for limited operations. Incrementalism, however, is the form long used by nearly all campus administrators, with bold exceptions like Robert Hutchins of the University of Chicago, Frank Aydelotte of Swarthmore, and Arthur Morgan of Antioch. And it is still the pattern employed by 90 percent of American academic management.

To this day, most education administrators who are skeptical or cynical about planning have a view of some sort of management science in their heads and say they prefer the "realism" of incrementalism (which many do not perceive as being a form of planning). Confusion is rampant. But then planning itself has been in turmoil.

Management science has two wellsprings, one philosophical, the other empirical.

The philosophical underpinnings were laid by Claude-Henri de Rouvroy, Comte de Saint-Simon (1760–1825), who propounded the vision of technocracy, a society whose main organizations and institutions would be led by educated industrialists, scientists, social engineers, and social science scholars.[12] Rational, farsighted, methodical planning and administration would replace the acquisitive, day-by-day stumbling forward of capitalist politics and administration. The thoughtful administration of things would displace the politico-military rule of people. The latest technical, economic, and social science knowledge would be applied to social affairs by experts in a systematic, reasonable way. France's revolutionary government in 1795 had founded the Ecole Polytechnique in Paris, a special college to train the professional technicians. Saint-Simon was influenced by the new college, next to which he lived for several years; and in turn he influenced many others at the college and elsewhere through his urgings to adopt the technocratic vision.

The empirical godfather, especially for the United States, was Frederick Taylor (1856–1915), the founder of time-studies and efficiency engineering, who not only formulated the principles and methods for the rationalization of industrial work but believed he had discovered the "scientific principles" that would head off most social conflicts.[13] Though American capitalism had a string of executives who gradually brought intelligent management to the corporate sector,[14] it was Frederick Taylor, more than any other person, who disseminated the idea that management could be scientific. High-strung, he hated waste, sloppiness, and rule of thumb. When he walked, Taylor counted his steps to figure out his most efficient stride. Hundreds of companies rearranged their production at the urging of Taylor and his disciples.

During World War II the British and Americans adapted the outlook of Saint-Simon and the techniques of Frederick Taylor to develop operations research, the heavily mathematical search for the most efficient ways to handle scarce resources against the enemy. For example, half a dozen professors attached to the Fighter Command devised systems for selecting the most favorable locations in England for radar installations, fighter plane bases, and maintenance crews, and the most efficient communications networks. They doubled the Royal Air Force's chances of intercepting Nazi bombers.[15] And Americans used operations research to allocate resources, sequence activities, and assure an integrated system of people, supplies, and weapons for any offensive strike. Operations research had a number of stepchildren: Norbert Weiner's cybernetics, Claude Shannon's information theory, Warren McCulloch's neuropsychology, and John von Neumann's game theory and automata theory, which laid the groundwork for the digital or analogical procedures of electronic computers, which were introduced commercially in the mid-1950s.

With the advent of computers in the 1950s, numerous scholars tried to capitalize on the machine's ability to handle vast quantities of data and to analyze complex systems in organizations and societal units. So "systems analysis" was born, as were management information systems and institutional research systems. Such systems might, for instance, diagnose the existing educational system of a community—its schools, colleges, libraries, museums, community centers, adult education facilities, educational toys and games outlets, television programs, and the like—to see where the weaknesses or needs were. Or an information system could monitor quantitatively the productivity and some kinds of measurable quality of various units of an organization.

To enterprising scholars in administration, management, and organization circles, the world suddenly seemed pregnant with the possibilities of more systematic, data-based management. Within four years three new scholarly journals were born: *Operations Research* in 1952, *Management Science* in 1954, and *Administrative Science Quarterly* in 1955. Political scientist Harold Lasswell began talking about the possibility of a whole new academic field called policy sciences, the application of systematic analysis to the formation of major executive decisions and the creation of strategic policies for political, business, military, and nonprofit organizations.[16] By 1960, Herbert Simon confidently proclaimed the coming triumph of managerial science in all sorts of organizations with his book *The New Science of Management Decision*. In 1963 the International Institute for Educational Planning was opened to help nations handle their expanding education systems.

Then, in 1965, two Canadians trained in economics and the new field of computer science, Richard Judy and Jack Levine, wrote a report to the Association of Universities and Colleges of Canada called *A New Tool for*

Educational Administrators, extolling the advantages of this more systematic approach tó university decision making. The book was widely touted
and nudged hundreds of reluctant academic executives to establish offices
of institutional research in the late 1960s. Its message was persuasive. For
decades, universities had been run by intuition, executive preferences,
faculty wish lists, and campus gossip. Now the amazing new computers
could help collect, store, and provide all the necessary information, simulations, and forecasts to make rational, data-grounded decisions. Judy and
Levine warned, "Information deficiency means excess capacity here and
shortages there; it means unsubstantiated budgets; it means emergency
appeals for funds."[17] In the late 1960s Purdue University used systems
analysis for scheduling its courses for students, the University of Illinois
used it for a campus vehicle parking network, and other institutions used it
for such activities as plant maintenance programs and bulk purchasing
arrangements.[18]

Two alert Johns Hopkins political scientists noticed that American
higher education in the 1960s was going through "a shift of managerial
perspective of a very dramatic kind" and, after a quick survey, published
The Managerial Revolution in Higher Education. They wrote, quite percep-
tively:

> In place of the loose, unstructured, and somewhat casual methods of man-
> agement practiced in colleges and universities in the past, we have seen a
> growing commitment to the use of automation in the routine processing of
> administration, an increased resort to data gathering and research as a basis
> for policy making, and an expanding effort to develop objective criteria for
> making decisions on the allocation of resources instead of leaving matters
> entirely to the play of campus pressures or the forces of tradition. . . .
>
> In cumulative effect, these innovations will certainly be regarded by
> historians of higher education as giving an entirely new character to univer-
> sity administration. . . . From now on the government of these institutions
> will reflect a much more conscious effort to plan the course of their develop-
> ment, to relate means to ends, and to seek a maximum return from univer-
> sity resources. . . . A new world of computer management and control lies
> ahead in higher education.[19]

A half-dozen computer modeling schemes were rapidly created for
higher education. Judy and Levine and their systems research group at the
University of Toronto in 1965 composed the CAMPUS model (Comprehensive Analytical Method for Planning in University Systems), which could
calculate the resources necessary—faculty, equipment, space, dollars—for
various enrollment levels. George Weathersby helped develop a "cost
simulation model" for the University of California at Berkeley in 1967–68.

The accounting firm of Peat, Marwick Mitchell and Company, with help from several foundations, put together the SEARCH model (System for Exploring Alternative Resource Commitments in Higher Education), mainly for smaller colleges. In 1969 Stanford, led by William Massy, fresh from MIT with a Ph.D. in management science, started Project INFO to design and test a computerized management information system to manage the university. And in the same year the American Council on Education commissioned a professor of planning to write a book for all campus executives about the new techniques available to them. The author said he was writing to campus administrators to "arouse their interest in the application of systems analysis, simulation, and computer models to university planning." He stated, "Systems planning provides an approach whereby key university problems can be stated in a form appropriate for mathematical analysis."[20]

Management science had moved so fast and become so large—an estimated $1 billion was spent by American organizations on long-range planning, systems and cost-benefit analysis, management information systems, and evaluations in the early 1970s—that one observer said we had entered a new age of "the prince and the pundit." Guy Benveniste cautioned, "The modern Prince, if he is wise, is aware of his increasing ignorance. . . . The social system is so complex and so interdependent that he has to rely heavily on analysis to discover the implications of alternative courses of action." The prince, whether governor, corporate executive, or university president, therefore needs pundits around him or her. "The pundit, the expert, the man or woman of knowledge, is a new breed of advisor. . . . They are concerned with the future, with what is to be done next. They are willing to provide advice; they have a domain of expertise. . . . The canons of their approach include team work, interdisciplinary research, a penchant for problems that can be quantified, and continued long-term involvement in policy, evaluation, and planning."[21]

Yet, despite the momentum and explosion of creativity, the management science approach curiously failed to take hold at most campuses, like blueberries planted in sand. The paraphernalia was there. There were new institutional research people and computer programmers in the administration. Computers seemed to get faster and smaller every year. But while the financial accounts and often the student records went onto computers, the planning and decisions at most institutions in the 1970s remained what they always had been. It almost seemed that the new piles of light green and white computer printouts only reinforced most deans' and presidents' views that management definitely was a matter of experience and "feel," not careful analysis and quantification.

One of the reasons that management science had a hard time taking root in higher education was the thick, deep adherence by campus department chairmen, deans, vice-presidents, and presidents to incrementalism. While management science is rational-economic, incrementalism is partisan-political. Incrementalism holds that the world is not rational and people are often not rational. Life is essentially political. George Santayana once wrote, "The working of a great institution is mainly the result of a vast amount of routine, petty malice, self-interest, carelessness, and sheer mistake. Only a residual fraction is thought." Incrementalists subscribe to that hypothesis. Change comes about, say incrementalists, through hundreds of tiny little steps, no one of which is heavy-footed enough to rock the boat. The steps need to appear as remedies, as small, reasonable responses to great pressures. They need to consider self-interest and people's territories. They often require bargaining. Incrementalism is usually consensual and, in a way, democratic.

The incremental approach to running an organization dodges values and theories because they create cleavages and feuds. Also, there is no one right way; at best there is enlightened partisanship. Organizational change is the art of the possible, often ignoring costs, consequences, and new developments in the environment. The approach also avoids speculations about the long run. To incrementalists no one can predict the future, so forecasting is, as Henry Ford said about history, bunk. As one campus president said to me, "He who lives by the crystal ball often eats broken glass." One job, one year, one election at a time. Besides, planning is too time-consuming. And collecting all that data and doing all those forecasts and simulations is conducive to blizzards of paperwork and is too expensive.

The person who has provided the most articulate explanation of the incremental approach is a squinty-eyed, bearded political economist at Yale, Charles Lindblom. In 1953, he and another political scientist at Yale, Robert Dahl, wrote in a book:

> Patching up an old system is the most rational way to change it, for the patch constitutes about as big a change as one can comprehend at a time. The ultimate result of "patching" is a transformation of the social system. Capitalism was only a series of patches on feudalism. Within limits, all change tends to be incremental in nature. The codes and norms of the operating social organizations defy attempts at abrupt transformations into a brave new world that exists only in the blueprints of social engineers.[22]

In 1954 Lindblom spent a summer doing research at the Rand Corporation in California, at that time a hothouse of new management science, systems analysis, and strategic defense thinking. As Lindblom told me, "I was amazed at the synoptic bias there, and the astonishing confidence those bright young people had in rational, long-range planning and their own ideas of what ought to be done. They seemed oblivious that comprehensive socialist planning had been a failure wherever it was tried, and that we lived in a pluralist democracy with constant compromises, deals, and mutual adjustments." Lindblom decided he had to pinpoint the flaws in management science and explain why incrementalism is as "rational" as the allegedly more rational new systems planning approach.

In 1959 he published an article which has become famous and is much mentioned in planning circles, "The Science of Muddling Through."[23] Lindblom argued that "the rational-comprehensive method" is in fact irrational. "It assumes intellectual capacities that man simply does not possess, and it is even more absurd as an approach to policy when the time and money . . . is limited, as is always the case." Human beings, he said, can't see into the future, can't grasp all the complex variables in any major social decision, and can't imagine all the possibilities for improvement latent in any situation. Also, the notion that one should select values and goals and then seek the best among several courses of action for realizing them is folly. "One chooses among values and among policies at one and the same time," Lindblom contended. Values and means cannot be separated neatly. Also, it is nearly impossible to get agreement on which means is best.

To Lindblom, it was actually the partisan-political approach that was rational. It recognized the realities of human nature, the tremendous difficulties and hostilities to social change, and the way things work in a democratic, free society. Also, he said incrementalism is "a method or system; it is not a failure of method." Indeed, it is "a common method of policy formulation" and "certainly superior to a futile attempt at superhuman comprehensiveness." Muddling through, with bit-by-bit social changes to the existing political situation or organizational predicament, to Lindblom, was the only method that made sense in a democracy and that preserved a modicum of harmony.

Three years later Lindblom sought to reinforce his argument by teaming up with Albert Hirschman, an economic development scholar then at Columbia, to write another article that has been well quoted and influential. This piece sought to demonstrate that recently some social findings were "converging" to bolster their claims for incrementalism.[24] The pair said that there is a kind of rationality and productivity in what appears to be duplication of effort, selfish pork-barrel politics, and disregard for values and the future; that Edmund Burke was right and some things should be left to a "wise and salutory neglect"; that goals keep changing and improvisation is productive; that the pursuit of rational efficiency to cut costs can often be uneconomical and stifling; that most problems are too complex for a single mind to plan through; and that "a rational problem solver wants what he can get and does not try to get what he wants." Above all, they advocated that leaders should "move away from ills rather than toward known objectives."

The Lindblom view of how to proceed in organizations is still very much alive, especially in political organizations and among political practitioners and close-in analysts of the endless trade-offs and power plays of democratic electoral politics. For example, Aaron Wildavsky wrote only a few years ago that "nowhere are plans fulfilled. No one, it turns out, has the knowledge to predict sequences of actions and reactions across the realm of public policy, and no one has the power to compel obedience." He said, "We may be smart but life is smarter." What seems so rational—to define your objectives and pursue them strategically—is really not so, because in reality our "objectives depend on resources" not values, shrewd visions, or even reasoned goals. Yet, despite his deep skepticism about planning and deference to power politics, Wildavsky allowed analytical intellect and foresightful planning in the back door. "Policy analysis," he admitted, "is about calculation and culture. What combination of social interaction and intellectual cognition, planning and politics, leads us to figure out what we should do and how to do it?"[25] Like many others in the past decade, Wildavsky is groping for a new third way.

The search for a third way in planning, one that eschews the arrogant excesses of the highly quantitative management science experts, their disregard for human frailties and politics, and their reams of computer printouts, but also the supine accommodations of the highly political brokers, their neglect of costs, values, and the future, and, their ready excuses about how so-and-so "won't buy it," has become the central quest of planning in the past few years. And it has led directly to the creation of the new field of strategic planning.

Strategic planning attempts to use the best wisdom of both approaches; it tries to encompass both the rational-economic and the partisan-political. As one practicing education planner has written, "A new approach to policy formulation is needed in American education that takes into consideration the constraints that affect the legitimacy and effectiveness of decision strategies and is sensitive to inevitable value trade-offs. Policy makers must attempt both to make the right decision and to make the decision right."[26]

The struggle for a new third way in planning has been accelerated by the barrages of criticisms that have been aimed at both management science and incrementalism.

To those who had held fast to the dogmas of management science, critics have pointed out the wide gaps between planning and implementation. Thousands of well-drawn plans sit gathering dust particles on shelves all over America's cities, government agencies, corporate headquarters, and colleges.[27] Howell Baum, a professor of community planning at the University of Maryland, says that is so because "most planners have seen their job as one of developing logical, beautiful schemes. They tend to overlook people's egos, politics, and traditions, and the need to have their plans enacted. But the new wave of planners is more interested in getting good things done than in merely conceiving of them."

Others like Peter Drucker have reminded the systems analysis protagonists of the critical role of entrepreneurship. Ideas need champions, people who carry ideas into history. Much of the change in history comes from dynamic, charismatic, or visionary leaders, as Joseph Schumpeter said.[28] But administrative science often confuses technical competence with leadership. The best-laid plans turn to damp and shadows without entrepreneurial acuity. Business historian Alfred Chandler, Jr., recounts that "at DuPont, General Motors, and Jersey Standard, the initial awareness of the structural inadequacies caused by the new complexity came from executives close to top management, but who were not themselves in a position to make organizational changes. In all three, the president gave no encouragement to the proposers of change. . . . In all three companies, it took a sizable crisis to bring action. Yet all three presidents had received proposals for reorganization before the crisis made their usefulness apparent."[29] The Soviet Union might not exist today if Lenin's vigorous, ruthless dedication had not championed the plans of a communist society. General Motors might have been a smaller, different company without Alfred P. Sloan.[30]

Management scientists have been told that they use a mechanical model that does not fit reality. That is, they usually propose to take an organization from an undesirable steady state to a more desirable steady state. But life is organic, continuous, and ever-shifting, not a freight train of steady states. And since life is Darwinian, the model of change must be a biological one, of a crab in a tidal pool. Continuous, flexible planning, not mathematical plans in books, is what is needed, say these critics.[31] Also, the mechanical model is internally driven, disregarding external factors. Yet evidence mounts that organizations are shaped by outside forces and by their markets at least as much as by internal determinations.[32] As one scholar put it, "This is an era of ecology. . . . We can no longer profitably discuss our world and its future in simple linear terms . . . for the evidence all around us is of multi-dimensional, complex interactions."[33]

Too often those devoted to quantitative planning and modeling forget the human factor, critics charge. They tend to ignore people, as Jane Jacobs once pungently reminded methodical city planners and their government sponsors. They overlook the intricate social webs people weave to protect themselves against hurt, neglect, and loneliness.

James March, one of the nation's leading organization psychologists, told a group in Washington, D.C., in March 1982 that scientific planners tend to underplay the emotional side of organization behavior, and all the preening and protecting and strutting and undercutting that goes on every day. He believes ritual, myth, and habit are terribly important in the way organizations work. "Decision making is an arena for symbolic as well as rational action," he claims. "Meaning controls most actions, and meaning seldom comes from information, computers, and analysis." He reports that there are growing indications from scattered research that gossip is as influential in executive decisions as data. And in one of his own studies he found that many managers who collect lots of information do so for "ritualistic assurance" and "representation of competence and reaffirmation of social virtue" more than for farsighted management. The information collected often has "little decision relevance."[34] Organizations, he reminds management scientists, are also theaters; many decisions are symbolic acts, dramatic gestures, or ritualistic cover-ups.

Related to March's strictures are the criticisms of journalists and literary persons against strategies based largely on quantifiable knowledge. One valiant economist, Benjamin Ward, for example, has written of the critical importance of "storytelling" in economics, organizations, and social actions. Though storytelling is viewed by most social scientists as a "prescientific remnant," it adds something indispensable to our view of reality. Formal, statistical systems can provide a greater sense of the overall picture; but, Ward says, "There are always unique features to an economic event which make its representativeness somewhat dubious." Storytelling supplies the unique to complement the general condition supplied by numerical analysis. Even the language of storytelling offers a sense of the peculiar, a feeling for the richly complex, a recognition of the role of character and the special interplay within one group of people, an inkling of the crocodiles beneath the surface of any firm's apparent situation or immediate problem.[35] Storytelling is the microscope that teams up with the telescope. To know about Walden Pond is not basic to hydrography, but it is not insignificant either. Management scientists, like most social scientists, tend to pass over the unique and the special, what Ward calls the "gentlemen's agreement to ignore interpersonal comparisons." Yet each college and university has a unique history, collection of persons, and set of hopes.

Then there is the dismal record of forecasting, on which much of management science stands. Economists have consistently failed to call the turns in the economy; economist Robert Solow has admitted that their "predictions are often wrong." Not one economist predicted the condition known as "stagflation." Demographic forecasts too have been unpredictable. Kenneth Boulding wrote a few years ago that "in the United States we had a period of high fertility (1947–61) which was quite unpredicted; now we are in a phase of low fertility which was equally unpredicted." Several studies have found that judgmental forecasts perform as well as econometric ones. Futurists like Herman Kahn failed to predict the large increase of women in the U.S. work force, the energy crisis of 1973–74, and the rise of the Middle East as a tempestuous area. And one analyst who has examined the evidence finds, "Political forecasting . . . is the weakest link in the whole range of forecasting trends."[36] Moreover, attempts to tune the forecasting models more finely run smack into the paradox that Tjalling Koopmans, who won the Nobel Prize for economics in 1975, discovered. Beyond a point, the introduction of more variables and added complexity actually reduces the reliability of econometric forecasts. Less is more.

Last, management scientists and comprehensive planners have had to endure the stings of a large number of cynical dart-throwers. One noted, "After successive disasters of comprehensive planning in other areas in which it has been applied, it is somewhat peculiar to see these techniques optimistically and unselfcritically grasped in education policy-making."[37] Ohio State's president Harold Enarson grumbled in print, "Planning . . . is definitely art, but mostly bad art." He added, "The value of a truly educated person is no more to be weighed and measured than is a sonnet or a smile."[38] A third commentator thought that long-range planning was America's "new religion," or worse, a "contemporary astrology of futurism," where "counting replaces reality." Worse, scientific management, which claims to help reduce costs, is actually adding to costs and robbing money from other programs: "In most states it is very probable that the new costs of data manipulation have been met largely by reducing the support of the activities which are measured."[39]

The incremental approach has also had its bevy of critics, many of whom feel it is a form of tiptoeing naked and buttocks-first into history. Several have given the U.S. intervention in Vietnam as an example of the results of "muddling through." A few are now beginning to point to the inability of American leadership—in any area of society—to come to grips with the massive, impending crisis in the Social Security System, despite the known actuarial and financial realities, as an example of the weakness of incrementalism and its accommodations. And a growing number in higher education worry about campuses trying to "muddle through" the 1980s.

Charles Lindblom admitted to me, "There is no question that incrementalism has shortcomings. It is much less valid in times of war, serious crises, and radical change. And its small-scale rationality can sometimes add up to large-scale irrationality. But compared to the dangers of centralized planning, it is still preferable, especially if we can institute *speedy* incrementalism, that is, lots of little changes in a relatively short time."

Incrementalism depends on bargaining. But the critics charge that bargains are more easily made in good times and in situations where there is something extra to divide up or "sweeten the pot." It is far more difficult to bargain over scarcity or where to retrench. In times of scarcity hard choices, priorities, and courage are needed because parties are unyielding and deals get extremely hard to arrange. Also, bargaining usually results in drift and purposelessness, and in dangerous ends which no one intended or examined. Charles Schultze says, "It is . . . naive to think that in areas of tremendous complexity, the pure bargaining process can translate a loosely developed set of general values into meaningful operational objectives. While it is often strategically and tactically important for participants in the bargaining process to conceal their objectives from their adversaries, it hardly behooves them to conceal them from themselves. Ends, as well as means, need systematic examination and analysis."[40]

To some critics incrementalists are inconsistent and perhaps upside-down in their approach. Many managers and political leaders will use long-range planning for, say, their own political careers, specific product introductions, or foreign policy but not for energy policy, financial solvency, or allocation of resources. Or an incrementalist will rant against planning in important areas, then demand that his university's football coach have better strategies and game plans. David Ewing claims that at its best football can be an exemplar for planners:

> In football, a key step in the game is taken before the whistle is ever blown. It comes when the coaches review the game films of the coming opponent and the condition of their own team, and then talk with the players about strategy for the forthcoming contest. What kind of game should they expect? How should they try to play it? . . . Will it be a wide-open, high-scoring game from the start, with the possibility of its being won early on some "long bombs"? Are the opponent's conventional defenses to be expected, or some-

thing new in the way of blitzing the passer or position-jumping? The success with which coaches and players answer these questions has no small part to play in how the team performs during the game.

   Similarly, in planning it is helpful to know what kind of action to expect when the work gets under way.[41]

Though incrementalists tend to downplay the use of models, proponents of computer models claim that models provide information that policymakers need and can get no other way. Without models, incrementalists fall into what Harold Enarson once called "the beagle fallacy." Beagles have a superb nose but poor eyesight, and they will often miss a rabbit that is staring at them. Jan Tinbergen says that while "model building has become a vogue," the best new models provide something quite valuable. "Precise knowledge about interrelationships can be obtained only by the technique of models."[42] Not only do incrementalists miss the interrelationships of a problem and fail to weigh adequately the likely consequences of their decisions, their keen noses often prompt them to let their eyes go unused. Life is flux, yet we need to stop it and see it at rest momentarily to get a picture of it. This is what models, like ancient myths, do, helping us to see our condition amidst the rush and constant flow. As Erich Jantsch says, "Both models and myths are man-made stilts with the help of which we may temporarily lift ourselves out of the stream of evolution . . . and orient ourselves as to which direction to take."[43]

Critics also charge that incrementalists are deficient in imagination. For incrementalists, what is, is real. They are loathe to imagine alternatives, to see possibilities, to envision things as different from the way they presently are. They are prosaic, dull tinkerers who nervously inch their way, wanting what they believe they can get rather than attempting to get what they want and need. Philosopher-scientist Michael Polanyi, for example, has argued that each of us has within us a shaping and integrating force he calls "tacit power," the ability to perceive, intuit, discover, invent. To him, life is potential as well as actual. Tacit power, he says, is "an imaginative thrust toward discovering these potentialities,"[44] and the source of all creativity. Like beautifully muscled illiterates, incrementalists, it is alleged, have overdeveloped powers of political calculation and underdeveloped powers of social imagination.

There are several other criticisms of incrementalism. One is that incrementalists tend to be nonintellectual in that they are so caught up in the political gamesmanship in their organizations they fail to use much of the best research from social science and history that pertains to their decisions. One team of investigators found that "there is little evidence to indicate that government planning offices have succeeded in linking social research and decision making," even though federal expenditures for applied social research have grown considerably since the early 1960s. In education too, "applied research . . . has not significantly increased the objective information base for decisions."[45]

Herbert Simon has charged in a commanding article: "We do not, in our colleges today, make use of *any* learning principles in a considered, systematic, professional way. We do not design the college as a learning environment. We do not give anyone a specific responsibility for bringing to the college the best available professional and scientific knowledge for designing that environment. We are a community of scholars, of amateur teachers."[46] Incrementalism, as it is widely practiced in government and higher education circles, is usually less sensitive to new evidence and research than the more scientific management practiced by many business organizations.

Another criticism flows from the flood of books on Japanese management, many of which purport that Japanese industry has been very successful in recent years because of its rapid assimilation of contemporary American management and long-range planning scholarship and techniques. American incrementalists are focused on the annual profit sheets, it is said, while many Japanese firms analyze, prepare for tomorrow, and plan and conduct research to make profits for the long term.

But perhaps the most telling criticism of all is that incrementalism, with its gradualist horse trading and little adjustments here and there, is unsuited for a period of drastic change and fiercer competition. Even Charles Lindblom acknowledges that his inherently conservative approach may be flawed in times of serious trouble, when rapid action and nimble changes of direction are called for. Both the U.S. economy and higher education have to be far more competitive than they were in the 1950s and 1960s. Cunning, farsightedness, and thoughtful strategies, say the critics, are what is now needed, not wheeler-dealer pragmatism—less Lyndon Johnson and more Ulysses. As one sociologist of education observed: "The dominant pattern of decision making in education is by incremental change. [This] seems to be a common pattern in most organizations, but in education it is dominant. [But this] does not suit a rapidly changing and demanding environment. . . . If education is to meet successfully its many demanding tasks and missions, it will have to find new and more dynamic decision strategies."[47]

The task for the advocates of planning was clear. Sociologist Amitai Etzioni saw it early on: "What is needed . . . is a strategy that is less exacting than the rationalistic one, but not as constricting in its perspective as the incremental approach; not as utopian as rationalism, but not as conservative as incrementalism; not so unrealistic a model that it cannot be followed, but not one that legitimizes myopic, self-oriented, non-innovative decision making."[48]

Political scientist Richard Neustadt, a hard-nosed incrementalist who has served as part-time adviser to Democratic presidents, also sees the need for leaning more toward a third way:

> "Backward mapping," as some of my colleagues call it, is one method . . . to make a start on estimating what if any gap exists between the way an institution works, on average, and the way it would have to work in order to contribute to a given outcome. . . . Inching forward is what most people do: with some sort of an aim in mind one thinks about the obstacles, especially those nearest, pondering one's resources for getting over, under, or around them, formulates a first step, tries it, looks and listens, reassesses, and then formulates another step (or maybe another aim).
>
> Not unreasonably, this is how most bureaucrats and politicians in our public life—and three Presidents that I myself have seen—appear to plan. . . It is a far cry from mapping backward. But I often urge on students headed toward the public sector that when they get into government they try to mix the two, working backward every now and then, enough to notice where forward motion takes them.[49]

The third way, strategic planning, slowly emerged, not surprisingly, from the world of business. Managerial science had roots in military planning, where political and consensual considerations could be largely dismissed and rational schemes ordered. Incremental "muddling through" had its roots in democratic politics, where bargaining was essential and rational, and long-range planning was extremely difficult. But business organizations operate in both the rational-economic world and the partisan-political world. And as corporations have become more internationally competitive, oriented to long-run growth, politically regulated, and aware of the psychological and political needs of their increasingly white-collar and professional work force, they have had to become more aware of persuasive incrementalism as well as bottom-line strategies. On the other hand, governments and quasi-political nonprofit organizations, pressed increasingly to come to grips with financial realities, huge deficits, and ethical issues raised by environmentalists, religious groups, and radical reformers, have had to take larger cognizance of the rational-economic side of their organizational lives. Thus, a new convergence is going on in the field of planning.

The convergence is being driven by another force: the growing tension between productive performance in large organizations and long-term viability of the same organizations. To achieve their goals economically and efficiently, many organizations, from trade unions to universities, have united and become larger. They try to show excellent results or profits each year. But as they get bigger, they become more decentralized, more bureaucratic, and more variegated in mission. The Wharton School may or may not subscribe to the overall style and goals of the Ivy League University of Pennsylvania of which it is a part. Each unit has its own special objectives, its own demands to produce annually. And in each unit bureaucrats have their special Dostoevskian propensities. But organizations need to change continually to pull together as a recognizable entity, to respond quickly and flexibly to new markets, new circumstances, new environmental conditions. They need to get ready for the future, develop strategies against aggressive new competitors, and plan how to best take advantage of emerging opportunities.

In sum, organizations have *both* localized, short-term, and bottom-line demands and all-organization, long-term, and investment-strategies-for-the-future demands. They must live for the familiar today, yet also must be forever looking out for how to live in a very different tomorrow.

This tension between today's bottom line and the long-term plans for a better tomorrow has crowded organizations into a middle area. Myopic, cautious organizations, whether auto manufacturers or colleges, are becoming more farsighted and strategic. Visionary organizations, whether transportation agencies or genetic engineering firms, are becoming more immediately productive and politically astute. Politics and planning, productivity and vision are converging. Strategic decision making, as some business firms have tried to practice it, is therefore capturing attention as something nearly all bodies now need to learn.

The scholar who first drew attention to the quiet, little-known struggles of numerous leading corporations to deal strategically with their product lines, organizational structure, finances, and growth-and-retrenchment cycles was Alfred Chandler, Jr., a business historian at MIT, and later at the Johns Hopkins University and at Harvard Business School. His 1962 study *Strategy and Structure: Chapters in the History of Business Enterprise* set out to investigate how business administration has changed over the years and stumbled on the fact that many corporations had been wrestling with strategies for what they wanted to accomplish and how they planned to get there. The company structures were in large part determined by these executive strategies.

The book, which contains superbly detailed storytelling, went through several printings. And in the 1960s—at exactly the same time the new PPB system was receiving fascinated study—the idea of strategic direction of an organization, like strategic direction of an invading military unit, began to seize the attention of both practicing executives and business scholars. Chandler's volume also jostled both management scientists and incremental muddlers who read it from their narrow paths. In a recent book on "strategic management," the editors write in their introduction, "Chandler contributed the basic concept of strategy, at least to academe, and from his seminal work has sprung much of the research reported and discussed in this volume."[50] In 1965 two other scholars, H. Igor Ansoff and Kenneth Andrews, sought to expand and refine the concept of strategy,[51] one year after Daniel Bell had tried to codify the available modes of predicting the future. Says Bell, "This is an era in which society has become 'future-oriented' in all its dimensions. A government has to anticipate future problems; an enterprise has to plan for future needs; an individual has to think of long-range career choices." He added, "A future-oriented society necessarily commits itself more and more to the idea of planning." But he noted, "Surprisingly, there are few studies extant of the planning process."[52]

Shortly after Bell wrote the last sentence, there was an explosion of interest—among corporations, military bodies, government agencies, and business schools—in the planning process, especially in a process that was neither rigidly remote like management science nor blindly cozy like incrementalism. General Electric introduced formal strategic planning in 1970; Richard Cyert attempted it at Carnegie-Mellon University; Peter Drucker, a former economic journalist, introduced it to the public with his best-selling books; and dozens of scholars sought to figure out how strategic planning was working, how it conceivably could work, and how it should work. Professors such as Henry Mintzberg and James Brian Quinn contributed first-rate reports on how strategic planning was actually being introduced,[53] while others reported on how not to implement it.[54] Business leaders and academics collaborated on making analyses of the external environment and the changing markets a crucial part of internal policy-making.

Occasionally there have been mind-stretching donations to the subject: the advertising world's microscopic dissection of the market, Graham Allison's marvelous study of decision making,[55] Michael Porter's innovative analysis of competitive strategies,[56] and the deft invasions of Japanese business into sections of the American market through carefully contrived strategies. These inevitably caused a stir and new debates and efforts. Once in a while a rather good state-of-the-art report about strategic planning has also appeared, such as those of David Ewing and that of William King and David Cleland.[57] Though several earnest attempts have been made,[58] the books and articles on strategic planning for higher education have been regarded by most educators as not quite what they feel they require.

Today, after 15 years of searching and experimentation, the outlines, if not the precise details, of strategic decision making are clear. It now has its parameters and its basic requirements. Ways of bringing planning and organizational politics together and methods for uniting strategy formulation and strategy implementation are being constructed, though the techniques are still crude. There is fairly solid evidence about what won't work, which means there is a checklist of no-nos and must-haves.

The third way—strategic planning—could not have been devised at a better time for American higher education. Colleges and universities across the land are realizing that they must manage themselves as most other organizations in society do; they are different and special but not outside the organizational world. Money, markets, competitors, and external forces matter as well as traditions, academic freedom, devotion to ideas, and internal preferences. Students are better off if they are pointed to a probable future as well as to the intellectual and artistic past. Design is better than drift. Thought is preferable to squabbling. Academic creativity and freedom need a solid tomorrow as much as a defiant today.

The time has arrived for college and university leaders to pick up management's new tools and use them.

PART II

CHAPTER SIX

Before Planning: Information, Quality, People

The tragedy of the world is that those who are imaginative have but slight experience, and those who are experienced have feeble imaginations. Fools act on imagination without experience. Pedants act on knowledge without imagination. The task of the university is to weld together imagination and experience.
ALFRED NORTH WHITEHEAD

The sine qua non *of innovative policy is controversy.*
RICHARD NEUSTADT

Some problems are so difficult they can't be solved in a million years—unless someone thinks about them for five minutes.
H. L. MENCKEN

GIVEN A DECLINING NUMBER of students, the acute financial situation, intensifying competition, and the need for changes in the content, distribution, and style of delivery of the academic offerings, what should a college do?

For any college or university that hopes to survive in the period ahead and perhaps emerge a bit stronger and better, there appears to be one overriding answer—the answer that the more alert and forward-looking institutions have already begun to give. Colleges need to strengthen their managements and shape academic strategies for themselves.

Each institution needs to see itself as if for the first time and ask, What business are we really in? Of the 3,100 colleges, universities, technical institutes, seminaries, and two-year community colleges, what special role do we play in America's higher education network? What attractive and important set of services does our institution provide that people cannot obtain elsewhere better, faster, or cheaper? What comparative advantages do we have over approximately similar places? What academic fields and college services will be most needed by the country and our region in the next decade? With our traditions, endowment, location, and collection of faculty and administrators, what should our campus be building toward? What should our college aspire to be 10 years from now? Clearly, an academic strategy is imperative.

But before an institution begins to shape an academic strategy for itself, it should be sure that it is well managed. It needs to tighten up before it tries to reach out and move ahead. It needs to be certain it has adequate information on which to base decisions. It needs to be sure that there is quality in the teaching, research, and service it is currently providing. And an institution needs to have the best people it can possibly get to carry out its intentions. No baseball team, army, business firm, or university can succeed, no matter how devoted to strategy, without adequate data; without high-quality equipment, programs, and performance; and without talented, dedicated personnel.

I once called on an elderly, well-known planner who had recently retired for the third time. I asked him what wisdom he had to impart after his lifetime of disappointments and achievements. He said, "A thousand little things. A thousand little things. Forget the grand plan. Of course, you must have a direction, but concentrate on the details. Make sure your airplane is in excellent shape before you take off into the sunrise. I've seen too many great plans crash because organizations didn't straighten out the details of their operation first."

Just as a university can be plodding and contentious, it can be ambitious beyond its means or capability. A college may not be ready to plan. First things first. Before strategic planning, it is wise to concentrate on good management.

College and university management, however, is a peculiar activity. Though it has elements of business management, political management, even military management, it is unique. It is closer to managing a hospital or research laboratory than to managing a nail factory or a bank. What I call "management" in higher education actually has four main components, and management unfortunately is also one of the components. The four parts cannot be neatly separated but they are somewhat distinct.

1. *Administration.* In the United States college presidents and their aides are known as "the administration." They are expected to *minister* to the needs of the faculty and students, providing scientific equipment, residence halls, records of students' progress, sports and recreation programs, paychecks for the faculty and staff, and a suitable library. Raising funds is part of administration; so is getting the mail in and out.

Administration is the provisioning and coordinating of activities for the principals of the campus: the professors, key staff, and students. It is vitally important, and all presidents or chancellors spend at least half their time on administration. Some unwisely spend nine-tenths of their time on it. Institutions are frequently regarded as "good" if their administration is excellent: things run smoothly; the horticulture and buildings are attractive; the admissions program is aggressive but high-toned; the faculty are energetic, dutiful, and approachable; the library is well organized and the staff is helpful; the courses are well scheduled; the alumni program is first-rate; faculty complaints or suggestions are handled promptly, courteously, and appreciatively. Well-administered places are seen as efficient campuses, where limited funds are spent with maximum effect and with a taste and manner befitting a university that espouses the best in thought, art, and sensibility.

This is the area for attention to "a thousand little things," and campuses can take a great leap forward by doing nothing more than improving the administration of their current operations. One genius at administration was Henry Wriston, the president of Lawrence College and then Brown University. His taste, devotion to quality, and concern for people led him to pay close attention to everything from the quality of food in the student cafeteria to the chemistry department's latest request for new equipment. His book *Academic Procession* is a diamond mine of sage advice to college administrators. Wriston believed, "Nothing that touches the life of a faculty or student should be alien to the interest or thought of the president. . . . Good administration facilitates good education."[1]

2. *Management.* It is not enough to see that the academic machine is well oiled, synchronized, and responsive, however, because the world changes as we walk on it. New threats pop up. New opportunities for growth or funding appear. Advances in technology compel changes in information handling and delivery. Society becomes more scientific, religious, or rebellious. Governments become more friendly or more suspicious toward higher learning. Departments stumble downhill in quality and programs become outmoded. New competition elbows in, pulling in a portion of an institution's students. Students plead for relevance and courses that are useful; parents and employers then demand a return to basics and courses that teach young persons to write, think, speak, and calculate well.

A university president, therefore, must also be a manager of change, a navigator who steers his or her institution through the treacherous channels of constant transformation. He or she needs to ask about each program every year, "Is this still worth doing?" and "What should we be doing now about higher education's likely developments?" He or she needs to ask about tomorrow's academic necessities as well as today's leaky faucets.

While administration sees that things are done right, management sees that the right things are done. While administration seeks for efficiency in the present structure, management strives for effectiveness through an improved structure. As management, the president, his or her aides, and the deans must foresee the future and the best of the new in order to bend the organization, in cooperation with leading faculty members, in the right direction. Management is the entrepreneurial element. It works to make things better and appropriately different. It seeks to raise productivity and keep the university at the cutting edge of new knowledge and new forms and content of academic service.

Most important of all, the president must give direction to the college and devise the strategies, make the hard decisions, and allocate the resources that will support movement in that direction. And as support for the direction, the president should play a direct part in selecting the key people for the institution and monitoring the performance of the various units.

Naturally, this cannot be done alone. In an organization with many highly educated professionals with considerable expertise of their own, the president needs to encourage and help develop management skills throughout the institution, strengthen the deans and department chairmen, and help each professional be his or her own planner and innovator. As one study found, "Innovative organizations are those which have mechanisms to infuse and stimulate ideas."[2] This means support in keeping up with the best through literature, visiting lecturers, conferences, and special trips. It means periodic retreats to evaluate, plan, and agree on strategies. And it means encouragement for a rapid flow of ideas up and down the organization. In academically strong universities, the faculty will usually be innovative and entrepreneurial. In weaker institutions, presidential coaching is imperative.

Management is the most neglected part of the contemporary college and university presidency. It is also the most neglected part of the contemporary provost's or academic vice-president's role, the deans' roles, and the roles of the department chairmen. Department chairmen have a special difficulty with management because they often believe they are spokesmen for their colleagues in the department to the deans and presidents "upstairs" rather than managers of their departments' futures, innovativeness, and quality. Although the picture is changing fast, few presidents spend enough time on this part of their task; some spend almost no time here. One business executive told Dartmouth's James Brian Quinn, "If I'm not two or three years ahead of my organization, I'm not doing my job"; and others agreed.[3] More college presidents need to think like that and double or triple their attention and energy to managing the organization's future, particularly in these hazardous times.

Some observers contend that every campus president has his or her own interests and style and must be allowed to stress what he or she feels most comfortable with. Therefore, if some campus leader wants to administer and govern but not manage or lead, that is up to him or her. This is very dangerous thinking, for it contends that stasis and drift are acceptable in a time of turbulent external change; it implies that the future will take care of itself; and it suggests that quality education and long-term excellence are reached by serendipity. Presidents should, and do, stress those components of their position that fit their experience, interests, and temperaments. But they cannot afford to neglect any of the four parts, least of all management, without damaging the institution. Peter Drucker believes that "managing the service institution is likely to be the frontier of management for the rest of this century."[4] Managing a university is certainly tough work. And it is a frontier the exact patterns of which are still being sculpted. But it is a task no president can evade with the limp contention that it doesn't fit his or her personality.

3. *Leadership.* At any college or university, spirits will flag. At some campuses the mood is one of tiredness and complaint. As Hirschman and other investigators have reminded us, people and organizations tend to run down. Presidents tend to wear out too. Henry Wriston claims, "Boredom is the bane of administration. . . . I have known more presidents to suffer from that administrative disease than any other."[5] Duty replaces entrepreneurship; what Herbert Simon calls "satisficing" replaces improvements and the quest for something finer; mere routine seems acceptable. So every institution needs a continuous stream of leadership to refresh itself, to remind itself of its goals and expressed intentions. Colleges, like cars, need to have their batteries recharged.

A president should supply the emotional injections that jolt faculty, students, and staff out of their tendencies to coast. He or she needs to hold out visions of potentialities and worthy objectives that motivate others to perform beyond the ordinary. Leadership is the poetic part of the presidency. It sweeps listeners and participants up into the nobility of intellectual and artistic adventures and the urgency of thinking well and feeling deeply about the critical issues of our time. Sometimes presidents don't quite have it: they are good administrators, managers, and governors of their republics of scholars, but poor writers and speakers, with tongues of felt. Or they may have had it early in their incumbencies, but have now lost it. Then, an academic vice-president or the chairman of the board or a few devoted members of the faculty will need to jump in to inject the spiritual force and reveal the dream in people's pockets.

In politics, John F. Kennedy provided leadership as Harry Truman and Dwight Eisenhower did not. In scholarship, Professor Mark Van Doren of Columbia stimulated scholars and furnished leadership for liberal education as others could not.[6] The University of Chicago's Robert Hutchins and Lawrence Cremin of Columbia's Teachers College are leaders, one almost spiritual about the great books and pure contemplation, the other dazzlingly intellectual about the new tasks of teaching and schools in an electronic age. A particularly winning example is that of Howard Lowry, who, as president of Ohio's Wooster College (1944–67), year after year through talks, baccalaureate speeches, articles, and addresses, gave fresh meaning to the purposes of higher education in a Christian setting.[7] The Reverend Theodore Hesburgh, a president for 30 years, has wedded moral values to intellect for many at the University of Notre Dame. Recently Father Hesburgh said, "Higher education and every other enterprise moves forward when there is good leadership; otherwise it stagnates. We need people with vision, *élan, geist,* people who have standards and a certain toughness. . . . Of course you need money. But if you have money and no vision, you just squander it."[8]

Leadership is that intangible ability to touch people's nerve endings and cause them to act. It is what a university president must provide, quietly or with fire in his breath, if he is to dignify the enterprise, rouse the disparate faculty and staff into a united drive toward excellence, and defend the work of higher education with cogency and ardor against unknowing or unappreciative assailants.

4. *Governance.* One thing that distinguishes the management of a college or university is that, unlike a business, military, or religious organization, it is a republic of sorts. That is, the faculty are politically partners in the management of the vital heart of the enterprise, its academic portion. Campuses usually have faculty senates. Some have all-college or all-university senates, which include students, staff, and even employees. These more inclusive bodies derive from the 1960s, when there was a passion for participatory democracy with direct rule by "the people." But a majority have already become vestigial since their purpose approximates that of the college's management but they lack an appropriate staff such as the president has.

A president absolutely must consult with, seek advice from, and be guided by his or her professors in anything pertaining to academic matters. And the president should also consult on matters that touch on the central teaching and research activities, from admissions policy to industrial grants for the university. Just as a hospital administrator should not make medical policy without counsel and approval from most of the chief resident physicians, so a college president must seek the concurrence of his or her professional colleagues. At the same time the president, or the dean of a college, must remember that he or she is solely responsible for the quality of the unit. So the final word in a contested policy is with the president or dean, or in some cases with the trustees.

Governance today is tricky. The old faculty senates are now ragged, poorly attended oratorical bodies in most cases. At some campuses, senior scholars have been forming new faculty councils to provide wiser, speedier consultation with the president, provost, and deans than the more inclusive, theatrical, and debate-oriented senates or all-college assemblies. At a growing number of campuses, presidents have recently forged a new kind of governance mechanism that contains representatives of the faculty, administrators, and perhaps students to help insure prompt deliberations and give wise advice on important matters. This new mechanism has the special virtue of tying academic issues to finances and long-range plans, rather than raising academic issues in splendid theoretical isolation.

Whatever the means, campus management must be tied somehow to acceptable governance procedures. A university is a quasi-political body. Faculties have been known to vote, like parliaments, no confidence in their president. The balance of power is shifting toward the president. Faculties are becoming more interested in reviewing, criticizing, and modifying policy than in making policy. But in a knowledge organization, where many faculty members often have more expertise in some areas than their management, the academic executives should not fail to share in some locally appropriate way the major decisions about academic matters.

These four components of academic management are usually interwoven. But academic executives on any campus need to keep each of the four in mind, with special attention in the coming years to the most neglected component: management. A person worth studying because he took a pretentious, provincial, religious college, shook it up, and launched it on its way to being one of the world's great universities, is Charles Eliot, president of Harvard from 1869 to 1909. Here is how two sociologists summarize his blending of administration, management, and governance:

> More and more Americans were going to Europe to study. A large number of those were attending the new German universities . . . in which it was possible to study any of a number of new sciences. In other words, American colleges were not competing effectively. . . .
>
> At this time Harvard had not suffered as much as other New England colleges; its enrollments were keeping pace with the growth of population.

The selection of Charles Eliot, the first president who was not a clergyman, represented a sharp break with the past. He had studied science and, at the time of his selection, was teaching chemistry at a newly founded college, Massachusetts Institute of Technology. Eliot was young, only 35 at the time. . . .

Within the first two years Eliot introduced a series of changes. . . . He doubled the size of the faculty, hiring mostly young men trained in the new academic disciplines. Instead of relying on the existing faculty to make recommendations, Eliot went out of his way to secure men with different intellectual perspectives. He introduced not only men of the new sciences but also men of the new social sciences such as economics.

The power structure was altered in several ways by Eliot. He created the new position of dean and delegated considerable authority to him. Eliot attended faculty meetings and increased the number of these meetings, with many complaints being registered by the old faculty. If Eliot met resistance to a particular idea, he would let the matter rest and bring it up at a later date. In these meetings, the majority vote counted. Thus there was a decentralization of decision making.

A number of student regulations were eliminated; the rules manual was reduced from 40 pages to five. Compulsory chapel was eliminated. Perhaps the most dramatic change was the abolition of the fixed curriculum instruction. Gradually the concept of electives was introduced into American education.[9]

As for leadership, James Ford Rhodes, a contemporary of Eliot who wrote a seven-volume history of nineteenth-century America, said in 1902, "For 12 years past no public addresses, save those of the Presidents of the United States themselves, have been so widely read throughout the country as have those of President Eliot."[10]

What is worth noting is that along with an academic strategy to turn Harvard from a small classical college into a larger university which conducted forefront scholarship in all the major disciplines of the period and provided training for each of society's leading professions, Eliot concentrated on information, quality, and people. He personally recruited deans and young faculty members in the new fields. He changed the rules of student life, reorganized the curriculum, and, by such inventions as the sabbatical leave, raised teaching quality by forcing professors to renew themselves by travel, talks with distant scholars, research, and wider reading. And his speeches and papers reveal the attention he paid to accurate, up-to-date information on which to base his decisions.

Eliot was not a pleasant person. He fought the spread of public higher education, wanted to incarcerate prostitutes, and had a grim earnestness and lack of human sympathy behind his high purpose. He was blunt and to the point, which he called "the small virtue in me to speak plainly." And he was moralistic and Victorian. He once said, "I made a bad speech last night. I was garrulous and diffuse. In fact I was intoxicated. I had taken a cup of coffee."[11] Eliot was Alfred P. Sloan, Lenin, John Dewey, and John Silber (the current president of Boston University) rolled into one. But he was ahead of his organization, in tune with his times, courageous, daring, deferential to faculty, and strategic in his moves.

Before any college or university executives begin to shape an academic strategy, they need to gather the proper information on which to base the strategy; satisfy themselves that the campus is operating at the highest quality possible given its recent past and the present structure, finances, and programs; and battle to obtain the finest people available as well as employ the existing people in the right ways. Information, quality, and people: these are the critical items for strategic planning to be effective.

All four components of management need to be employed in order to elicit fresh efforts on these items. In turn, improvements in information, quality, and people make the execution of each of the four components easier. For example, forward-looking management is easier with innovative scholars and an enterprising staff; so is administration and governance. And the demands for prodding, pulling leadership are lessened.

There are also political reasons to concentrate on information, quality, and people before attempting the wrenching experience of devising an academic strategy. One of the epiphanies of the third way, strategic planning, is that planning and implementation should be concurrent, not divorced. If they are done in two entirely separate steps, plans tend to go unused by the unconvinced or wary line officers. Planning should ooze out of meetings and encounters almost unnoticed; and parts of any strategy should be championed by the very people who will need to implement it. That is, a college's or university's leading people need to be psychologically prepared for faster change, for new ventures, for zesty initiatives, and should be involved in the creation of a strategy. The powerful centers of political resistance to adaptation to new realities need to be neutralized or, if possible, convinced of the urgency of altering their attitudes. A consensus needs to be hammered out for a new kind of forward movement so that the seeds of strategy fall on fertile soil.

In his important book and articles summarizing how several of the best corporate executives he studied manage strategic change, James Brian Quinn found that they "artfully blend formal analysis, behavioral techniques, and power politics," and they "consciously and proactively move forward incrementally." They set up good formal and informal networks to get accurate information, not just the favorable data and news that their aides tend to give out. They keep pressing for better quality, growth, new approaches, and greater efficiency. And they search for outstanding persons, both within and outside, for their firms.

In my visits to colleges and universities around the country, I have found a strikingly similar approach among the best academic leaders. They are careful to multiply awareness through such devices as enrollment projections, technological forecasts, and financial likelihoods and lay solid groundwork for more concentrated planning efforts. Quinn observes that numerous people have spoken of the "cognitive limits" to long-term planning. But, he says, "Of equal importance are the process limits—that is, the timing and sequencing imperatives necessary to create awareness, build comfort levels, develop consensus, and select and train people—that constrain the system yet ultimately determine the decision itself."[12]

Also, while strategic planning can be scoffed at, it is much more difficult to argue against improvement in the existing operation. Nearly everyone will agree that new financial, demographic, and competitive factors require that every dollar be used more effectively, that every unit operate with greater quality, that only the best people be rewarded, promoted, and selected from outside, and that the institution have thorough information about itself and the external environment in order to pinpoint internal strengths and weaknesses and alert people to emerging external conditions. Quinn found that among strategically oriented corporate executives, "beginning moves often appear as tactical adjustments in the enterprise's existing structure. As such, they encounter little opposition."[13]

For the faculty, it is especially awkward to take stands against stronger information about one's institution and societal trends, greater quality, and better appointments. This does not mean that some professors won't object and try to paint the efforts in this direction as Taylorism or a touch of 1984. Who hasn't been on a search committee where a few colleagues push for someone who fits in rather than someone who is brilliant or innovative? But it is awkward, and for the best minds, downright embarrassing. When I visited the University of California at Berkeley, one faculty member pointed out how Chancellor Ira Heyman is consolidating a fragmented biology department and pressing to raise its quality and improve its facilities. He said, "Some people don't like the intrusion and changes. But at Berkeley it's hard to argue against factual appraisals and especially hard to fight against any efforts to foster the very highest quality."

So before embarking on the formulation of strategies, a president or dean should move where movement is easiest and traditionally acceptable, and in doing so get everyone ready for the longer, more difficult voyage.

Information. At one campus I know, the president was visited by a disgruntled group of engineering professors who informed him that while enrollments in engineering had gone up by one-fifth in the last three years the number of faculty positions had not. They were surprised that he was surprised to learn of this condition. A week or so later I mentioned this incident to a leading historian at the same university. He quickly put his forefinger between his lips, urging quiet. "The history department," he said, "has lost one-third of its students since the early 1970s and we still have the same number of faculty."

Many presidents today have a surer grasp of the internal movements of their campus than this president. But information about what exactly is going on within a college or university is still underdeveloped at numerous campuses. Though things are improving fast, institutions of higher education tend to be backward about gathering useful information about themselves. Outsiders find this peculiar given academia's thirst for data and knowledge. Improving the management information system is therefore an indispensable step in improving the everyday operation of the campus as well as a requisite for strategic planning.

A first act, if it has not been done, is to gather a task force to recommend what pieces of data are vital for excellent decision making. Such a group can sometimes galvanize people into asking themselves such questions as: What is the connection between policy and information? What kinds of decisions are critical for a college or university? and How much should information be shared and by what means? This often leads nicely into better self-monitoring in several quarters and begins to elicit fruitful comparisons, news of significant changes, and fresh perspectives. One president I recall kicked off a modernization of his college's institutional research office by saying he wanted to find out if the college was bothering the faculty for too much data. After early cheers, the faculty and administration discovered they knew pitifully little about their operations and recommended a move to more and better data—for budgets, decisions, quality reports, reallocations, and financial health.

MIS, or management information systems, is a large subject. But I should indicate some of the categories of information that are important and point to those where colleges are particularly deficient.

Clearly, information about campus internal operations is crucial: space utilization, facility and equipment use and needs, patronage of the library, the bookstore, the student center, and the like. And information about costs and the flows of dollars is equally important. These tend to be fairly highly developed at most campuses.

Curricular and program data also are moderately well attended to, though evaluation of courses by students and recent graduates is rare except at the better universities and colleges. Information about the faculty, except at the finest institutions, is often thin. A president and his provost and deans should know the publications, papers, and research of their professors, the quality of their teaching (from student evaluations and visits), their honors, and their professional activities. I have witnessed noticeable changes in activity at several second-tier institutions after the academic vice-president asked each department to submit detailed annual progress reports with lists of faculty activities and then circulated them in compiled form for all of the faculty to see and compare.

As for information about students, it is both superb and astonishingly meager. What is superb are the data on characteristics, abilities at entry, rates of dropout, financial help, and the like. What is meager is the information in two areas. One is market research and analysis of students, such as the Consortium on Financing Higher Education does so well for its elite members. The other area is that of student outcomes. Since the main "product" of a college is the refined student who was once raw talent, you would think that institutions would keep good statistics on what the value-added achievements are. Such is not the case. The leading proponent for reform in this area is Alexander Astin of UCLA. To Astin,

> A high-quality institution is one that knows about its students. . . . Further, the high-quality institution has a method for gathering and disseminating this information, enabling it to make appropriate adjustments in programs or policies when the student data indicate that change or improvement is needed. In other words, quality is equated here not with physical facilities or faculty credentials but rather with a continuing process of critical self-examination that focuses on the institution's contribution to the student's intellectual and personal development.[14]

As Astin said to me, "Universities must monitor what they get paid to do. It is irresponsible for an institution not to know what the students are learning, what impact the college is having, what suggestions the students have for change." Astin, incidentally, dissents on the direction of most current education planning. In his view planning should focus not on a more prestigious faculty, new buildings, more money, or greater research, though these are important, but on improvement of the education process for the paying students. He says,

> With enrollments going down and costs up in the 1980s, I would invest in absolutely first-rate undergraduate learning. I would concentrate on excellent student services, superb teaching, and rigorous studies, so that my college had a great number of highly satisfied customers, and a steady stream of superbly trained young people. Parents would love a place where

young students received lots of attention and learned more than they thought they could. Such a campus would have great word-of-mouth advertising, and that is the best marketing and competitive strategy.

Central to any such campus is a careful monitoring of student time, activities, and outcomes: improved information about the student's educational progress.

Three other areas for improved information are cross analyses of educational data and cost data, trends about the environment outside the institution, and facts about chief competitors. The first—cross analyses—is especially urgent, given the financial crunch. Information such as per student costs per academic program is essential for decision making. The need for better information about the environment is also growing fast. Victor Baldridge believes that most change in higher education today comes from external pressures and shifts. He said to me, "In the 1980s universities will need to create an information capability for the outside happenings affecting higher education nearly as complete as their present institutional research operations for internal affairs." And, since much innovation at any college is purloined from other colleges, a campus should work harder to get information on the best new additions at other comparable institutions.

When he was planning at the University of Michigan, Donald Lelong found that "in a small minority of situations, the factual and evaluative information assembled in the course of a particular planning activity paints such a clear picture of the need for change that it alone is sufficient to precipitate a decision to act."[15] Good information not only facilitates more rational decision making; it also motivates toward more strategic decision making.

Quality. Quality-mongering can also stimulate. It can be threatening to the less able and less productive faculty members. But like better information, raising quality at a university is a movement hard to oppose. Thus, it is an area that academic management can work on with both hands—and certainly should.

Nearly everyone in higher education is agreed that academic quality will be an especially huge concern in the next decade or two. In a time of enrollment growth, access is the key word; but in a time of enrollment decline—at least in the traditional 18-to-22-year-olds category—competition increases, and schools that give great intellectual value and superior training for their tuition will fare best. Quality throughout a college's operations is therefore a condition of survival and a must for academic management. But in the process of building new levels of excellence, a tone is set, aspirations are raised, and the foundations for strategy are laid. As Quinn found: "Successful managers . . . build the seeds of understanding, identity, and commitment into the very processes that create their strategies. By the time the strategy begins to crystallize in focus, pieces of it are already being implemented. . . . Constantly integrating the simultaneous incremental processes of strategy formulation and implementation is the central art of effective strategic management."[16]

To pursue quality, a president and the rest of academic management should see that the entire institution speaks of taste, care, and thought to a visitor or enrolled student. The signs around the campus ought to be clear and handsome, not a hodgepodge of bad typography. The admissions office must not have art reproductions on the walls like those in cheap motels, hospital-green paint, and a gum-chewing receptionist. A few departments cannot be allowed to remain known weak spots, offering "gut" courses to keep enrollments up. The alumni magazine ought to be first-rate like those of Brown, Johns Hopkins, Harvard, Pennsylvania, and Notre Dame. (Quality helps pay the bills too. MIT's well-edited *Technology Review* sells at newsstands; the *Notre Dame Magazine* brought in $200,000 in gifts from readers to support it in 1981.) Henry Wriston once said that since nearly every undergraduate complains about the food, there is no cheaper, more direct way to improve morale and gain good word-of-mouth publicity than serving up exceptional food in attractive, well-run dining halls—especially since friendships and romances often bloom there and discussions of Hazlitt's prose, Brecht's dramas, Thomas Sowell's economics, or the role of genes in human behavior take place over bean sprouts or warm bagels. A thousand little things.

Quality cannot be imposed. It must be elicited. Lack of quality, however, should be sternly and surgically dealt with. Nothing corrodes as much as the tendency in some universities to carry their incompetents the way some football-devoted universities carry their athletically gifted semiliterates. Concentrate on work and results, and their quality. As Peter Drucker emphasizes, for executives "relations must be task-focused rather than personality-focused."[17]

In my experience, two methods of eliciting quality have often proven especially effective. One is incisive questioning. The managerial questioning needs to show real curiosity and wear no underclothes of judgment or reprimand. For instance, a president or vice-president can meet with his or her director of admissions and financial aid and ask, "What are you doing about the expected 10 percent drop over the next decade in high school graduates within our own and the surrounding states? How are you handling the swelling needs for financial aid? Are you satisfied with the performance of everyone on your staff? Are our black alumni helping us recruit more talented black students?" It often helps if the administrator asks for a short paper in 30 days with proposed initiatives from the admissions director, especially one that suggests steps the college should be taking to help the admissions office attract the finest students. Of such encounters is quality raised, management improved, and strategic thinking begun.

I once heard, in vividly remembered detail, of a dean lunching with a small but important department and saying to the assembled faculty something like the following. "I keep hearing things about this department. Can anyone explain why, with all this talent, there have been only two small research grants and no books in the past four years? Are we letting you down or not supporting you in the way we should? And why are enrollments dropping in this important field?" It turned out—as the dean already knew—that the chairman was going through a divorce, one senior department member had begun drinking heavily during the day, one junior member was a wretched teacher, and several others were capable but coasting. However, several of the faculty fixed the blame on lack of the dean's monetary support, especially for salaries and travel to more conferences. Two years later, the department turned around.

Raymond Bacchetti, an ex-philosophy professor and the vice-provost for budget and planning at Stanford, who is a bear on detailed data about the internal workings of each department, is said to be a particularly penetrating questioner despite his relaxed, dryly humorous, self-deprecating manner. He uses the annual budget requests to query chairmen, deans, and directors in a gentle but piercing way. As he told me, "More than a few scholars are averse to data about their operations. We make it hard to avoid or dismiss the facts. And we keep trying to help every unit become as nationally significant as it should be."

The other effective method for eliciting quality is through asking persons for suggestions about how to achieve higher quality in their area. This forces people to think methodically about the subject and discuss it; it lets them know you care for both quality and their ideas about how to reach higher. This is becoming a more popular method because of its use in some Japanese corporations where the entire staff is said to be encouraged to help the management improve quality. The Japanese have made great leaps in quality since the early 1950s when "Made in Japan" meant cheap and shoddy. Charles Kepner, a management consultant, recently reported to a group in Baltimore that in 1980 at the Toyota Motor Company 48,757 employees made 859,039 suggestions, about 90 percent of which were useful. The estimated savings to the company for that year was $30 million.

At the University of Maryland, Baltimore County, library where I did my research for this book, there is a prominent suggestion box right next to the checkout desk. Every suggestion is typed up, read and answered by the library staff, and posted on a large bulletin board nearby. The suggestions are taken seriously, and specific action, with dates, promised. Many are implemented. The librarians treat everyone—pimply farmboys; ghetto youths; nonbookish young scientists; adult mothers working on a graduate degree in English; bearded professors with bulging, stained leather bookbags—like visiting foreign ministers of education, the way the professional waiters at New York's Russian Tea Room, next to Carnegie Hall, treat everyone from shop girls to Isaac Stern. It is one of the best small university libraries I have ever seen. One study found that UMBC has the highest rate of library usage by students of any college or university in the state of Maryland.

Incidentally, one of the people who brought quality to Japanese industry is W. Edwards Deming, a statistics professor from NYU. There is a quality-control prize in Japan known as the Deming Award now given annually to honor this prophet of quality. Deming is a quirky and opinionated man. Nevertheless he told several of us in January 1982, "If anybody needs quality control it's the service industries, including universities. College presidents, like most executives, fail to see that improving quality is their main business. We're in a new economic era. Quality is the key to higher productivity because approximately 20 percent of the cost of things, from automobiles to college educations, is a charge for waste." Deming's procedure is simplicity scrubbed: locate the shortcomings or defects, scrutinize them, trace the sources of the problem, make corrections, and then record the new results. So, if the engineering students lack adequate mathematical skills, or if alumni annual giving is very low . . .

Of course, rewards help, both monetary and nonmonetary, as when thoughtful notes are sent to faculty for articles published or when troubled parents are made comfortable. So do nonthreatening teaching workshops for stale or dull instructors, and dozens of other devices. Whatever the preferred methods, quality must be attended to, both for good management and as preparation for planning. The alternative may be a quality audit by the new state board of higher education, which states like New York, Louisiana, and Illinois have instituted.[18] Or it may be an enrollment decline.

People. Andrew Carnegie is said to have ordered for his tombstone: "Here lies a man who knew how to bring into his service men better than he was himself." Every university search committee should have that message in its packet of instructions. There is no more important task than selecting people for positions at a college or university. Again, bright, energetic, flexible men and women who care about ideas, research, and the spread of culture and learning not only add immediately to the good functioning of a campus but they facilitate the task of institutional transformation and renewal for the future. Such extraordinary persons are less inclined to be defensive and argumentative about change—though I have found they are inclined to be slightly more territorial than those with less of a domain of accomplishment to protect.

Presidents themselves must take an interest in all key appointments, and the provost or academic vice-president must be meticulous about tenure approvals. Though faculty departments make recommendations for promotion and tenure, the evidence is overwhelming that, except in the exceptionally well-disciplined departments, the professors are far too tender-hearted and philanthropic to their colleagues. They have little stomach for nonapprovals. And many deans are almost as weak. The hurdle for tenure should be: is there anyone *in the nation* better qualified than this man or woman who would be willing to teach at this level, at this institution? If there is, tenure should not be granted. This is tart medicine. But a good college is a meritocracy. It should not be permitted to be a home for the amiable or an employment bureau. Academic executives must care for people, but they must care more for what academic life stands for.

Alfred P. Sloan, who took a small, anarchic, almost bankrupt little automobile company and shaped it into the coordinated organization known as General Motors, wrote, "An administration may also be measured by the caliber of the men brought in or retained by it."[19] Mr. Sloan would often chair personnel meetings himself and was known to spend several hours of his crushing schedule on the appointment of some chief mechanic or financial supervisor. President Cyert of Carnegie-Mellon agrees with Sloan, though he is more modest about his success rate: "One of a manager's most important and time-consuming tasks is judging people. Like most managers, I think I'm an excellent judge of other human beings. Yet I estimate I haven't beaten random chance by much in my appointments."[20]

In my experience, a decisive difference between the noted colleges and universities and the less-noted ones is the attention they pay to the selection of their people, from the landscaping chief, cooks, and technicians to the art curator, resident poet, and chairman of the physics department. While mediocre campuses have a faculty that reads the best books and articles, the best campuses have a faculty that takes pains to correspond with and get to know the scholars who produce them. To the avaricious about talent go the spoils.

One of the most dramatic success stories in American higher education is the rise of Stanford University between 1955 and 1975 from a mediocre university with an excellent engineering school but terrible library, provincial faculty, and shabby facilities to a campus of world eminence. It is a fascinating story of daring, toughness (they moved an angry medical school—"Wally's Folly"—and killed a school of architecture!), ingenuity, fund raising, great leadership (as late as 1967 Stanford had no faculty senate), a treasure hunt for good people, and brilliant strategy.[21] The strategy had three prongs. The largest and central one was to recruit over several years 150 of America's finest minds for Stanford. The second prong was a sequenced emphasis on first those areas where Stanford had a comparative advantage (engineering and physics), next the social studies, then the humanities, stressing graduate work and the professional schools. The third prong was massive fund raising to provide facilities, equipment, and attractive housing to lure the talented scholars.

The genius in the drive under President Wallace Sterling was Provost Fred Terman, the former dean of engineering who not only inspired "Silicon Valley" and helped bring hundreds of millions of dollars in federal research grants to Stanford but also was a tenacious hunter and recruiter of outstanding people for his deans and faculty. When a new professor was being considered, Terman made exhaustive investigations. He often visited the person's campus to examine his or her career and work on the spot. He urged departments to make lists of the ablest people in their fields and try to tell them about Stanford. As Terman recalled in 1979, he had to "show our department heads how to recruit faculty, and also graduate students. Sometimes the deans too did not know how to get the best men. . . . When I became provost, few members of the faculty had national reputations, nor was there anybody who was a member of the National Academy of Sciences. Today there are 64 members of the Academy."

Once, when Neil McElroy of Procter and Gamble gave President Sterling a check for $25,000, Provost Terman and Sterling decided to use it to strengthen the chemistry department by adding some really creative people. Terman quickly convened a special panel consisting entirely of Nobel Prize winners for advice. The panel recommended the University of Wisconsin's William Johnson, whom they said was one of the most brilliant and promising organic chemists in the world. Johnson was approached, but he would come only if he could bring several of his research team and if Carl Djerassi of Wayne State University would also come to Stanford. Djerassi said yes, if Johnson was going and if he too could bring a few of his finest researchers. But Stanford had barely adequate facilities in chemistry and no room for the two top scientists and their research crews. Wallace Sterling later said,

> Fred Terman and I decided on a bold stroke. The operating budget at the time was less than $20 million. The so-called General Fund, the unbudgeted part of the University's resources, was around $600,000. Fred and I took our courage in our hands. We went to the trustees and asked for $500,000 out of the General Fund in order to provide the space and facilities for the two research teams. Not surprisingly, the trustees were skeptical of the wisdom of this.
>
> Meanwhile, Fred was on the track of possible donors. They were John Stauffer of Stauffer Chemical and his niece, Mitzi Briggs.
>
> July came and with it, the annual Grove encampment of the Bohemian Club, to which Fred and I went. Although I had been party to the negotiations with John Stauffer, I thought it would not violate the Bohemian Club's motto—"Weaving Spiders Come Not Here"—if I paid a call on Stauffer.
>
> I climbed the stairs to his camp, only to find Terman already there and the two men on their knees, examining the blueprints for Stanford's new chemistry building. By early fall, Fred had closed the deal, and we had the pleasure of handing back the half million dollars to the General Fund.
>
> The rest is history. The chemistry department went on to become one of the top three in the country.[22]

With precise information, real quality in most parts of the institution, and a nucleus of gifted, innovative people, the work of shaping an academic strategy can begin.

CHAPTER SEVEN

Shaping an Academic Strategy

Except for the elaboration and furtherance of the grand plan there is not need of a president. Almost everything else that he does could be done by some other officer, a good deal of it by a clerk.
SAMUEL CAPEN

There is nothing more difficult to take in hand, more perilous to conduct, or more uncertain in its success than to take the lead in introducing a new order of things.
NICCOLÒ MACHIAVELLI

Policeman: *Lady, do you realize you are driving the wrong way on this one-way street?*
Lady: *Officer, have you considered that the one-way sign may be pointing in the wrong direction?*
ANONYMOUS

BEFORE YOU BEGIN to shape an academic strategy for your college, school, or university, it is important to make sure that the misconceptions and prejudicial debris are swept away. The idea of planning in higher education is anathema to some. The notion of strategic planning strikes many as something reserved for West Point generals and executives of multinational corporations, and an activity that restricts and confuses leaders of good judgment, strong vision, and wide experience. So it is important to understand what strategic planning is not.

1. *It is not the production of a blueprint.* The idea is not to produce a fat, detailed document that everyone should follow but to get all the key people thinking innovatively and acting strategically, with the future in mind. Strategic planning involves continuous adjustments to shifting conditions, with a central strategy in mind. The strategic plan may be very simple, like General George Marshall's core strategy of beating Nazi Germany first, then defeating Japan. It is often a matter of a few concepts on paper or a few pages of typescript.

2. *It is not a set of platitudes.* Often an institution's goals are given as the education of youth; the training of critical thinkers; or teaching, research, and service. This is like saying you believe in liberty or have faith.

Strategic planning means the formulation of succinctly stated operationa aims.[1] It is specific, not vague and vapid.

3. *It is not the personal vision of the president or board of trustees.* A strategy is based on calculations about the markets for your services and probable external conditions such as the economy's vitality, population changes, and the preferences of political leaders and state board of higher education officials, as well as your institution's traditions, academic strengths, and financial ability. An academic strategy will of necessity include a measure of the president's own vision, sometimes a huge measure, but never to the exclusion of considerations of other realities.

4. *It is not a collection of departmental plans, compiled and edited.* This form of bottom-up planning was a popular pastime in the 1960s and is still practiced at some places. But strategic planning is for the whole institution and for its long-term stature and excellence, not for satisfying dozens of separate internal hopes spun in isolation from a college's overall needs. A university is something more than the aggregate of its parts. A strategic plan is something more than a list of individual wants and aspirations.

5. *Strategic decision making is not done by planners.* As one planning official wrote, "First we ask: Who is leading the planning? If it is a planner . . . we are in trouble."[2] In strategic planning, the planner does not plan. He or she prompts and helps the line officers to plan with statistics, forecasts, institutional data, the best reports by outsiders and on competitors, and visits to your campus by other strategists, scholars, or consultants. The university planner's duties are two: arranging the process of planning and providing crucial information that helps key officers make decisions that are informed and sensitive to current and emerging realities. It is the president, provost, chairman of the board, financial vice-president, deans, and department heads who should decide on both the institution's strategy and its implementing tactics. Unless the chief operating officers subscribe—or at least feel they cannot ignore or torpedo the strategy—the plan will not sail.

6. *It is not a substitution of numbers for important intangibles.* Data are used. Computers are employed. Financial forecasts are made. Models may be tried. But these are introduced to sharpen judgments, analyses, and decisions, not to substitute for them. They yoke facts to the executives' feel; they bring more enlightened intuition. Quantification is provided mainly to enrich qualitative sagacity not replace it. The essence of academic strategy is decision making. And computers don't make decisions, people do.

m of surrender to market conditions and trends. Formulating
s not entail giving up all your college stands for in order to
,yers or to go with the flow. It does require you to be aware of
narkets for higher education, the new forms of delivering
inforn.. n, and the developing conditions that will affect your college
and its goals in a profound way. But the Juilliard School does not switch
out of music when the arts are in the doldrums, and Illinois's Wheaton
College did not drift away from its Christian evangelism moorings during
the secular hedonism of the 1965–75 decade. If you intend a wilderness
trip, it is wise to have maps and the right equipment and clothing; it does
not mean you have to live like primitive people or animals in the wild.

8. *Strategic planning is not something done on an annual retreat.* It is
ongoing, continual, not an activity done separately, away from the class-
rooms, budgets, laboratories, and libraries. Special sessions are necessary
during the formulation stage and when special threats arise. But planning
itself is integral not occasional.

9. *It is not a way of eliminating risks.* If anything, strategic planning
increases risk taking. It fosters an entrepreneurial spirit, a readiness to
start new ventures. It encourages boldness about opportunities and ag-
gressiveness in the face of threats. In doing so, it often causes disruption.
But it recognizes with the prophetic economist Joseph Schumpeter that in
our new world of rapid technological advance and shifting international
conditions the competition is less and less from small differences in price,
size, or quality and more and more "from the new commodity, the new
technology, the new source of supply, the new type of organization—
competition . . . which strikes not at the margins of profits and outputs of
existing firms but at their foundations and their very lives."[3] A clear
strategy helps a university take more calculated risks, more risks with a
purpose, and proper, necessary risks that enhance the long-term viability
and quality of a campus.

10. *It is not an attempt to read tea leaves and outwit the future.* Of course, the
future is unpredictable. But it is not a random walk. There are likelihoods,
built-in dynamics, national character, and even a few near-certainties.
Strategic planning is an effort to make this year's decisions more intelligent by looking toward the probable future and coupling the decisions to
an overall institutional strategy. It is not a phantasmagoria about tomorrow. It is a set of decisions that need to be begun now if there is to be a
secure future—decisions based on the best evidence there is about the
unpredictable but not wide-open future.

If strategic planning is none of these, what is it? The answer to that question cannot be given in a neat definition any more than an answer to such questions as What is teaching? or What is management? can be captured in a one-sentence response.

There are, however, six features that distinguish strategic planning from such predecessors as systems analysis, incrementalism, management science, long-range planning, and doing what you have always done.

1. *Academic strategic decision making means that a college, school, or university and its leaders are active rather than passive about their position in history.* To be strategic is to take positive, vigorous steps to overcome the enemy, as Alexander the Great so brilliantly did, as Machiavelli's Prince was urged to do, and as George Patton did, the enemy for a campus being the vicissitudes of life, sharp changes in the course of intellectual inquiry or educational demand, or challenges from television, home computers, or an innovative rival in the region. It entails a belief that you can to some extent shape your own destiny as well as be shaped by external forces.

Colleges tend to be extraordinarily docile before the forces that affect them. They prefer to complain about the niggardly legislature, parents who no longer send their offspring to their kind of institution, the urban decay near their campus, the athletics-happy alumni, federal government aid policies, inadequate corporate support, newfangled technology, and creeping philistinism or careerism or hedonism in society. There is little reason for this docility and perennial grumbling except the dogma that institutions of higher learning do better if they go unmanaged, muddle through incrementally, and remain superciliously aloof but verbally persistent about public and private support for their learned labors. Yet nearly all the finest colleges and universities were actively pulled into eminence by vigorous strategic leadership. Andrew White, Daniel Coit Gilman, and William Rainey Harper aggressively designed new houses of learning at Cornell, Johns Hopkins, and Chicago. Charles Eliot and Nicholas Murray Butler tugged and shoved their classical, local colleges—Harvard and Columbia—into the modern world of science, social science, and research and attracted students nationally and internationally. Frank Aydelotte lifted a little Quaker campus into a high-powered Swarthmore. John Hannah transformed an aggie college into an important university, and at one time he had the second largest number of National Merit finalists at Michigan State because of his opportunistic nationwide recruiting for them. Herman Wells lifted Indiana University close to the top ranks.

To think strategically is to look intensely at contemporary history and your institution's position in it and work out a planning process that actively confronts the historical movement, overcomes it, gets on top of it, or seizes the opportunities latent in it. A campus with an academic strategy has a battle plan to get stronger and better in the teeth of historical conditions. It reads the face of history—or, to change disciplines, the ecological environment—skillfully and then devises a scheme to survive in it and transcend it. With an academic strategy a college or university leaves the passive mendicant order and becomes an active knight-errant.

The research suggests that strategic activists in organizations come in three varieties.[4] One is the group called "the defenders." These leaders fight for stability, quality, order, and continuity. They fend off threats with active defensive maneuvers. But they have trouble with change. They tend to be efficient, protective, and pay lots of attention to running an excellent corporation or university.

A second variety is dubbed "the analyzers." These managers and their organizations are anxious to keep up with changes but are cautious. They let others go first, watch them, then move fast behind the innovators if the move is successful. They keep analyzing their environment, the competition, their finances, their next actions. They can get clobbered if they are too cautious, as Timex, the world's largest maker of finished watches, did by the solid-state revolution in digital display watches by American semiconductor companies and Japanese firms.[5]

Third, there are "the prospectors," who aggressively seek to find and exploit new services and markets. They usually have a large R & D operation, alert management, and financial acumen. These leaders tend to build too diverse an organization like ITT or too thin an organization like Antioch College, with its numerous branch campuses in major cities, or to be very successful like Merrill Lynch.

There is also a fourth variety of managers in the research typology that is a huge, widespread one: "the reactors." These are actually nonstrategists. These leaders and organizations are always reacting, putting out fires, defending turf, changing uncertainly. Leaders and organizations of this kind are often quite responsive to external pressures but inconsistent, unaware of their own historical or market situation, and lacking in direction.

Strategic thinking leads one into being an active defender, analyzer, or prospector rather than a passive reactor. It means being highly conscious of the imperatives of strong management in higher education and the advantages of a shrewd strategy. McGill's Henry Mintzberg says, "The manager's effectiveness is significantly influenced by his insight into his own work."[6] The institution's effectiveness is also influenced by such insight.

2. *Strategic planning looks outward and is focused on keeping the institution in step with the changing environment.* This is strategic planning's single most important contribution to organizational decision making. For decades most colleges and universities have been inner-directed, formulating their aims on the bedrock of their own religious commitments, traditions, faculty desires, and ambitions for growth, largely ignoring the world outside. The language in the college catalogues still reflects that narcissism and disregard for market conditions and external forces: "Jove College has since its founding been devoted to . . . "; "You will be part of our distinguished tradition that . . . "; "The unique mission of Buena State has never wavered."

But perhaps three-quarters of all change at most institutions of higher learning is now triggered by outside factors such as directives from the state board of higher education, an economic recession, migration patterns, a change in the supply of gasoline, the wider use of records and cassettes, a governor's change of politics, a new law from Washington, a sweeping court decision about a major affirmative action case, and the shifts in the job markets. The more aware institutions have realized that and have moved swiftly to improve their data collection and monitoring of the society external to their campus gates. They are becoming other-directed, to use the labels from David Riesman's 1950 sociological study of our changing national character, *The Lonely Crowd.* Colleges are switching from a self-assertion model of their existence to a biological model of continuous adaptation to their powerful, changing social environment.

An academic strategy asserts that neither willfulness nor acquiescence to the fashions and temporary external conditions is an appropriate course. Rather, a university's own direction and objectives need to be shaped in the light of the emerging national situation and new external factors as well as the perennial needs of youth, truth, and intelligence. And because the external environment is in constant flux, strategic planning must be continuous, pervasive, and indigenous, not a blueprint or the work of a planning officer or a one-time experiment at some mountain retreat.

F. Scott Fitzgerald wrote in 1936, "The test of a first-rate intelligence is the ability to hold two opposed ideas in the mind at the same time, and still retain the ability to function."[7] While an institution's own hopes and the outside forces of history are not exactly "opposed," anyone planning strategically for a college, school, or university needs to keep two incongruous bodies of facts and ideas—internal aspirations and external conditions—in mind at the same time and act to move the institution ahead nonetheless.

*strategy making is competitive, recognizing that higher educa-
...t to economic market conditions and to increasingly strong com-
p...*   is is the most recently added—and least developed—piece to
academic strategy thinking. It will be a vitally important one in the
stringent period ahead, with too many colleges and universities chasing a
dwindling number of students. Military strategy is, of course, competitive,
with a specific enemy, potential enemies, or unfriendly neighboring countries.[8] And U.S. business firms have always had to think competitively.
Most democratic politicians constantly think of competitive ploys and
short-range strategies.

Astonishingly, colleges and universities have until recently seldom
thought in competitive terms, except in obvious ways. Private, or independent, colleges compete with public, or state, colleges. An old state university may resent the rise of a second, new state-supported university. And
Harvard and Yale poke fun at each other. But a deep awareness of the
market for higher education or one's own market segment has not been
developed. State universities and colleges, for instance, have almost totally ignored the spectacular multiplication of community colleges in their
areas as a new factor in the market.

This is surprising because if there is anything that distinguishes American higher education from that of all other countries it is the vast number
and variety of institutions of higher learning. As long ago as 1870, there
were more institutions in the United States awarding bachelor's degrees,
more law schools, and more medical schools than in all of Europe combined.[9] Ten years later, President Frederick Barnard of Columbia won-
dered how England, with a population of 23 million, managed with only
four degree-granting institutions, whereas the state of Ohio, with a population of only three million, supported 37 colleges and universities.[10] And
Max Weber observed in 1909, after his visit to America, "The constitution
of American universities and much else about them is affected by the fact
that American universities, to an even greater degree than the German,
are institutions which compete with each other."[11] Yet, somehow, the little
competition that existed has been muted and certainly non-strategic.

The reason the 3,100 American colleges, universities, schools, seminaries, and institutes have not been strategically competitive until the past
few years is that the market for higher education has been expanding
almost uninterruptedly since the Civil War, even through the depression of
the 1930s. Abundance breeds magnanimity. It is scarcity that draws out
competition and combativeness. Now higher education faces scarcity. The
number of colleges closing is accelerating. Between 1960 and 1969, 95
colleges closed; between 1970 and 1979, 135 colleges ended their lives.[12]

Therefore, it is logical that comparative advantage has suddenly become a major new interest in higher education. What strengths and advantages over other colleges and universities do you possess that your competition does not? Here is how Carnegie-Mellon president Richard Cyert explained it to the learned audience at an American Council on Education workshop in October 1981:

> The planning unit must determine what its comparative advantages are. Comparative advantage means comparative to other departments, colleges, or universities with which that unit is competing. We must face the fact that colleges and universities are in a competitive market.
>
> Comparative advantage may stem from a location. It may be based on particular strengths in the organization that have developed over the years, or may be based on a particular person or group of persons who have flourished at the institution. It may be based on the historical traditions of the organization.
>
> The point is that there are some elements which the school can build on to create an organization that has, if not unique characteristics, special characteristics that only a few can match. The aim of strategic planning is to place the unit in a distinctive position.

It is also logical that colleges and universities pay closer attention to the shrinking market for traditional students and the new markets for adults. Hundreds of colleges and universities have recently begun to conduct market research, set up marketing committees, and rewrite their publications in livelier prose with students and market segments in mind. Marketing is closely related to competitive strategies. In a breezy booklet on "positioning," two marketing executives recently stressed that the old messages about how unique, caring, high-quality, and terrific your college is are increasingly falling on deaf ears. "Find comparatives, not superlatives," they counsel. They urge institutions to forget the trumpets and banners about how wonderful they are. (Most higher education public relations efforts are shamelessly boastful and hyperbolic.) Instead, campuses should learn what positions in the higher education market and in people's minds they own, and then improve and build upon those. Comparative market strategy, or what they call "positioning strategy," is a growing concern in the face of increasingly confusing competition.[13]

When Marcus Sieff, also Baron Sieff of Brimpton, grandson of Michael Marks, the Polish peddler who founded Marks and Spencer, England's finest and most successful department store chain, was queried recently by an American reporter, he revealed his corporation's use of competitive analysis and comparative advantage strategy:

Q: "When Sears [Roebuck] has been so successful selling insurance in its hundreds of stores throughout America, why . . . has Marks & Spencer not done the same?"

We of course study Sears' operations, just as they study ours, and we have seriously considered mounting a similar insurance business, which, we have no doubt would be very large and quite profitable. But our research convinced us that we could not do a better job than our best English insurance companies are now doing. And, as you know, we believe that in the long run this company's interests are best served if we only do for our customers what we can do better than others.[14]

4. *Strategic planning concentrates on decisions, not on documented plans, analyses, forecasts, and goals.* Strategic planning is action-oriented. It constantly asks: What shall we do? How shall we decide? Where do we put our attention and energy? It especially emphasizes the allocation of resources, asking how shall we decide now to spend our money and employ our people, buildings, and equipment? It therefore has revived the Charles Hitch invention of the planning, programming, and budget system, because PPBS so neatly links strategies, university programs, and the operating and capital budgets. Strategic planning spends on what it believes; and what it believes derives from the academic strategy to advance the institution. Strategic planning is *people* acting decisively and roughly in concert to carry out a strategy they have helped devise.

Neither systems analysis nor traditional long-range planning nor management science nor incremental muddling through is decision-oriented. Rational analytical planning is keen on the right approach, the proper concept, the factually rich analysis. But the decision to implement or to act upon the rational plan is left as a separate matter for the more political decision makers. Incrementalism is keen on reasonable compromises, on trade-offs that provide the least acrimony. It wants controversies resolved, differences lessened. It seeks immediate harmony, not long-range excellence. It avoids decisions, consciously made and sometimes unpopular, but necessary for long-term health or new levels of quality or prosperity. Incrementalists prefer to "arrive at" a position; they tend to duck from the hard choices. Strategic planning is more surgical. After careful analysis and discussion, and using experience and prognoses, strategists decide to cut, amputate, graft, inflate, or strengthen with injections of new blood or vitamins. For strategists, the decision's the thing.

5. *Strategy making is a blend of rational and economic analysis, political maneuvering, and psychological interplay. It is therefore participatory and highly tolerant of controversy.* Just as the finest scholars blend facts, interviews, historical wisdom, comparative analyses, insights, and bold speculation in their depictions of a situation, so collegiate strategies combine

computer modeling, favorable and unpleasant facts, research, discussions among many people, market and competitive analyses, and large spoonfuls of ingenuity, judgment, and daring to come up with a course for the institution's future.

Strategic action recognizes that human nature is an amalgam of intellect, power plays, and emotions such as fear, envy, anger, compassion, greed, and desire for purpose and meaning. So it gathers the best information and forecasts; struggles to overcome political jealousies, inertia, and sabotage; and builds psychological awareness and commitment. Unapologetically, it marries rationality and artfulness, financial facts and politics. Good timing is essential for the sequencing of these and for capitalizing on a sudden retirement or death, a budget crisis, or a competitor's sharp decline in leadership or quality.[15]

Because the politics and psychology are important, strategy making must be participatory, though not in a wide-open way. Several colleges have tried the Athenian forum approach, with disastrous results. But most of those with management responsibilities on campus need to be part of the meetings and deliberations. Nor should strategy making be done without an agenda or persistent pressures for decisions. Factual background materials, environmental reports, forecasts, and financial likelihoods are imperative to pull people away from their own concerns, viewpoints, and emotional preferences toward the larger world of historical, economic, and educational reality and institutional purpose. Executives can guide the discussions and must keep pressing for decisions that benefit the whole institution. But politically most of the key people need to be on board the strategy train when it leaves the station. Participation is imperative. There need not be a full consensus. There seldom is. Dissent must be permitted, although sabotage should not be. The president, however, is the final arbiter, the ultimate shaper of strategy. He cannot act if his staff and aides are split or heavily opposed. He may need to wait as Eliot of Harvard did at faculty meetings and come back after the situation worsens. But academic leaders should not fail to act if there is a rough concurrence. Enthusiasm for a course of change is almost unheard of. And most deans and vice-presidents expect that the president and his board of trustees will put the refined touches on the strategic advance anyway.

Should the board of trustees be involved in strategy formulation? It depends on the activism of the trustees. Several campuses I visited have included one or two board members in key strategy sessions. The governing board obviously has a role to play in major policy decisions. But because board members are usually busy executives themselves, they often prefer to make more rapid yes-no decisions and let their chief executive work out the slow, careful deliberations. President David McLaughlin of Dartmouth says he has an annual retreat with his senior officers and all the trustees in late August where discussions exclude monthly business and explore instead long-term needs, strategies, external threats and opportunities, and major changes. No decisions are made, says President McLaughlin, but trustee thinking and preferences are uncovered for use in campus strategy formulations. This appears to be a useful way of informing trustees and involving them in strategy development, as well as giving campus presidents an additional chip to use against the recalcitrants and reactors. Unless the trustees themselves are the recalcitrants and reactors.

To encourage participation in strategy formulation, the academic leaders need to have a high tolerance for argument and controversy. The innermost feelings and wildest thoughts of principals should be permitted to slip out. If the emphasis is clearly placed on facts, important concerns, ideas, honest doubts, and imaginative initiatives and not on personalities, everyone gradually realizes that it is the institution's strategy and welfare that is the issue, not each other's reputations. In his wise book *Men Who Manage,* Melville Dalton wrote, "Conflict is typical. . . . We are currently so busy hiding conflict that we quake when we must simultaneously deal with it and pretend it doesn't exist." As Dalton says, "Perpetual harmony is alien to all life," and, "Conflict and cooperation are usually intermingled in all advances, especially in democracies."[16] And numerous other experts on organizational change concur. Chris Argyris, for example, says that academic executives must couple their "advocacy with an invitation to others to confront one's views, to alter them, in order to produce the position that is based on the most complete and valid information possible and to which people involved can be internally committed."[17] To Argyris, "The probabilities of implanting educational processes that threaten the *status quo* are always low and disheartening," but the chances are increased if, in trying to change a university's strategy, the president recognizes that he needs to change the attitudes of its main actors.[18]

An instructive book to read in this regard is Thomas Kuhn's *The Structure of Scientific Revolutions,* wherein the author describes how difficult it is to change a scientific view, or paradigm, and how many scientific revolutions have been made only with fierce controversies, international name-calling, and the dissolution of old friendships.[19] To enter the house of strategy, one must to go through the doorway of debate and catharsis.

6. *Strategic planning concentrates on the fate of the institution above everything else.* In *Three Thousand Futures: The Next Twenty Years in Higher*

Education, Clark Kerr and his staff discovered a fascinating fact:

> Taking as a starting point 1530, when the Lutheran Church was founded, some 66 institutions that existed then still exist today in the Western world in recognizable forms. [These are] the Catholic Church, the Lutheran Church, the parliaments of Iceland and the Isle of Man, and 62 universities. Universities in the past have been remarkable for their historic continuity . . . and have come out less changed than almost any other segment of their societies.[20]

Universities in Western Europe have had extraordinary staying power. Many of America's earliest colleges are also still alive and well. Colleges and universities clearly have won a special place in Western society as an indispensable institution, one worth guarding and fighting for as one would a religion or a parliament. The changes within those venerable institutions have been many and radical, but the organizations of learning themselves have endured in recognizable form. The great British observer of America James Bryce once remarked that "a university should reflect the spirit of the times without yielding to it." Institutions of higher learning have done just that, although not always very promptly. The endurance of universities is a truly remarkable fact about Western civilization.

When you think of it, it is peculiar to want to perpetuate something abstract like a business corporation, a religious organization, a national state, or a university. Many great leaders—Lenin, Charles de Gaulle, Mao Tse-tung—have not worried about successors. And great corporations sell out, collapse, or become mere fragments of themselves. Among America's largest business enterprises in 1909 were: Lake Superior Corporation, Central Leather, American Writing Paper, Baldwin Locomotive Works, United Copper, and Calumet and Hecla.[21] It takes a special devotion to a college or university as an organization to keep it vibrant for century after century. The Venetian republic has not survived but the University of Bologna has. French kings have gone, but the University of Paris goes on.

Strategic planning places the long-term vitality and excellence of a college or university first. It cares about traditions, faculty salaries, and programs in Greek, agriculture, and astrophysics. But it cares about institutional survival more, so that there will be places for scholars of Greek, agriculture, and astrophysics to teach and do their research. Scholars cannot easily hang their shingle out like physicians or architects. They need a *universitas.* In medieval times *universitas* and *societas* meant a body of people operating as a single person; both words were used to designate the medieval guilds.[22] Professors still need to unite as a *universitas.*

Surely there are colleges and universities that are marginal in quality or that should never have been started or that have lost their flavor and reason for being. Not every existing institution of higher learning will, or should, survive the 1980s, or the twentieth century. It may surprise some, but according to a 1981 study of the National Association of College and University Business Officers, fewer than 50 of America's 3,100 colleges and universities have endowments of $100 million or more, and fewer than 200 have an endowment larger than $10 million. Nine out of ten institutions in the United States, therefore, are precariously financed, and many live at the brink of jeopardy and instant retrenchment.

Yet the older and the superior campuses deserve to live on. And the nation needs a rich variety of higher education institutions to help preserve pluralism and freedom of choice. Strategic planning attempts to keep an eye on the long-run viability of these institutions.

As you get set for the actual formulation of a strategy, you need a conceptual framework to help assemble an academic plan for your institution. This is the more rational and analytical portion of strategic decision making; it needs to be used in conjunction with the political and psychological-behavioral segments. But in some ways the conceptual framework is the heart of strategy formulation.

Since the fundamental aim of strategic planning is a Darwinian one of linking the forward direction of your organization with the movement of historical forces in the environment, the two critical areas for analysis are one's own organization and the environment. You need to look inside and outside. And in each of these searches there are three elements, as presented schematically in the chart.

Traditions, Values, and Aspirations	Strengths and Weaknesses: Academic and Financial	Leadership: Abilities and Priorities

ACADEMIC STRATEGY

Environmental Trends: Threats and Opportunities	Market Preferences, Perceptions, and Directions	The Competitive Situation: Threats and Opportunities

In effect, you need to examine the internal traditions, values, and states of mind of your organization, the strengths and weaknesses of its programs, faculty, location, size, and finances, and the qualities and desires of the president, provost, trustees, deans, and department chairmen. That is, you need to have an intimate knowledge of your organization, its values, and its leadership. You need to come to know your campus as if for the first time.

As important, you need to take a careful look at the external world. What are the likely developments in electronics, high school populations, energy costs, federal policy, and the national and regional economy? How will they affect you? What new opportunities might they open up? What are likely to be the frontiers of academic research and study? Who are your competitors and how are they responding to these frontiers, and to their threats and opportunities? And what segments of the higher education market do you now serve? How do the various segments of the market perceive your institution, and its strengths and weaknesses? What are the growing and declining demand areas for your programs?

In short, you need to know what your college or university can or cannot do, and what it wants to do. Then you need to discern what it might do, and should do. Last, you need to decide what it will do. Your academic strategy, at least its more rational components, should exude from this compound of internal and external considerations.

It may be helpful to describe in greater detail each of the six elements for analysis:

1. *Traditions, values, and aspirations.* Every college, school, or university has embedded in its tissues an intangible set of traditions, values, and hopes. Sometimes these are a fairly unified set of values. Colleges such as Berea, Reed, Agnes Scott, and St. John's are examples; so are universities such as MIT, Baylor, Howard, and Iowa State. Some campuses have an "organizational saga," an institutional mythos, that dominates the place.[23] At other campuses there may be divisions of opinion between, say, the faculty and the students, or the older trustees and alumni and the newer trustees and present professors, or the faculty and the administrators. Also, there may be divisions about what the institution should be like 10 years from now. These qualitative factors need to be revealed fully and examined candidly.

A strategic plan may bend or redirect a college's traditions and values, and it may alter its aspirations. But the strategy will never be effective if it tries to ignore these powerful intangibles. Values are like tides, invisible but mighty. The University of Texas could not become a smaller institution stressing the arts and humanities any more than Carleton College could switch to career training or Millsaps College could transform itself into a science and technology institute for women. An institution's traditions, values, and aspirations may no longer be in step with current realities and may be very difficult to maintain in the probable environment ahead. Your academic strategy may need to revise or update the values of the institution. But it should do so knowingly, tenderly, tactfully. Strategies work best when they are roughly consonant with, or in some way an extension of, an institution's traditions and ambitions,[24] though obviously some traditions and expectations, like old clothing, no longer fit.

2. *Academic and financial strengths and weaknesses.* Is your campus accomplished in computer science, like Carnegie-Mellon, MIT, and the University of Illinois? Is it strong in music, like Oberlin, Atlanta University, and Indiana University? Is your institution unusually well endowed, like Rice University, Smith College, the University of Delaware, or Berry College in Georgia? And where is your campus deficient?

You need to examine the pros and cons of your location, scholarship aid for students, ambience, tuition levels, physical plant, size, alumni loyalty, salary scales, and student achievements. Above all, you must evaluate the strengths and weaknesses of the institution's faculty and programs. There are numerous indices for evaluating the faculty; this has become a popular activity in the past two decades.[25] Program reviews have also grown in importance recently as higher education has had to reduce its scale, as some campuses have begun to concentrate on their comparative advantage, and as more institutions realize that they need to cut back to move ahead. As one strategic planning study put it: "To grow in quality in a time of fiscal constraint, universities need to accept the principle of substitution. That is, to race out into the academic growth fields of the 1990s, it is necessary to trim or discard some of the programs of the 1950s."[26]

As a shorthand way of looking at college programs, some institutions use the now-famous grid devised by the Boston Consulting Group. The grid is a thumbnail way of doing quick and gross portfolio analysis for a corporation. It divides all the firm's products into four categories: "stars," those with good growth potential and market share; "cows" (for cash cows), those with weak growth potential but good market share; "question marks," those with high growth potential but poor market share; and "dogs," which have poor growth prospects and poor market share. "Stars" should be nourished; "dogs" should be divested or phased out. An academic adaptation of this four-box grid is shown. Some analysts prefer to make this a nine-box grid, adding medium quality and moderate potential student demand. I prefer the larger grid.

ACADEMIC PROGRAMS

High Quality   Low Quality

STARS	QUESTION MARKS	High Student Demand
COWS	DOGS	Low Student Demand

One of the best simple rating schemes for programs is that developed for the State University of New York at Albany in the mid-1970s. It has 12 basic criteria for evaluating each academic program and different rating categories.[27]

	Evaluative Criteria	*Rating Categories*
QUALITY	Quality of Faculty	Exceptional, Strong, Adequate, Weak
	Quality of Students	High, Medium, Low
	Quality of Library Holdings	Excellent, Adequate, Insufficient
	Quality of Facilities and Equipment	Excellent, Adequate, Insufficient
NEED	Centrality of Mission	Yes, No
	Present Student Demand	High, Moderate, Low
	Projected Student Demand	Growing, Stable, Declining
	Demand for Graduates	High, Medium, Low
	Locational Advantage	Yes, No
	Comparative Advantage	Yes, No
COST	Cost/Revenue Relationship	Good, Adequate, Poor
	Other Costs and Benefits	(Listing)

This part of the strategic analysis can be somewhat painful for colleges and universities that have a weak tradition of honesty and frankness or are not used to institutional introspection. But it must be done, being sensitive, of course, to the threatening nature of this inquiry to some people. There is little value in basing a plan for the future on rhetoric, pieties, or unnecessarily negative or inflated beliefs. As David Ewing has said, "Perhaps most important in organizational appraisal is focusing on *abilities* rather than aspirations, on *strengths* rather than status, on *aptitudes* and *values* rather than verbalizations."[28] In my experience, universities often are much better in certain areas than they realize and a lot worse in other areas than they pretend to be. This element in the analysis tests the institution's vaunted "search for truth" claims.

3. *The abilities and priorities of the leaders.* John Millett, one of the most distinguished and experienced analysts of academic management, makes no bones about it: "The planning effectiveness of a campus depends on the planning effectiveness of its presidential leadership. There is no escape from this situation."[29] It is also Millett's view that "few governing boards have the competence or the inclination to be innovative, to be experimental, to chart new courses. By their very nature governing boards tend to conserve what is and seek new paths only when a crisis is clearly at hand."[30] This suggests that, although trustees must make the final decisions, the initiative for planning must come from the president and provost, along with the financial vice-president, deans, and leading members of the faculty. I agree, though I have known single trustees to play an influential or propelling role. And occasionally a board of trustees will take its own planning initiative, as did the trustees of Indiana's Hanover College, who organized a Long-Range Planning Committee, won a grant from the Lilly Endowment for their work, and conducted their own two-year study between 1980 and 1982. President John Horner says, "The Board believes that the future of the college cannot be left to chance. It must be planned as much as possible." But this is unusual. Therefore, an unjaundiced and nonroseate analysis of the abilities, weaknesses, and personal leanings of the campus leadership is imperative, as is a penetrating look at who exactly makes the key decisions on campus and how.

The entire strategy may have to be tailored considerably for the top leadership if the strategy is to get off the ground. Lawrence Lynn, in an interview about policy analysis, said:

> Let me take the example of Elliot Richardson, for whom I worked, or Robert McNamara, for that matter. These two individuals were perfectly capable of understanding the most complex issues and absorbing detail—absorbing the complexity, fully considering it in their own minds. . . . An analyst could actually get away with being somewhat sloppy and still make the point because these men had exceptionally capable minds; they were highly rational.
>
> On the other hand, and I do not want to use names, you will probably find more typical the decision makers who do not really like to approach problems intellectually. They may be visceral, they may approach issues with a wide variety of preconceptions, they may not like to read, they may not like

data, they may not like the appearance of rationality, they may like to see things couched in more political terms, or overt value terms. And an analyst has to take that into account. . . .

I can give you an example of what I mean by that latter one. . . . Joe Califano was very different in the way he could be reached than an Elliot Richardson, or even Caspar Weinberger. Califano is a political animal and has a relatively short attention span—highly intelligent, but an action-oriented person. And one of the problems his analysts had is that they attempted to educate him in the classical, rational way without reference to any political priorities, or without attempting to couch issues and alternatives in terms that would appeal to a political, action-oriented individual. . . .

I think it is not that difficult to discover how a Jerry Brown or a Joe Califano or a George Bush or a Teddy Kennedy thinks, how he reacts. All you have to do is talk to people who deal with them continuously, or read what they say and write. And you start to discover the kinds of things that preoccupy them, the kinds of ways they approach problems. And you can use that information in your policy analyses.[31]

Strategies need to have a keen sense of the particular strengths and prejudices of the key implementers. Strategies should not be built, however, entirely around one or two individuals, because presidents turn over, deans retire or leave, and provosts can move on to take a new position elsewhere. The welfare of the institution must remain the highest priority. But in the short run, trimming, adjustments, and substitutions may need to be made so that the academic managers have a saddle that they find comfortable for riding into the future. There is little profit in concocting a bold, ingenious strategy for new quality if the president feels, "We have a good little college here. Our only problem is that people don't love it enough."

4. *Environmental trends: threats and opportunities.* Though many methods have been tried here, from the Delphi technique of the early 1970s to the Trend Analysis Program, or TAP, the Washington-based unit that monitors journals, government statistics and reports, and scholarly papers and books to attempt to discern the major trends and issues of the next decade for the Institute of Life Insurance (400 top insurance executives), no agreed-upon set of procedures for scanning the environment exists. Major universities and the best colleges have a faculty, of course, who can be extremely useful for this analysis. Indeed, more and more corporations are hiring professors to do issues analysis and forecasting for them, to alert top management of upcoming, unsuspected issues in society and new outside threats to and opportunities for the business. But each institution needs to devise its own way of approaching this very important analysis.

There are generally agreed to be five areas about which a campus needs to do forecasting.

a. *Technological forecasting.* What is likely to happen with computers, telecommunications, transportation? What will your campus do about, say, the advent of word processing: capital purchases, retraining, printing services, new academic programs?

b. *Economic forecasting.* Has the United States entered a prolonged period of slight economic decline and intensified international competition? If so, what does that do to the structure of our economy and its manpower needs? What about inflation, and family incomes? Are there changes in consumer spending on the horizon? Are there opportunities for new educational services or new kinds of research?

c. *Demographic forecasting.* What exactly will the high school graduation cohort be like for each of the next 18 years—in your state, your region, and nationally? How will immigration patterns affect enrollments? Interstate migrations? What are the trends in adult education?

d. *Politico-legal forecasting.* What are the probabilities of federal government support for research, scholarship aid, equipment, graduate studies? What trends can be found in recent court decisions pertaining to education? What are the likely political developments in your state and county? Which require opposition, which support?

e. *Sociocultural forecasting.* Are there likely shifts in public values, moral tenets, life-styles, the arts? David Ewing said a decade ago that we need to think also of "the trends we take no account of at all, such as changes in attitude toward authority, organization, technology, society, and man himself."[32] Might higher education itself soon come to be seen as too expensive and drawn-out a process?

These questions are but a few that should be raised in each category. Though the procedures for gathering these forecasts are still crude and likely to remain so, this must not deter skillful guesswork based on data, insights, and shrewd speculation. It is a common flaw among the highly learned in academe to prefer to do very little until near-certainty and rigorous methodologies have been worked out. But life does not allow such delays. We must act, doing the best we can with what we have. Herodotus and Thucydides wrote the first histories without a tidy method. Environmental scanning too should proceed regardless, adjusting regularly to new conditions.

5. *Market preferences, perceptions, and directions.* David Riesman and other higher education watchers have suggested that colleges have entered a new period of student consumerism, one that will have radical consequences for the way institutions approach and deal with their clienteles. Already advertising has increased; admissions materials are being rewritten and newly designed; graduate students are being treated differently; more universities are using direct mail, market research, and close analysis of students who get accepted but elect to go elsewhere and students who drop out.[33]

Marketing has so far developed three major concepts: segmentation, perceptual mapping, and positioning. Segmentation seeks to break down the market into discrete blocs of clients or potential clients. Perceptual mapping attempts to find out what adolescents, parents, alumni, business leaders, community influentials, and other groups perceive to be the nature of your college or university and its strengths and weaknesses. Positioning, which relies on segment analysis and perceptual mapping, tries to help build on widely held perceptions about your organization with the right audiences. As one pair of practitioners write, "Start with the mind of the prospect. Instead of asking what you are, you ask what position you already own."[34] It is essential to know precisely what your institution's strengths and weaknesses are. But it is also important to know what the public thinks are your strong and weak points, what image of your campus the market holds in its mind. For example, MIT has a sizable and quite good liberal arts program and it has long been strong in economics and business. But the institution is perceived almost totally as an applied science and engineering campus.

Marketing, which has a sleazy ring to it for most academics, is not to be confused with selling or advertising. Generally, higher education does too much selling and too little marketing. In marketing, the effort is a more scholarly one of systematically understanding who it is your university is serving, why they come, why they don't come, and how you might serve your students better and position yourself more self-consciously in the complex network of 3,100 colleges and universities. Marketing is an invaluable tool in helping to improve your institution's communications with outsiders and establish your comparative advantage. As the French marketers say, *"Cherchez le creneau,"* or "Look for the hole." Your campus needs to look for the special hole, or market niche, that you already hold or wish to occupy. To be trite, no college can be everything to everybody.

6. *Competitive situation: threats and opportunities.* Every college and university competes for good students and excellent professors, as well as for

research contracts, foundation grants, and financial contributions from alumni (a large portion of whom are alumni of more than one school that seeks their dollars) and other donors. When I have reminded campus executives of this, the usual response is, "Of course. I know that." But it is rare that a college takes the competitive situation into consideration in its plans, strategies, hiring, construction, or recruiting. Many U.S. state universities have yet to consider the impact on them of the expansion of the state colleges and the addition of new community colleges over the past 30 years.

But this too is changing fast. In the 1980s and beyond, universities will almost certainly increase scanning expertise in this area. You simply cannot design a fruitful strategy without an astute understanding of your institution's competitive situation. Michael Porter of Harvard Business School, who has written the first methodical book on the subject, *Competitive Strategy*, says, "The goal of competitive strategy . . . is to find a position in the industry where a company can best defend itself against these competitive forces or can influence them in its favor."[35]

Colleges and universities need to set up a system for competitor evaluations: collecting annual reports, student newspapers, budget presentations, alumni magazines, admissions literature, weekly calendars of events, lectures, and social occasions, and other revealing materials. Fortunately, colleges are far more open about sharing information and techniques than commercial firms. Indeed, a few institutions, in order to preserve their own integrity, scale, and competitive edge, have helped other campuses get started.

For example, in the 1960s the leaders of the University of Toronto decided that for academic reasons it should not grow beyond 15,000 students. But the city of Toronto and the province of Ontario had a rapidly growing population. So the university actually helped the province start several new campuses, lending faculty and guiding the new places toward forming their own personalities during the first several years. Toronto now has some new competition such as York University, but it finds this preferable to gradually becoming as large as, say, Ohio State or the University of Texas at Austin, and losing its distinctive educational position, advantages, and reputation.[36]

Once you have good information on the colleges and universities with which you most frequently compete, you can plot your competitive situation as we did during a strategic planning study at the University of Maryland. Such a depiction can be only roughly accurate, but it can help provide a crude sense of which institutions are close competitors and in which direction you might wish to improve.

← *low* ACADEMIC QUALITY *high* →

QUALITY OF LIFE (← *low* / *high* →)

Harvard
Princeton ●   ● Harvard
                    ● MIT
                              ● U. of Pennsylvania
Bryn Mawr ●
Swarthmore ●
              ● U. of Virginia
                              ● U. of North Carolina
        ● Lehigh
Gettysburg ●   ● Bucknell
Goucher ●
Hood ●
Washington ●   Lafayette
Western Maryland ●
                              ● Johns Hopkins
Towson State ●   Virginia Tech   ● Georgia Tech
Loyola ●   ● U. of Maryland, College Park
Howard ●   U. of Delaware   ● Georgetown
St. Mary's State ●   ● St. John's
Frostburg State ●   ● Carnegie-Mellon
Salisbury State ●   West Virginia U.   ● UMBC
Morgan State ●
        ● Montgomery C.C.

● Baltimore C.C.

When the University of Illinois sought to consolidate its two campuses in Chicago, Chicago Circle and the Medical Center, into one stronger institution, it was a competitive analysis that turned out to be one of the most persuasive pieces of information. Developed by James Elsass, now associate vice-chancellor for academic affairs at the Medical Center, the award-winning instrument is called *An Identification of College and University Peer Groups.* It examines 27 institutional variables, using factor analysis; then, using cluster analysis on the factors, it clusters the more than 1,000 colleges and universities studied into 18 peer groups for public institutions and 27 for private ones. When Chicago Circle's objective comparative standing in the competitive analysis turned out to be much lower than the campus's subjective claims, the revelation acted as one of the catalysts for merger.[37]

According to Michael Porter, there are three "generic" strategies of competition. One is "overall cost leadership." This is where a firm provides good quality at a lower cost than competitors. It is what Black and Decker does in power tools and Panasonic does in consumer electronics;

and it is what Berkeley and UCLA provide for Californians, Cooper Union for New Yorkers, and the University of Florida for Floridians. Several outstanding community colleges also offer excellent values in their limited areas. A second generic strategy is "differentiation," where an organization provides a distinctive product or service—Levi's pants, L.L. Bean's outdoors goods, American Express, Berlitz. Most colleges and universities fit this category—or should. Third is the strategy of "focus," when an institution furnishes a special product or service for a particular segment of the market: Mercedes-Benz, or Grumbacher paints and brushes for artists. In this category are institutions such as Gallaudet College (for the deaf), the Webb Institute of Naval Architecture, Oral Roberts, University of California at Davis (the enology program), and many schools of music, art, and technology.

Central to the formulation of an academic strategy is a knowledge of where you stand in the competition and a decision about exactly what competitive position you will strive to establish. Porter advocates that each organization decide emphatically which of the three it will emphasize. He says, "A firm that is stuck in the middle is in an extremely poor strategic situation," although "there seems to be a tendency for firms in difficulty to flip back and forth over time among the generic strategies."[38]

If the key persons at your college or university plant these three elements of internal analysis and three elements of external analysis firmly in their minds, and if the institution can openly discuss, perhaps even with occasional acrimony, where the organization should fit in and then build out, you are on your way toward deciding your own academic future—one that is rationally grounded in the internal and external factual realities yet one that is psychologically and politically convincing to most of the campus principals. The final strategy will surely involve some compromises because of certain people or conditions, but at least the compromise will not be reached on the basis of power plays and horse trading alone; it will have considerable rational and economic components too. Your university will have some agreed-upon objectives for action now and in the near future. You will need to make frequent adjustments as internal and external conditions change, but you will be able to manage, through holding people to the strategy, by objectives.

In their book *The Art of Japanese Management,* Richard Pascale and Anthony Athos argue for a renewed emphasis in America on what they call the "soft" aspects of Japanese management: the right management staff; the consultative style of the organization; the special skills of an organization that other organizations do not possess; and "superordinate goals," or guiding concepts that the entire organization understands, accepts, and behaves according to.[39] As Richard Chait has pointed out in a delightful article, American colleges and universities have long concentrated on what are now suddenly regarded as the sources of Japanese management success: participatory management, lack of autocratic rule, quality controls, specially selected people, and lofty aims.[40] But American higher education is only now beginning to think in terms of academic strategies that will contribute to long-term health and quality. With slightly stronger and controversy-tolerant central management and strategic decision making added, the better colleges and universities should continue to prosper and contribute mightily to the quality of life and people of this nation for many more centuries.

CHAPTER EIGHT

Different Campuses, Different Processes

*Don't be afraid to take a big step if one is indicated.
You can't cross a chasm in two small jumps.*
DAVID LLOYD GEORGE

*There has always been room for innovation and fresh
starts in American higher education, even if this freedom, which rested partly on expanding enrollments
and funds, is more circumscribed now. What is really
lacking is strong and visionary academic leadership.*
DAVID RIESMAN

Q: *How does one make love to a porcupine?*
A: *Very carefully.*
ANONYMOUS

IF A COLLEGE OR UNIVERSITY is persuaded that it
should move promptly toward better management and strategic planning,
where does it begin?

The stimulants for such a change in academe are fairly clear. They
derive from three sources. One is a major crisis in finances, enrollments,
or quality that mandates quick, decisive, intelligent action. Another is
strong pressure from outside, by a governor or legislature, influential
alumni, the press, key trustees, or a state higher education agency (if it is
reputable and not just political or aggrandizing). The third is a vigorous,
farsighted leader, usually the campus president, but sometimes the academic or financial vice-president, and more rarely a chairman of the board
of trustees or one or two deans and a few senior faculty members.[1]

About two-thirds of America's institutions of higher learning currently
have, and others will very soon have, the first impeller. Many institutions,
particularly public ones, are also pressed by the second one. But relatively
few colleges or universities today possess forceful, visionary leadership.

Looked at another way, academic change is stimulated by either Marxist and Darwinian forces, where objective factors, economic conditions,
and the external environment compel people and organizations to alter
their structures and ways, or by Hegelian and Weberian factors, where the
charisma, intellect, energy, or values of extraordinary individuals pulls

people and organizations in new directions. Max Weber, for example, proposed that dozens of powerful Protestant leaders succeeded in instituting a new "Protestant ethic," which made possible a frugal, hardworking "spirit" for the creation of a capitalist society. And Hegel suggested that there are "great historical men," who have influenced the course of history: "Such individuals had no consciousness of the general Idea they were enfolding while prosecuting those aims of theirs. On the contrary, they were practical, political men. But at the same time they were thinking men, who had an insight into the requirements of the time—what was ripe for development."[2]

Most colleges today have two of the three forms of impetus available to use for a drive for better management and strategy. The main problem is with the third, although, as I have described, a new breed of stronger academic executives with planning interests is coming into existence.

Academic strategy must begin, therefore, with a change of heart and mind in the academic executives—or a change of academic executives. Simply put, campus presidents need to shift the focus of their attention and energy gradually to the long-term interests of their institutions and their increasingly competitive and difficult environments. Just as America's corporate executives have been lambasted for their intense concern for annual profits at the expense of the long-term health and competitiveness of their corporations,[3] so college and university leaders may be faulted for their preoccupation with daily administration. They need to spend more hours worrying about future threats and opportunities.

American higher education is famous for its variety. Colleges and universities differ immensely. Amitai Etzioni once observed that where tradition is strong and commitment to an organization is high, exceptional central management is not so imperative; but where an organization is new, weak, or declining, the role of the top executives becomes critical.[4] Some campuses have lively faculty governance; others have almost none. Some large universities are enormously complex and cumbersome to unite; some small colleges are relatively easy to gather together for a strategy. Also, leaders differ in their strengths and proclivities. As there are many different kinds of institutions of higher education, there need to be many different kinds of strategic planning processes and styles of management. You will need to analyze your own situation and devise a tailored process.

Yet there are some constants. Every institution needs to have a forcible champion of good management and planning. It should be the president. But if he or she is not able to be, the president must support unwaveringly the provost or whoever else is the active leader for better quality controls, academic management, and strategy making. More efforts at improvement and better planning collapse because of the lack of consistent advocacy by the top leadership and persistent monitoring of divisional plans than for any other reason. As Donald Lelong found in his office's attempts to stimulate better planning at the University of Michigan, "Many academic administrators went to the president or academic vice president, asking in effect: Whose idea is this, really, and how seriously are we to take it?"[5] That is, unit heads will stonewall, drag their feet, or give mere lip service to better management and strategic policymaking unless they are fully convinced that the president (and his or her board of trustees) really means it and is prepared to get tough with laggards.

Deans and academic middle managers are not especially reactionary. They are just human and dedicated line officers. The psychologist William James said in 1892:

> In all the apperceptive operations of the mind, a certain general law makes itself felt—the law of economy. In admitting a new body of experience, we instinctively seek to disturb as little as possible our pre-existing stock of ideas. We always try to name a new experience in some way which will assimilate it to what we already know. We hate anything absolutely new. . . .
>
> In later life this economical tendency to leave the old undisturbed leads to what we know as "old fogyism." A new idea or fact which would entail extensive rearrangement of the previous system of beliefs is always ignored or extruded from the mind in case it cannot be sophistically reinterpreted so as to tally harmoniously with the system. We have all conducted discussions with middle-aged people, overpowered them with our reasons, forced them to admit our contention, and a week later found them back as secure and constant in their old opinion as if they had never conversed with us at all.
>
> We call them old fogies; but there are young fogies too. Old fogyism begins at a younger age than we think. I am afraid to say so, but I believe in the majority of human beings it begins at about 25.[6]

It is one of the supreme agonies of our time that many educated Americans are children of the Enlightenment, adhering to notions of progress, change, and liberation, to the need to discard the past and tradition, and to the urgency of reform and greater rationalization; but they behave for the most part as obdurate conservators hostile to alterations in their personal lives and in their organizations. We proclaim the urgency of renovation and say the new is superior to the old; yet we are annoyed with anyone who would disturb our nests and change our daily routines.[7] Academic officials and professors are not exempt from the foibles of human nature.

But there is also an inevitable tension between stability and change in organizations, between the innovators and strategists and the line officers and operators. Executives with responsibility for production and the effective operation of their areas work hard to achieve smooth, harmonious conditions. They seek peace and stability to get their jobs done, and done well. To them, long-range strategists and planners are creators of turbulence, askers of nasty questions, bringers of upsetting news about new external forces, and wreckers of solid performance. Line officers often squirm and scheme to escape from strategy sessions: "How much longer will this go on? I've got an operation to run." Their very dedication to unruffled productivity this month, or this year, leads to their distaste for change, innovation, and strategic shifts. Planning only throws sand into the pistons.

Yet especially in our time, the absolute rule is "Thou shalt not calcify." The continued health of the operations of any organization depends on clever adaptation, alert changes, daring innovations.[8] Therefore, as one analyst put it, "The problem of striking the right balance between strategic and operating considerations is one of the central problems in the whole management process."[9] And Fred Crossland, for years an officer promoting change for the Ford Foundation, wrote during the heyday of management science, "It is especially important to prescribe proper dosages of planning for colleges and universities. Too little, and the debilitating systems of institutional drift, ad hoc-ism, and crisis management become more acute. Too much, and creativity may be replaced by formulas, process may become more important than product, managerial arteriosclerosis may set in, and all the unattractive side effects of advanced bureaucratitis may become evident."[10]

This means that balance is critical in academic management. Since the present situation in higher education, however, is one tending to stalemate and muddling, with the normal wariness toward change reinforced by the prospect of hard times, which causes people to dig in with all 10 fingers against cuts or changes, the need is for much more active management, a new emphasis on innovation and adaptation to new conditions, and a push for the creation of an academic strategy to weather the lightning and heavy rains. Special steps are in order to establish a new "planning culture."[11]

Michael Kami, who has served as director of planning for both IBM and Xerox, believes such a planning culture can grow only if all three parties—president, planners, and line executives—do their part. Presidents must give one-third of their time to the long-run strength and quality of the organization, feel comfortable with risk, controversy, and change ("to accept, love, and promote change"), and be ready to make the hard decisions. Planners need to help with the process with vital information and facts. They should coordinate, stimulate, and encourage planning in all divisions rather than plan themselves, and keep planning simple and low-key. Line officers have to be prepared to take responsibility for innovations and strategies of their own that embellish the main strategy, as well as running their day-to-day operations. They need to see that continued smooth operations and good performance in their areas absolutely demand that they look ahead and outward as well as directly in front of them and inward.[12]

Three things seem to help nearly every college or university in its strategic struggle for stability and greater quality.

One is a venture capital fund. University leaders will never convince line officers of their commitment to change and to fresh approaches unless they make dollars available for important new ventures or areas of bright intellectual potential. George Weathersby told me: "Colleges talk a lot about developing new ideas and information. But it is startling how few actually set aside money for promising new ventures. One way to find out quickly if a university means what it says about its creativity and pushing out the frontiers of knowledge is to ask how much of its budget is set aside annually as risk capital to sponsor good new ventures. Every really good college and serious university should have a venture capital fund."

Bluntly, an institution espousing alertness, flexibility for new opportunities, and strategic initiatives needs to put some of its money where its mouth is. The University of Michigan, for example, until the financial crisis, had a Priority Fund, where all units contributed one percent of their budgets to a central pool for reallocating resources and providing seed money for enterprising new ventures.[13] Other universities have recently instituted similar special funds. Sometimes budget cuts can provide an occasion for new venture money. Indeed, Richard Cyert believes that retrenchments should at all possible times be accompanied by "positive programs." He says no college should ever allow itself to get in a position of unrelieved trimming, pulling back, and economizing at every turn. "Danger stems from too great an emphasis on survival. . . . The university must not only survive, but it must survive fruitfully."[14]

When Emmett Fields, now president of Vanderbilt University, was president of the State University of New York at Albany, he was forced to make program cuts because of financial shortfalls in 1975 to 1978. A dedicated planner, Fields cut slightly deeper than absolutely necessary into programs like nursing, speech pathology, and astronomy and used some of the dollars saved to invest in programs of superior quality, in one or two new ventures, and in programs that were most central to SUNY

Albany's academic strategy of using to advantage its location in the state capital: policy studies, political science, criminal justice, and social welfare. According to Fred Volkwein, the assistant to the president, "The faculty was obviously not happy. But they were able to take pride in the fact that the university was still moving ahead, sharpening its mission, and supporting fresh opportunities even in a time of terrible cuts."

It is urgent that hard times not kill all advances and initiatives. One state university I know recently declared that as of the fiscal year 1983–84 all proposals for new funding would not be considered until further notice. This is to proclaim slow death by self-strangulation because the academic management, like Christian Scientists, refuses to do any minor surgery. Certainly, an academic strategy and an advance in quality are impossible at such a university. To foster change, have a venture capital fund ready to support those on campus who are the most creative and entrepreneurial.

A second form of help is a consultant. Consultants, like auto mechanics, come in all shades of expertise. But the best of them in higher education— and there are as yet relatively few superb ones except in the fund-raising area—can inject a wealth of fresh and stimulating perspectives. Also, by being outside the internal bureaucracy and satrapies, they can transcend local rivalries and speak impartially about the good of the whole institution. In his study of 49 liberal arts colleges that had received planning grants from the Exxon Foundation to improve their academic management, Victor Baldridge learned that "in the Exxon colleges, it appears that the most successful projects used outside consultants well, linking them with knowledgeable people within the institutions."[15]

The problem with consultants for academic management is that those expert in business management and strategic planning, like those with McKinsey or Arthur D. Little, often are said to have an inadequate feel for higher education as an enterprise, while education consultants tend to be experienced incrementalists, sometimes wise but seldom attuned to the new strategic and financial planning needs of the 1980s. Still, a few truly discerning outside minds can jolt the campus into looking at realities or attractive possibilities as insiders would not dare to do and could not afford to do.

A third form of assistance for an institution wishing to improve its academic management and strategic decision making is the growing number of courses, workshops, and programs available to campus executives. Some institutions like Carnegie-Mellon and Harvard have summer institutes in higher education management, and hundreds of campus administrators, mostly middle-level executives, have attended. Some of the national higher education associations now run workshops and short institutes. And several universities have begun their own in-house programs for upgrading management expertise, planning capabilities, and computer modeling techniques.

Such training programs should multiply in the 1980s as the management of higher education organizations is increasingly viewed as a critical factor in an institution's ability to endure and continue to grow in excellence in the more competitive and difficult period ahead. As Ohio University's President Charles Ping has written, "What is required is not a simple transfer of technique from business to higher education but rather a translation of the business model for organizational planning into references and values of the campus."[16] Colleges and universities should avail themselves of the training available, or set up their own little Rand Corporation on campus to study what are the best ways to structure the university, enhance learning on campus, and manage nonprofit organizations. Just as Frederick Taylor and his disciples believed that the efficiency of the operations of the workers held the key to productivity and excellence in manufacturing firms, so the evidence seems to be gathering that good principals and professional, visionary academic managers may be the key to productivity and excellence in schools, colleges, and universities.

Nobel laureate Herbert Simon put it this way:

> A substantial part of this nation's resources are being devoted to higher education. The nation has a right to expect more than talented amateurism and an occasional Mark Hopkins in return.
>
> A college president who tries to make education professional should not expect a unanimous vote of thanks from his faculty, or even his students. But if a man's first aim in life were to be comfortable and to be liked, he would choose an easier occupation than college president. Leadership that persuades an institution to seize the opportunities before it can be a source of deep satisfactions, satisfactions that will repay the effort, stress, and even conflict required to achieve them.[17]

CHAPTER NINE

Tomorrow's Professors and Administrators

Our college cause will be known to our children's children. Let us take care that the rogues shall not be ashamed of their grandfathers.
DANIEL WEBSTER

Many great civilizations in history have collapsed at the height of their achievement because they were unable to analyze their problems, to change direction, and to adjust to new situations which faced them by concerting their wisdom and strength.
KURT WALDHEIM

He who defends everything defends nothing.
FREDERICK THE GREAT

EVERYONE KNOWS THE REALITIES of trying to run a college or university and the actual behavior of organization executives are opposed to the near-heroic and rationally decisive normative behavior drawn in textbooks about management. For example, despite the fact that more than 80 percent of all campus presidents have been faculty members, Cohen and March found in their investigations: "Educational policy, in so far as it is a matter for the general faculty, tends to be a fairly straightforward 'log-roll' among the major faculty groups. . . In general, the president's role has been relatively unimportant in recent years except in a few cases where he has entered the educational policy arena with limited objectives. . . . Although presidents are educators by experience and by identification, they are not educators by behavior."[1]

Academic administrators are frequently patronized and mocked, and regarded as necessary evils or carbuncles on the faculty collective's neck. This is especially so at the superior institutions. Thorstein Veblen expressed the anarchic longing of some faculty 65 years ago: "The academic executive and all his works are anathema, and should be discontinued by the simple expedient of wiping him off the slate."[2] And during the student uprisings of 1967–72 Veblen's feelings were echoed by many other professors, including some illustrious scholars. Noted journals like *Daedalus* published professorial statements such as this: "Trustees, presidents, deans, registrars, secretaries, janitors, and the like are not, strictly speaking, part of the university at all. . . . They are ancillary to the real business of the university, and only the supplanting of the community model by the corporation model has put them in their present dominant position."[3] By the early 1970s the attitude toward administrators held by numerous faculty members, confident because of rising enrollments, increasing grants and dollars for research, earnings comparable to businessmen, and new public respect for science and intellect, began to resemble the attitude of the nouveau riche industrialists in the early 20th century toward the professors they supported with their contributions and patronized as quaint if sometimes radically noisy "eggheads."

This supercilious mind-set toward the management of their own institutions, a management which is usually composed of ex-professors and often recent colleagues, still persists among faculties, though in diminished form, despite the old and new realities of faculty funding and behavior. In the same year as the *Daedalus* remark, the noted political scientist David Truman wrote: "There has been a kind of atrophy of intra-institutional contacts and identifications. We now have a situation, perfectly familiar in most universities, where a man will have more intimate and close contact with colleagues 3,000 miles away and will share more loyalty and affection with them than he will with a colleague who occupies an office three doors down the corridor. There has been, in consequence of this, a weakening of concern for the collective educational enterprise that spans any such professional boundaries or should span them."[4]

The erosion of institutional collegiality is often combined with the long-famous reluctance of most professors to come to closure, to choose priorities, or to decide anything irrevocably and with their reluctance about change within a college or university. The academic department is the dominant educational influence on most campuses. Yet J. B. Lon Hefferlin found that in 1968, as the student rebellions were expanding, only 73 of the 426 academic departments he studied, or 17 percent, were receptive to curricular changes of any kind.[5]

Thus, there is the reality that presidents can't act and faculties won't act. This, at the very time that higher education faces the most serious enrollment, financial, and public confidence crises of the century, as well as radical changes in program demands, the use of technology, and client markets.

There is also the reality of executive life. Managers, including academic managers, work a punishing number of hours. They prefer the telephone, informers, and short, personal meetings over facts, reports, and information about the environment. There are tedious ceremonies and constant interruptions. They become prisoners of their daily calendars and mail trays, and compulsives about dealing with every crisis, no matter how small. They behave not too differently from some presidents of the United States, as Richard Neustadt described them:

> A President's own use of time, his allocation of his personal attention, is governed by the things he *has* to do from day to day. . . . These doings may be far removed from academic images of White House concentration on high policy, grand strategy. There is no help for that. A President's priorities are set not by the relative importance of a task, but by the relative necessity for him to do it. He deals first with the things that are required of *him* next. Deadlines rule his personal agenda.[6]

In his study of corporate managerial work, Henry Mintzberg discovered: "It was rare to see a chief executive participating in abstract discussion or carrying out general planning. . . . Clearly, the classic view of the manager as planner is not in accord with reality."[7] Indiana's George Weathersby said to me, "The quality of management in most American colleges and universities is not high. Many presidents spend much of their time trying to anger the fewest people rather than trying to produce something really good—for their students, their faculty, their institution." In my own experience, university presidents will often accept needless engagements or take peculiar trips rather than thrash out an issue thoroughly or pry a hard decision affecting the future of their campus out of their colleagues and aides. These evasions reduce controversy but deprive deans and vice-presidents of guidance, direction, and clear-cut strategic preferences.

Henry Wriston once quipped that "the duty of the dean is to make the college what the president has long asserted it already is." It often works out that way. There is churning administration and a fair amount of governance, both below with the faculty and above with the trustees. But, except among rare individuals, presidents in American higher education tend to avoid management and leadership like a poison ivy patch.

Must this continue to be so? I think not. Moreover, I believe that unless new patterns of leadership, such as I have shown are already being crafted, become more prevalent, U.S. higher education will have an even more tearing time in the coming decade than many expect. This would be a tragedy for American scholarship and for the nation, which increasingly depends on an intelligent, innovative, internationally competitive populace.

A major obstacle is the unwillingness to recognize that a college or university can no longer claim to be like a snug little boarding school community and the concomitant unwillingness to accept the fact that colleges and universities are organizations, and often large, complex, expensive ones at that. The main point is not to prod the contemporary university to behave more like a business, but to nudge it to behave more like an organization. Or better, to get it to behave like an organism that must feed itself, change, and adapt to its environment.

Contributing to the obstacle is a curious notion among some academics that thought is somehow quite separate from activity in life, and that management is ugly because it attempts to be thought-in-action, because it is practical. William James reminds us all that "the brain, so far as we understand it, is given us for practical behavior. Every current that runs into it from skin or eye or ear runs out again into muscles, glands, or viscera, and helps the animal adapt to its environments. . . . We cannot escape our destiny, which is practical; and even our most theoretic faculties contribute to its working out."[8]

No one railed against the precious view of university intellectuality more than the philosopher Alfred North Whitehead. He wrote in his preface to *Aims of Education,* "The whole book is a protest against dead knowledge, that is to inert ideas." He stormed on, "Every intellectual revolution which has ever stirred humanity into greatness has been a passionate protest against inert ideas. . . . Pedants sneer at an education that is useful. But if education is not useful, what is it? Is it a talent to be hidden away in a napkin?"[9]

American scholars have, to their glory, forged some valuable knowledge about organizations, group psychology, planning, and management. This knowledge should not remain inert, unused. It is applicable to colleges and universities, who need all the aid they can get against the troublesome period ahead. Faculty professionals should see that enlightened academic executives who are employing the new knowledge to cope with fiercer conditions are not a freshly armed enemy but activist colleagues.

But college and university presidents and other administrators also present an obstacle in that they often believe organizational administration means that they have to eschew thoughtful analysis, intellectual digestion of important data and forecasts, and new ideas for their life of practical, nose-in-the-grit duties. "I have to be practical," presidents have said to me, as if practicality excluded thought, foresight, and vision. Whereas some professors grow disdainful with inert ideas, some academic executives grow frenetic with mindless activity.

There is nothing so important for American higher education now as the reemergence of thoughtful educators, of academic executives who are farsighted statesmen and not just card-carrying members of the firemen's union. And the new forms of strategic analysis and decision making provide sharp new tools to exercise academic management of an order never before practiced.

The probable linchpin for organizational renovation on campus is a new form of governance that is also a new form of management. Mary Parker Follett, the first American woman to write about problems of organization and management, hinted at the new form in her book *Dynamic Administration,* wherein she described a process that included both greater clarity of decision making and increased consultation among the "primal authorities" in the organization.[10] You can watch it being born in the new policy and budget committees and planning and priorities committees sprouting up among American colleges and universities. The new committees bring together faculty, deans, and administrators; thought, numbers, and action; financial considerations, long-range plans, and programs; this year's budget, fund-raising goals, and competitive strategies. They are the policy boards in which central academic strategies are most likely to be shaped in the future.

"The scarce factor is attention," Herbert Simon said.[11] There never seems to be enough time for academic managers to give adequate attention to planning for their institutions' survival and added quality. Yet when the students were in turmoil in the late 1960s and early 1970s presidents found ways to devote one-fourth or more of their time to pacification efforts. And when capital campaigns come along, presidents somehow manage to spend one-third or more of their time telling their cases to the affluent, visiting foundations and corporations, and traveling to enlist new support.

Now good management and academic strategy making is as vital as peace and new endowment funds. Indeed, the quest for support in the future is likely to become increasingly dependent on an institution's ability to prove it is well run and has intelligent plans and fresh initiatives to deal with its more inimical, storm-prone environment.

It is instructive to look back at the late-nineteenth-century giants of higher educational leadership. They were not only daring, creative academic managers and fund-raisers, but they remained scholars, public servants, and education reformers. President Noah Porter of Yale wrote a massive textbook, *The Human Intellect,* which went through 30 printings, and edited the first edition of the monumental *Webster's International Dictionary of the English Language.* James Burrill Angell of the University of Michigan was a president of the American Historical Association and made time during his presidency to serve as minister to China under U.S. President James Garfield and minister to Turkey under William McKinley. Minnesota president William Watts Folwell wrote a four-volume history of Minnesota that remains a useful social history of the region. Andrew Dickson White of Cornell helped develop the field of modern European history; served as minister to Germany (1879–81), minister to Russia (1892–94), and ambassador to Germany (1897–1903); and wrote a major book defending science against attacks that it was destructive of religion. Princeton president Woodrow Wilson went on to become a U.S. President.[12]

Surely there were daily crises at the universities in those days too, although educational institutions were less busy and complex. But the style of academic leadership was different. The style of academic management today tends to be far more administrative in a busy, routine way and far less managerial and strategic. Who but Yale's President Giamatti has spoken about today's threats to science and objectivity? Who is leading investigations into the alleged decline of education in schools?

What is needed is a rebirth of academic management, one that combines educational policy and planning with financial administration, one that shows passionate concern for the long-term health of America's best colleges and universities, one that has an agreed-upon strategy for an institution's role and objectives for action.

The philosopher Whitehead saw the need early on, as clairvoyant scholars sometimes do, and addressed it this way in 1928:

> In the modern complex social organism, the adventure of life cannot be disjoined from intellectual adventure. Amid simpler circumstances, the pioneer can follow the urge of his instinct, directed toward the scene of his vision from the mountain top. But in the complex organizations of modern business the intellectual adventure of analysis, and of imaginative reconstruction must precede any successful reorganization.
>
> Today business organization requires an imaginative grasp of the psychologies of populations engaged in different modes of occupation. . . , It requires an imaginative grasp of the interlocking interests of great organizations, and of the reactions of the whole complex to any change in one of its elements. It requires an imaginative understanding of the laws of political economy. . . . It requires an imaginative vision of the binding forces of any human organization, a sympathetic vision of the limits of human nature and of the conditions which evoke loyalty of service. . . . It requires a sufficient conception of the role of applied science in modern society. It requires that discipline of character which can say "yes" and "no" to other men, not by reason of blind obstinacy, but with a firmness derived from a conscious evaluation of relevant alternatives.[13]

Whitehead added, "A university is imaginative or it is nothing—at least nothing useful. . . . The whole art in the organization of a university is the provision of a faculty whose learning is lighted up with imagination."[14]

With astute analysis and participatory discussion, each faculty and its management can decide on an imaginative academic strategy for its competitive future, adjusting it as new conditions arise. Working together and using the new tools of management and strategic planning more self-consciously, scholars and executives can steer their institution's way through the turbulent waters ahead and emerge even stronger and finer.

It is critical that America's colleges and universities do so. If we have become a knowledge-based society, these organizations are the factories and cathedrals of our age. They produce the new knowledge and well-educated leaders for all segments of our society that the United States must have. To the credit of those institutions that are cutting the new templates, the transformation of American higher education from "garbage can" administration to strategic management is under way.

NOTES

CHAPTER ONE: THE NEW TABLEAU OF HIGHER EDUCATION

1. See, for example: Richard Cyert, "The Management of Universities of Constant or Decreasing Size," *Public Administration Review*, 38 (July–August 1978), 344–49, and in the same issue, Charles Levine, "Organizational Decline and Cutback Management," pp. 316–25; Kenneth Mortimer and Michael Tierney, *The Three "R's" of the Eighties: Reduction, Reallocation, and Retrenchment* (AAHE/ERIC, 1979); Robert Behn, "Leadership for Cutback Management: The Use of Corporate Strategy," *Public Administration Review*, 40 (November–December 1980), 613–20; and James Mingle, ed., *Challenges of Retrenchment* (Jossey-Bass, 1981).

2. *Wall Street Journal*, 5 March 1982.

3. David Hopkins and William Massy, *Planning Models for Colleges and Universities* (Stanford University Press, 1981), ch. 2.

4. There has been a remarkable reshaping of the history of American higher education in the nineteenth century by recent scholarship. For an overview, James McLachlan, "The American College in the Nineteenth Century: Toward a Reappraisal," *Teachers College Record*, 80 (December 1978), 287–306. Among the important studies: Jurgen Herbst, *From Crisis to Crisis: American College Government, 1636–1819* (Harvard University Press, 1982); Mark Beach, "Professors, Presidents, and Trustees: A Study in University Governance, 1825–1918," doctoral dissertation, University of Wisconsin, 1966; an earlier work, George Schmidt's *The Old Time College President* (Columbia University Press, 1930); three pieces by David Potts: "American Colleges in the Nineteenth Century: From Localism to Denominationism," *History of Education Quarterly*, 11 (Winter 1971), 363–80; "Liberal Arts Colleges, Private," *The Encyclopedia of Education* (Macmillan; Free Press, 1971), 5, 496–505; and "College Enthusiasm! As Public Response, 1800–1860," *Harvard Educational Review*, 47 (February 1977), 28–42; John S. Whitehead, *The Separation of College and State: Columbia, Dartmouth, Harvard, and Yale, 1776–1876* (Yale University Press, 1974); Sally Gregory Kohlstedt, *The Formation of the American Scientific Community, 1848–1860* (University of Illinois Press, 1976); Douglas Sloan, "Harmony, Chaos, and Consensus: The American College Curriculum," *Teachers College Record*, 73 (December 1971), 221–51; Natalie Naylor, "The Theological Seminary in the Configuration of American Higher Education: The Antebellum Years," *History of Education Quarterly*, 17 (Spring 1977), 17–30; James Findlay, "Agency, Denominations, and the Western Colleges, 1830–1860," *Church History*, 50 (March 1981), 64–80; Stanley Guralnick, *Science and the Antebellum American College* (American Philosophical Society, 1975); Colin Bradley Burke, *American Collegiate Populations* (NYU–Columbia University Press, 1982); Thomas Harding, *College Literary Societies: Their Contribution to Higher Education in the United States, 1815–1876* (Pageant Press, 1971); David Allmendinger, Jr., *Paupers and Scholars: The Transformation of Student Life in Nineteenth-Century New England* (St. Martin's Press, 1973); Daniel Boorstin, *The Americans: The National Experience* (Random House, 1966), ch. 20. Also see Carl Bode, *The American Lyceum* (Southern Illinois University Press, 1956).

5. W. H. Cowley, *Presidents, Professors, and Trustees* (Jossey-Bass, 1980), p. 52.

6. Potts, "American Colleges in the Nineteenth Century," p. 367.

7. Potts, "Liberal Arts Colleges, Private," p. 500; Findlay, "Agency, Denominations, and the Western Colleges, 1830–1860."

8. Cowley, *Presidents, Professors, and Trustees*, p. 138.

9. Allan Nevins, *The State Universities and Democracy* (University of Illinois Press, 1962); Richard Storr, *The Beginning of Graduate Education in America* (University of Chicago

Press, 1953).

10. Milton Mayer, in his delightful sketch, *Young Man in a Hurry: The Story of William Rainey Harper* (University of Chicago Alumni Association, 1957), p. 68.

11. Nathan Pusey, *American Higher Education, 1945–1970: A Personal Memoir* (Harvard University Press, 1978).

12. Earl Cheit, *The New Depression in Higher Education* (McGraw-Hill, 1971), p. 5.

13. David Henry, *Challenges Past, Challenges Present: An Analysis of Higher Education Since 1930* (Jossey-Bass, 1975), p. 16; Cheit, *New Depression in Higher Education*, p. 8; Howard Bowen, *Academic Compensation* (TIAA, 1978); Everett Ladd, "The Economic Position of the American Professoriate," paper delivered at a conference at the University of Southern California, 25–27 January 1978.

14. Cheit, *New Depression in Higher Education*, pp. 6–7. Cheit's influential report, though useful and informative, is a curious one. A scholar of business administration, Cheit never inquired to what extent the "new depression" in higher education was owed to shoddy financial management or weak academic administration. At one point, however, he observes, "It is remarkable how difficult it is for colleges and universities to provide precise amounts for the components of expense and income" (p. 103).

15. William Jellema, "The Red and the Black," *Liberal Education*, 57 (May 1971), 147–59.

16. Howard Bowen, "Financial Needs of the Campus," in *The Corporation and the Campus*, ed. Robert Connery (Academy of Political Science, 1970), p. 81.

17. Fred Crossland, "Learning to Cope with a Downward Slope," *Change*, 12 (July–August 1980), 18, 20–25.

18. *The Post–Land Grant University: The University of Maryland Report* (University of Maryland, 1981), p. 57.

19. Clark Kerr, "Administration of Higher Education in an Era of Change and Conflict," in *Conflict, Retrenchment, and Reappraisal* (University of Illinois Press, 1979), pp. 15, 18.

20. Ben Wattenberg, "This New Nation of Immigrants," *American Spectator* (February 1982), p. 39. For a sensitive portrayal of the new academic tensions, see Richard Rodriguez, *Hunger of Memory: The Education of Richard Rodriguez* (David Godine, 1981).

21. Daniel Bell, *The Reforming of General Education* (Columbia University Press, 1966), see especially ch. 6.

22. Bell, *Reforming of General Education*, p. 282.

23. William James, *Some Problems in Philosophy* (Longmans, 1940), p. 51.

24. George Keller, "The Search for Brainpower," *Public Interest*, no. 4 (Summer 1966), pp. 64–65.

25. Rodney Hartnett and Robert Feldmesser, "College Admissions Testing and the Myth of Selectivity," *AAHE Bulletin*, 33 (March 1980), 3–6.

26. *Three Thousand Futures: The Next 20 Years in Higher Education* (Jossey-Bass, 1980), p.30; David Riesman, *On Higher Education: The Academic Enterprise in an Era of Rising Student Consumerism* (Jossey-Bass, 1980); Philip Kotler, *Marketing for Nonprofit Institutions*, 2d ed. (Prentice-Hall, 1982); Edward Fiske, "The Marketing of the Colleges," *Atlantic*, 244 (October 1979), 93–98; "Hard Sell for Higher Learning: With Enrollment and Budgets Down, Colleges Cater to the Kids," *Time*, 2 October 1978, p. 80.

27. *Post–Land Grant University*, ch. 6; Martin Kilson, "Black Social Classes and Intergenerational Poverty," *Public Interest*, no. 64 (Summer 1981), pp. 58–78; William Julius Wilson, *The Declining Significance of Race*, 2d ed. (University of Chicago Press, 1980).

28. *Three Thousand Futures*, p. 22; Harold Hodgkinson, "Hodgkinson's Wonderful Slide Show," *AGB Reports*, 22 (January–February 1980), 58.

29. David Noble, *America by Design: Science, Technology, and the Rise of Corporate Capitalism* (Knopf, 1977), p. 171. See also Monte Calvert, *Mechanical Engineer in America, 1830–1910* (Johns Hopkins Press, 1967).

30. Noble, *America by Design*, pp. 178–88, 124–25. The kinetic interplay between American higher education, the federal government, and industry in lifting the United States into world eminence in science and technology has received expert attention in recent years. In addition to Noble's history, see especially, Daniel Kevles's exquisite *The Physicists: The History of a Scientific Community in Modern America* (Knopf, 1977), which has a comprehensive bibliographic essay. Also, such studies as: Don K. Price, *Government and Science* (New York University Press, 1954); Thomas Devine, *Corporate Support for Education* (Catholic University of America Press, 1956); A. Hunter Dupree, *Science in the Federal Government: A History and Policies to 1940* (Harvard University Press, 1957); Daniel Greenberg, *The Politics of Pure Science* (New American Library, 1967); Joseph Ben-David, "The Universities and the Growth of Science in Germany and the United States," *Minerva*, 7 (Autumn 1968), 1–35; William Nelson, ed., *The Politics of Science: Readings in Science, Technology, and Government* (Oxford University Press, 1968); Stanley Coben, "The Scientific Establishment and the Transmission of Quantum Mechanics to the United States, 1919–1932," *American Historical Review*, 76 (April 1971), 442–66; Edwin Layton, *The Revolt of the Engineers: Social Responsibility and the American Engineering Profession* (Case–Western Reserve University Press, 1971); Bruce L. R. Smith and Joseph Karlesky, *The State of Academic Science* (Change Magazine Press, 1977).

31. Barbara Culliton, "The Academic-Industrial Complex," *Science*, 216 (May 1982), 960–62.

32. *Three Thousand Futures*, p. 26.

33. Kim Cameron, "The Relationship between Faculty Unionism and Organizational Effectiveness," *Academy of Management Journal*, 25 (March 1982), 6–24.

34. Neal Gross, "Organizational Lag in American Universities," *Harvard Educational Review*, 33 (Winter 1963), 62.

35. Kerr, "Administration of Higher Education in an Era of Change and Conflict," p. 19.

CHAPTER TWO: THE GREAT LEADERSHIP CRISIS

1. Michael Cohen, James March, and Johan Olsen, "A Garbage Can Model of Organizational Choice," *Administrative Science Quarterly*, 17 (March 1972), 1–25; Michael Cohen and James March, *Leadership and Ambiguity: The American College President* (McGraw-Hill, 1974); James March et al., *Ambiguity and Choice in Organizations*, 2d ed. (Bergen, Norway: Universitetsforlaget, 1979).

2. Paul Lazarsfeld and Sam Sieber, *Organizing Educational Research* (Prentice-Hall, 1964), p. 13.

3. Clark Kerr, *The Uses of the University*, 3d ed. (Harvard University Press, 1982), pp. 35–37. See also Adam Yarmolinsky, "Institutional Paralysis," *Daedalus*, 104 (Winter 1975), 61–67.

4. Richard Hofstadter and C. DeWitt Hardy, *The Development and Scope of Higher Education in the United States* (Columbia University Press, 1952), pp. 129–30; Kenneth Lynn, ed., *The Professions in America* (Houghton Mifflin, 1965).

5. Paul Goodman, *The Community of Scholars* (Random House, 1962), p. 168. Also, for example, Daniel Griffiths, *Administrative Theory* (Appleton Century Crofts, 1959), p. 89: "It is not the function of the chief executive to make decisions. It is his function to monitor the decision-making process to make certain that it performs at the optimum level."

6. Hazard Adams, *The Academic Tribes* (Liveright, 1976), p. 5.

7. Quoted in Cowley, *Presidents, Professors, and Trustees*, pp. 23–24. Also, James Bryce: "A visitor from Europe is struck by the prominence of the president in an American university or college, and the almost monarchical position which he sometimes occupies towards the professors as well as the students." *The American Commonwealth*, 3d ed. (Macmillan, 1895), vol. 2, p. 670.

8. Cowley, *Presidents, Professors, and Trustees*, pp. 17–21; Walter Metzger, "Academic Freedom in Delocalized Institutions," in *Dimensions of Academic Freedom* (University of Illinois Press, 1969), pp. 10–11; Kevles, *Physicists*, pp. 86–87.

9. Many of the first professors of economics also had studied in Germany: J. B. Clark and E.R.A. Seligman of Columbia, F. W. Taussig of Harvard, Richard T. Ely of Wisconsin, and Arthur Hadley of Yale.

10. Charles Thwing, *The American and the German University* (Macmillan, 1928); Fritz Ringer, *The Decline of the German Mandarins: The German Academic Community, 1890–1933* (Harvard University Press, 1969); Burton Bledstein, *The Culture of Professionalism: The Middle Class and the Development of Higher Education in America* (Norton, 1976), pp. 312–18.

11. Thwing, *American and the German University*, p. 135.

12. Francis Rourke and Glenn Brooks, *The Managerial Revolution in Higher Education* (Johns Hopkins Press, 1966), p. 128.

13. J. Victor Baldridge, "Shared Governance: A Fable about the Lost Magic Kingdom," *Academe*, 68 (January–February 1982), 14.

14. Metzger, "Academic Freedom in Delocalized Institutions," pp. 1–2. See also *Post–Land Grant University*, ch. 4.

15. Robert Presthus, *The Organizational Society* (Knopf, 1962), p. 15.

16. See, for example, Lenin's *State and Revolution* of 1917 (International Publishers, 1932): "To organize the whole national economy like a postal system . . . all under the control and leadership of the armed proletariat—this is our immediate aim" (p. 44). "We do not at all disagree with the Anarchists on the question of the abolition of the state as an aim" (p. 52). "From the moment when all members of society, or even the overwhelming majority, have learned how to govern the state themselves, have taken this business into their own hands . . . the need for any government begins to disappear" (p. 84). "Under Socialism much of the 'primitive' democracy is inevitably revived since, for the first time in the history of civilized society, the mass of the population rises to independent participation, not only in voting and elections, but also in the everyday administration of affairs. Under Socialism, all will take a turn in management, and will soon be accustomed to the idea of no managers at all" (pp. 97–98).

17. Cowley, *Presidents, Professors, and Trustees*, p. 70.

18. Walter Metzger, "The Academic Profession in 'Hard Times,' " *Daedalus*, 104 (Winter 1975), 29.

19. Metzger, "Academic Freedom in Delocalized Institutions," p. 29.

20. Rourke and Brooks, *Managerial Revolution in Higher Education*, p. 129.

21. Glenn Brooks, "The Managerial Revolution in Higher Education: The Role of Information Systems," *Proceedings of the CAUSE National Conference*, 1976, p. 12.

22. Burton Clark, "Faculty Organization and Authority," in *Academic Governance*, ed. J. Victor Baldridge (McCutchan, 1971), pp. 236–50.

23. Cameron, "Relationship between Faculty Unionism and Organizational Effectiveness," pp. 6–24.

24. Metzger, "Academic Profession in 'Hard Times,' " p. 31.

25. Baldridge, *Academic Governance*, p. 13.

26. Kerr, *Uses of the University*, p. 23.

27. Gross, "Organizational Lag in American Universities," p. 71.

28. Clark, "Faculty Organization and Authority," p. 247.

29. Herbert Simon, "The Job of a College President," *Educational Record*, 58 (Winter 1967), 69.

30. Clark Kerr, "The Trustee Faces Steady State," *AGB Reports*, 17 (May–June 1975), 10.

31. Cowley, *Presidents, Professors, and Trustees*, p. 69.

32. Charles Levine, "Signpost: Hard Times Ahead," *University of Maryland Magazine*, 7 (Spring 1979), 19.

33. Behn, "Leadership for Cutback Management," p. 618.

CHAPTER THREE: NEW MANAGEMENT WINE IN OLD ACADEMIC BOTTLES

1. George Sabine, *A History of Political Theory*, rev. ed. (Henry Holt, 1950). For a memorable view of Machiavelli's precepts and the ineluctable tension between managing any state and personal liberty, see Isaiah Berlin, "The Originality of Machiavelli" in his *Against the Current: Essays in the History of Ideas* (Viking, 1980). An excellent detailed history of the rise of corporate management is Alfred Chandler, Jr., *The Visible Hand: The Managerial Revolution in American Business* (Harvard University Press, 1977); also Leslie Hannah, ed., *Management Strategy and Business Development: An Historical and Comparative Study* (London: Macmillan, 1976). Thorstein Veblen in *The Higher Learning in America* (Hill & Wang, 1957), published originally in 1918, says, "The place in men's esteem once filled by church and state is now held by pecuniary traffic, business enterprise" (p. 35). The birth of the study of management and organization behavior is chronicled in Daniel Wren, *The Evolution of Management Thought* (Ronald Press, 1972); and in the early chapters of Peter Drucker's *Management: Tasks, Responsibilities, Practices* (Harper & Row, 1974); and is mentioned analytically in a few articles such as Warren Bennis, "Revisionist View of Leadership," *Harvard Business Review*, 39 (January–February 1961), 26–36, 146–50. A fascinating attempt to create a bridge between the old political theory and the new organization theory is Mary Parker Follett's *The New State: Group Organization the Solution of Popular Government* (London: Longmans, Green, 1918), in which she wrote, "The potentialities of the individual remain potentialities until they are released by group life. Man discovers his true nature, gains his true freedom only through the group" (p. 6). A more recent attempt: John Galbraith, *The New Industrial State*, 3d ed. (Houghton Mifflin, 1979).

2. Kenneth Andrews, Introduction to *The Functions of the Executive*, by Chester Barnard, 30th anniversary ed. (Harvard University Press, 1968).

3. To compare for yourself: William Stearns Davis, *Life on a Medieval Barony* (Harper, 1923); *The Statesman's Book of John of Salisbury*, trans. John Dickinson (Knopf, 1927); P. Boissonade, *Life and Work in Medieval Europe* (Knopf, 1937); Carl Stephenson, *Medieval Feudalism* (Cornell University Press, 1942); Bede Jarrett, *Social Theories of the Middle Ages, 1200–1500* (Newman Book Shop, Westminster, Md., 1942); Marc Bloch, *Feudal Society*, trans. L. A. Manyon (University of Chicago Press, 1961), pts. 3–6. See also John P. Davis, *Corporations* (Capricorn Books, 1961), which depicts the common origins of universities and corporations in medieval institutions.

4. Frederick Herzberg, *Work and the Nature of Man* (World, 1966), pp. ix, 33.

5. Daniel Bell, *The Social Sciences Since the Second World War* (Transaction Books, 1982),

p. 50, and Bell's "The Social Framework of the Information Society," in *The Computer Age: A 20-Year View,* ed. Michael Dertouzos and Joel Moses (MIT Press, 1979), pp. 163–211. See also Daniel Bell's comprehensive *The Coming of Post-Industrial Society* (Basic Books, 1973); and Peter Drucker, *The Age of Discontinuity* (Harper & Row, 1969).

6. Patrick Montana, ed., *Marketing in Nonprofit Organizations* (AMACOM, 1978), p. ix.

7. Drucker, *Management: Tasks, Responsibilities, Practices,* p. 30.

8. Ibid., p. 8; and Theodore Levitt, "Management and the 'Post-Industrial' Society," *Public Interest,* no. 44 (Summer 1976), 69–103.

9. Douglas McGregor, "On Leadership," *Antioch Notes,* May 1954, pp. 2–3.

10. The new worker is increasingly seen like the hero Rowan in Elbert Hubbard's story *A Message to Garcia.* Rowan was asked to carry a message from the U. S. president to the insurgent Cuban general Garcia during the Spanish-American War. While he was given an objective, Rowan was expected to use his own pluck, ingenuity, and skills to get through. He did not have to obey a lot of specific directions. For a contemporary version of *A Message to Garcia:* Tracy Kidder, *The Soul of a New Machine* (Atlantic Monthly Press–Little Brown, 1981), a nonfiction account of how a team of young, brilliant computer scientists carry out the objective of designing a new-generation computer for Data General; and Herbert Kaufman's pioneering *The Forest Ranger: A Study in Administrative Behavior* (Johns Hopkins Press, 1960).

According to Daniel Bell, "In a postindustrial phase, there is a *knowledge* theory of value, not a *labor* theory of value, that is central. . . . The 'value added' components in a set of national income accounts are due, increasingly, to the contribution of knowledge workers, and the kinds of knowledge that these men can draw upon. . . . The major feature of a postindustrial society is the rise of the science-based industries—polymers, optics, electronics, telecommunications—that derive from the codification of theoretical knowledge" ("Liberalism in a Postindustrial Society," in *The Winding Passage: Essays and Sociological Journeys, 1960–1980* [Abt Books, 1980], pp. 237–38).

11. Douglas McGregor, *The Human Side of Enterprise* (McGraw-Hill, 1960); and Warren Bennis, Edgar Schein, and Caroline McGregor, eds., *Leadership and Motivation: Essays of Douglas McGregor* (MIT Press, 1966).

12. For a caustic look at how business management was pressed into school administration in the 1910–1930 period, see Raymond Callahan, *Education and the Cult of Efficiency* (University of Chicago Press, 1962); and Veblen's famous attack in *Higher Learning in America.*

13. The primary reason is economic. But it may be that management is being seen by many of the brighter students as a new kind of intellectually challenging field in postindustrial life. More students than ever are studying business and management:

Master of Business Administration degrees awarded

1960	4,643
1970	21,599
1981	54,000 (estimated)

And really superior students are going to the top four (Chicago, Harvard, Stanford, and the Wharton School of the University of Pennsylvania) and other fine graduate business schools such as Columbia, Dartmouth, and Northwestern. Dean Donald Jacobs of Northwestern says, "The 1970s and 1980s are the decades of management. At other times the cream of American youth went into science, became law professors, or went into government to reform the system. Now they are going to the *grandes écoles* of the M.B.A." ("The Money Chase: What Business Schools Are Doing to Us," *Time,* 4 May 1981, p. 58).

14. C. D. Ahlberg and D. D. Christenson, *Report on Phase I, The Kellogg Foundation Leadership and Management Development Project at Wichita State University* (Wichita State University, 1977); and Foster Buchtel, "Approaches of Medium-Sized Universities," in *Improving Academic Management*, ed. Paul Jedamus and Marvin Peterson (Jossey-Bass, 1980), pp. 602–25.

15. Robert Zemsky, "A View from the Trenches: Postsecondary Education Finance" (Higher Education Finance Research Institute, University of Pennsylvania, no date).

16. Joe B. Wyatt, James Emery, and Carolyn Landis, eds., *Financial Planning Models: Concepts and Case Studies in Colleges and Universities* (EDUCOM, 1979).

17. Kent Alm, Marina Buhler-Miko, and Kurt Smith, *A Future-Creating Paradigm: A Guide to Long-Range Planning for the Future* (American Association of State Colleges and Universities, 1978).

18. George Weathersby, "Scarce Resources Can Be a Golden Opportunity for Higher Education," *Change*, 14 (March 1982), 12.

19. Aaron Wildavsky, "The Uses of Adversity in Higher Education," speech delivered in Washington, D.C., on 2 March 1982, at the annual meeting of the Association for the Study of Higher Education. Amitai Etzioni says, "Crises serve to build consensus for major changes of direction which are overdue," in "Mixed Scanning: A Third Approach to Decision-making," *Public Administration Review*, 27 (December 1967), 391.

20. Levitt, "Management and the 'Post-Industrial' Society," pp. 73–74.

21. A revealing example is *Forty Years as a College President: Memoirs of Wilson Elkins*, ed. George Callcott (University of Maryland, 1981). Dr. Elkins presided for 24 boom years (1954–78) over the University of Maryland with integrity, dignity, and formality and with a remoteness and passive, easygoing manner. Among his views: "An administrator learns to listen to committees, not instruct them too much" (p. 51). "The departments determine what happens in a university" (p. 94). "It is very difficult for an institution to improve itself from within. There are too many vested interests" (p. 172).

22. Edward Gross and Paul Grambsch, *University Goals and Academic Power* (American Council on Education, 1968).

23. Rourke and Brooks, *Managerial Revolution in Higher Education*, p. 85.

24. Hopkins and Massy, *Planning Models for Colleges and Universities*.

25. Robert Zemsky, Randall Parker, and Laura Oedel, "Decentralized Planning," *Educational Record*, 59 (Summer 1978), 229–53.

26. Howard Bowen, *The State of the Nation and the Agenda for Higher Education* (Jossey-Bass, 1982), p. 183.

27. Rourke and Brooks, *Managerial Revolution in Higher Education*, pp. 104–5.

28. David Ewing, *The Human Side of Planning* (Macmillan, 1969), p. 136.

29. Richard Daft and Selwyn Becker, *Innovation in Organizations* (Elsevier, 1978), p. 154.

30. Alfred P. Sloan, Jr., *My Years with General Motors*, ed. John McDonald with Catharine Stevens (Anchor Books, 1972).

31. S. D. Warren Company Annual Report, 1966, p. 21. Quoted in David Ewing, "Corporate Planning at the Crossroads," in *Long-Range Planning for Management*, ed. David Ewing, 3d ed. (Harper & Row, 1972), pp. 51–52.

32. Rourke and Brooks, *Managerial Revolution in Higher Education*, chs. 2, 3.

33. Irene Rubin, "Universities in Stress: Decision Making under Conditions of Reduced Resources," *Social Science Quarterly*, 58 (September 1977), 247.

34. Sally Zeckhauser, "Models as Planning Tools: The Harvard Experiment," in Wyatt, Emery, and Landis, eds., *Financial Planning Models*, pp. 93–114.

35. Earl Cheit, "The Management Systems Challenge: How to Be Academic though

Systematic," in *Education and the State*, ed. John Hughes (American Council on Education, 1975), p. 170.

36. David Ewing, *The Practice of Planning* (Harper & Row, 1968), p. 139.

37. Peter Drucker, *The Effective Executive* (Harper & Row, 1967), p. 113.

38. Albert Hirschman, *Exit, Voice, and Loyalty: Responses to Decline in Firms, Organizations, and States* (Harvard University Press, 1970), p. 12.

39. See Abraham Zalesnik, "Managers and Leaders: Are They Different?" *Harvard Business Review*, 55 (May–June 1977), 67–78.

40. Ewing, *Practice of Planning*, p. 135.

41. See, for example, *Post–Land Grant University*.

CHAPTER FOUR: SLOUCHING TOWARD STRATEGY

1. Jeffrey Bracker, "The Historical Development of the Strategic Development Concept," *Academy of Management Review*, 5 (April 1980), 219; William Solebury, "Strategic Planning: Metaphor or Method?" *Policy and Politics*, 9 (October 1981), 419–37.

2. Leonard Berry and William George, "Marketing the Universities: Opportunity in an Era of Crisis," in Montana, ed., *Marketing in Nonprofit Organizations*, pp.159–71.

3. Drucker, *Effective Executive*, p. 109.

4. Dan Schendel and Charles Hofer, eds., *Strategic Management: A New View of Business Policy and Planning* (Little, Brown, 1979), p. 13.

5. Richard Anderson, *Strategic Policy Changes at Private Colleges* (Teachers College Press, 1977), p. xiv. The author found that private single-sex colleges had decreased in number from 515 in 1963 to 156 in 1973 (p. 2). During the same period institutions with a religious affiliation declined from 910 to 790.

6. Donna Shoemaker, "Institutional Strategies: Hood College," *Educational Record*, 63 (Winter 1982), 52–57.

7. Perhaps the most candid and thorough of all U.S. academic audits is Columbia's *Report of the Presidential Commission on Academic Priorities in the Arts and Sciences* (Columbia University, 1979).

8. Peter Magrath, "The State Connection," *Educational Record*, 61 (Fall 1980), 68–71.

9. "University decision making frequently does not resolve problems. Choices are often made by flight or oversight" (Cohen, March, and Olsen, "A Garbage Can Model of Organizational Choice," p. 11).

10. James March, "Footnotes to Organizational Change," *Administrative Science Quarterly*, 26 (December 1981), 575.

11. Raymond Haas, "Winning Acceptance for Institutional Research and Planning," in Jedamus and Peterson, eds., *Improving Academic Management*, pp. 539–54.

12. Bell, *Coming of Post-Industrial Society*, p. 488.

13. Frederick Emery and E. L. Trist, *Towards a Social Ecology: A Contextual Appreciation of the Future in the Present* (Plenum Press, 1973), p. 157.

14. Hirschman, *Exit, Voice, and Loyalty*, p. 15; Hirschman, *The Strategy of Economic Development* (Yale University Press, 1958), p. 12.

15. Herbert Kaufman, *The Limits of Organizational Change* (University of Alabama Press, 1971), p. 96. See also Rachel Elboim-Dror, "Some Characteristics of the Educational Policy Formation System," *Policy Sciences*, 1 (Summer 1970), 246–47.

CHAPTER FIVE: PLANNING: THE TURBULENT STATE OF THE ART

1. Michael Cohen and James March, "Decisions, Presidents, and Status," in March et al.,

Ambiguity and Choice in Organizations, pp. 193–94.

2. Lewis Mayhew, *Surviving the Eighties* (Jossey-Bass, 1979), p. 112.

3. Charles Hofer finds that "most of the research done to date has been descriptive . . . in character. Most of the future research . . . should be normative." Also, "Much more research has been done on strategy and strategic planning in businesses . . . . The potential for future research is even greater for non-business organizations" ("Research on Strategic Planning: A Survey of Past Studies and Suggestions for Future Efforts," *Journal of Economics and Business,* 28 [Spring–Summer 1976], 281). When a conference of strategic planning experts was held at the University of Pittsburgh in May 1977, not only did it resemble a flock of sandpipers explaining a rhinoceros but the papers were mainly bibliographic summaries commenting on each other's suggestive findings. See Schendel and Hofer, eds., *Strategic Management.*

4. Jacob Ernest Cooke, *Alexander Hamilton* (Scribner's, 1982).

5. Frank and Fritzie Manuel, *Utopian Thought in the Western World* (Harvard University Press, Belknap Press, 1979), p. 28.

6. The connection between socialism and planning is an intimate one. As John Plamenatz explained its rise: "The natural sciences make rapid progress, and their discoveries are used abundantly to improve productive techniques. As Marx puts it in *Capital*: 'Modern industry never regards or treats the extant form of the productive process as definitive. Its technical basis is, therefore, revolutionary; whereas the technical basis of all earlier methods of production was essentially conservative.' Voluminous records are kept, and the historical and social studies develop rapidly. Society changes more and more quickly, and men have this change brought home to them in every aspect of their lives . . . .

"This social order, in which everyone (though no one as much as the manual worker) feels insecure is more studied and discussed than any before it. There is, therefore, a rapid increase in knowledge (or what passes for knowledge) about society along with much greater insecurity and a weakening hold of tradition, so that the urge to control society and to change it grows more intense. The scale of production is vastly greater than before; there are often hundreds and thousands of workers under one management. The planning of production within the larger enterprises is elaborate and looks forward far into the future. The idea of a managed economy comes to seem less fantastic" (*Karl Marx's Philosophy of Man* [Oxford University Press, Clarendon Press, 1975], pp. 164–65).

7. Otis Graham, Jr., *Toward a Planned Society: From Roosevelt to Nixon* (Oxford University Press, 1976).

8. Stephen Cohen, *Modern Capitalist Planning: The French Model,* rev. ed. (University of California Press, 1977). According to Guy Benveniste, "In the post–World War II period, hundreds of national development plans were elaborated, more than 125 central planning offices were established in both rich and poor countries, and about a hundred specialized training centers gave courses in national and regional planning" (*The Politics of Expertise,* 2d ed. [Boyd & Fraser, 1977], p. 22).

9. "The Need to Plan," Editorial, *New York Times,* 23 February 1975.

10. Herbert Simon, *The Sciences of the Artificial,* 2d ed. (MIT Press, 1981), p. 60.

11. See Charles Schultze, *The Politics and Economics of Public Spending* (Brookings Institution, 1968) for a succinct, penetrating discussion of PPB and its critics.

12. Frank Manuel, *The New World of Henri Saint-Simon* (Harvard University Press, 1956); Ghita Ionescu, ed., *The Political Thought of Saint-Simon* (Oxford University Press, 1976).

13. See the collection of his writings in Frederick Taylor, *The Principles of Scientific Management* (Harper Brothers, 1947). For insightful descriptions of Taylorism, see Daniel

Bell, *Work and Its Discontents: The Cult of Efficiency in America* (Beacon Press, 1956); and Roger Burlingame, *Backgrounds of Power: The Human Story of Mass Production* (Scribner's, 1949), ch. 15.

14. Chandler, *The Visible Hand.*

15. John Pfeiffer, *A New Look at Systems Analysis in Our Schools and Colleges* (Odyssey Press, 1968), pp. 16–17.

16. Yehezkel Dror, "Prolegomena to Policy Sciences," *Policy Sciences,* 1 (Spring 1970), 135–50.

17. Richard Judy and Jack Levine, *A New Tool for Educational Administrators: Educational Efficiency through Simulation Analysis* (University of Toronto Press, 1965).

18. G. Ben Lawrence and Allan Service, eds., *Quantitative Approaches to Higher Education Management* (AAHE/ERIC, 1977), p. 8.

19. Rourke and Brooks, *Managerial Revolution in Higher Education,* pp. vi, vii, 18.

20. Juan Casasco, *Planning Techniques for University Management* (American Council on Education, 1970), pp. v, 1.

21. Benveniste, *Politics of Expertise,* pp. 5–7.

22. Robert Dahl and Charles Lindblom, *Politics, Economics, and Welfare: Planning and Politico-Economic Systems Resolved into Basic Social Processes* (University of Chicago Press, 1976), p. 86. Originally published in 1953.

23. Charles Lindblom, "The Science of Muddling Through," *Public Administration Review,* 19 (Spring 1959), 79–88. See also idem, "Still Muddling, Not Yet Through," *Public Administration Review,* 39 (November–December 1979), 517–26.

24. Albert Hirschman and Charles Lindblom, "Economic Development, Research and Development, Policy Making: Some Converging Views," *Behavioral Science,* 7 (April 1962), 211–22.

25. Aaron Wildavsky, *Speaking Truth to Power: The Art and Craft of Policy Analysis* (Little, Brown, 1979).

26. Frank Schmidtlein, "Decision Process Paradigms in Education," *Educational Researcher,* 3 (May 1974), 11.

27. "Innovations are seldom implemented as planned" (Paul Berman and Milbrey McLaughlin, "Implementation of Educational Innovation," *Educational Forum,* 40 [March 1976], 349); David Clark, "In Consideration of Goal-Free Planning: The Failure of Traditional Planning Systems in Education," *Educational Administration Quarterly,* 17 (Summer 1981), 42–60.

28. Joseph Schumpeter, "The Creative Response in Economic History," *Journal of Economic History,* 7 (November 1947), 149–59.

29. Alfred Chandler, Jr., *Strategy and Structure: Chapters in the History of the Industrial Enterprise* (MIT Press, 1962), p. 303.

30. Sloan, *My Years with General Motors.*

31. For example, Emery and Trist, *Towards a Social Ecology,* pp. 203–4.

32. Shirley Terreberry, "The Evolution of Organizational Environments," *Administrative Science Quarterly,* 12 (March 1968), 590–613; Kotler, *Marketing for Nonprofit Institutions;* Al Ries and Jack Trout, *Positioning: The Battle for Your Mind* (McGraw-Hill, 1981).

33. Derek Birley, *Planning and Education* (London: Routledge & Kegan Paul, 1972), p. 4.

34. Martha Feldman and James March, "Information in Organizations as Signal and Symbol," *Administrative Science Quarterly,* 26 (June 1981), 171–86; and the pioneering work: Richard Cyert and James March, *A Behavioral Theory of the Firm* (Prentice-Hall, 1963). For the role of gossip in decision making, see Henry Mintzberg, "The Myth of MIS," *California Management Review,* 15 (Autumn 1972), 92–97.

35. Benjamin Ward, *What's Wrong with Economics?* (Basic Books, 1972), ch. 12.

36. Seymour Martin Lipset, "The Limits to Futurology and Social Science Analysis," in Lipset, ed., *The Third Century: America as a Post-Industrial Society* (Hoover Institution Press, 1979), pp. 3–18; James Traub, "Futurology: The Rise of the Predicting Profession," *Saturday Review,* 6 (December 1979), 24–32; William Ascher, "The Forecasting Potential of Complex Models," *Policy Sciences,* 13 (May 1981), 247–67.

37. Stephen Dresch, "A Critique of Planning Models for Postsecondary Education," *Journal of Higher Education,* 46 (May–June 1975), 249.

38. Harold Enarson, "The Art of Planning," *Educational Record,* 56 (Summer 1975), 173.

39. Emerson Shuck, "The New Planning and the Old Pragmatism," *Journal of Higher Education,* 48 (September–October 1977), 594–602.

40. Schultze, *Politics and Economics of Public Spending,* p. 66.

41. Ewing, *Practice of Planning,* pp. 19–20.

42. Jan Tinbergen, "The Use of Models: Experience and Prospects," *American Economic Review,* 71 (December 1981), 18, 19.

43. Erich Jantsch, *Design for Evolution* (Braziller, 1975), pp. 192–93.

44. Michael Polanyi, *The Tacit Dimension* (Doubleday, 1966); and his "The Creative Imagination," *Chemical and Engineering News,* 44 (April 25, 1966), 85–93.

45. David Cohen and Michael Garet, "Reforming Educational Policy with Applied Research," *Harvard Educational Review,* 45 (February 1975), 19, 40.

46. Simon, "Job of a College President," p. 76.

47. Elboim-Dror, "Some Characteristics of the Educational Policy Formation System," pp. 246–47.

48. Amitai Etzioni, *The Active Society* (Free Press, 1968), p. 283. See also his "Mixed Scanning: A Third Approach to Decision-Making," 385–92.

49. Richard Neustadt, *Presidential Power,* rev. ed. (Wiley, 1980), p. 190.

50. Schendel and Hofer, *Strategic Management: A New View of Business Policy and Planning,* p. 9.

51. H. Igor Ansoff, *Corporate Strategy* (McGraw-Hill, 1965); and Kenneth Andrews et al., *Business Policy: Text and Cases* (Irwin, 1965). Later Andrews published his views separately as *The Concept of Corporate Strategy* (Irwin, 1971).

52. Daniel Bell, "Twelve Modes of Prediction," *Daedalus,* 93 (Summer 1964), 869, 870.

53. Henry Mintzberg, *The Nature of Managerial Work* (Harper & Row, 1973); and "Patterns of Strategy Formulation," *Management Science,* 24 (May 1978), 934–48; James Brian Quinn, "Strategic Change: Logical Incrementalism," *Sloan Management Review,* 20 (Fall 1978), 7–21; and his "Managing Strategic Change," *Sloan Management Review,* 21 (Summer 1980), 3–20.

54. For example, Lee Sproul, Stephen Wiener, and David Wolf, *Organizing an Anarchy: Belief, Bureaucracy, and Politics in the National Institute for Education* (University of Chicago Press, 1978).

55. Graham Allison, *Essence of Decision: Explaining the Cuban Missile Crisis* (Little, Brown, 1971).

56. Michael Porter, *Competitive Strategy: Techniques for Analyzing Industries and Competitors* (Free Press, 1980).

57. Ewing, *Practice of Planning; Human Side of Planning;* and Ewing, ed., *Long-Range Planning for Management;* William King and David Cleland, *Strategic Planning and Policy* (Van Nostrand Reinhold, 1978). The preface of the 1972 third edition of Ewing's *Long-Range Planning for Management* is revealing: "When I started working on the first edition of this anthology in 1957, informed colleagues told me it couldn't be done—there wasn't

enough material available. . . . By 1964, when the second edition came out, that situation had changed considerably. . . . Still the literature on planning was uneven. . . . Today the situation has changed dramatically. The neglected corner has become a favorite corner for nearly everyone. . . . Equally important, long-range planning is no longer exclusive to big business. Numerous small companies practice it. Leaders in federal, state, and local governments are working on it. Health and welfare organizations, art associations, and churches are experimenting with it" (pp. ix–x). Eight years later, in 1980, Kenneth Andrews could write in the preface to his revision of *The Concept of Corporate Strategy,* "Attention to strategic issues is now so common as to constitute a verbal fad" (p. iii).

58. Robert Cope, *Strategic Planning, Management, and Decision Making* (American Association for Higher Education, 1981); Philip Kotler and Patrick Murphy, "Strategic Planning for Higher Education," *Journal of Higher Education,* 52 (September–October 1981), 470–89; Jack Lindquist, *Strategies for Change* (Council for the Advancement of Small Colleges, 1978); John Millett, *Planning in Higher Education: A Manual for Colleges and Universities* (Academy for Educational Development, 1977); Robert Shirley, Michael Peters, Adel El-Ansary, *Strategy and Policy Formulation,* 2d ed. (Wiley, 1981).

CHAPTER SIX: BEFORE PLANNING: INFORMATION, QUALITY, PEOPLE

1. Henry Wriston, *Academic Procession* (Columbia University Press, 1959), p. 151.

2. Michael Aiken and Jerald Hage, "The Organic Organization and Innovation," *Sociology,* 5 (January 1971), 80.

3. Quinn, "Managing Strategic Change," p. 5.

4. Drucker, *Management: Tasks, Responsibilities, Practices,* p. 10.

5. Wriston, *Academic Procession,* p. 132.

6. Mark Van Doren, *Liberal Education* (Beacon Press, 1943).

7. Howard Lowry, *College Talks* (Oxford University Press, 1964).

8. Fred Hechinger, "Hesburgh Earned Respect the Hard Way," *New York Times,* 13 October 1981.

9. Jerald Hage and Michael Aiken, *Social Change in Complex Organizations* (Random House, 1970), pp. 82–85. See also Hugh Hawkins, *Between Harvard and America: The Educational Leadership of Charles William Eliot* (Oxford University Press, 1972).

10. Quoted in Bledstein, *Culture of Professionalism,* p. 132.

11. Ibid., p. 155.

12. James Brian Quinn, *Strategies for Change: Logical Incrementalism* (Irwin, 1980); Quinn, "Managing Strategic Change," pp. 3–20.

13. Quinn, "Managing Strategic Change," p. 7.

14. Alexander Astin, "Proposals for Change in College Administration," in *Maximizing Leadership Effectiveness,* ed. Alexander Astin and Rita Scherrei (Jossey-Bass, 1981), p. 162.

15. Donald Lelong and Martha Hinman, *Implementation of Formal Planning: Strategies for the Large University* (Center for the Study of Higher Education, University of Michigan, 1982), p. 67.

16. Quinn, *Strategies for Change,* p. 145.

17. Drucker, *Effective Executive,* p. 77.

18. Richard Miller, "Appraising Institutional Performance," in Jedamus and Peterson, eds., *Improving Academic Management,* pp. 422–23.

19. Sloan, *My Years with General Motors,* p. 109.

20. Richard Cyert, "Does Theory Help?" *Wall Street Journal,* 7 April 1980.

21. Donald Stokes, "The Sterling Touch: How Stanford Became a World Class Univer-

sity," *Stanford Observer,* October 1979, pp. 1, 3–4; and November 1979, pp. 6–8.
    22. Ibid., pp. 7–8.

CHAPTER SEVEN: SHAPING AN ACADEMIC STRATEGY

    1. Mortimer and Tierney, *The Three "R's" of the Eighties,* p. 55.
    2. David Craig, "The Personal Criterion in the Planning Program," in David Ewing, ed., *Long-Range Planning for Management,* p. 201.
    3. Joseph Schumpeter, *Capitalism, Socialism, and Democracy,* 3d ed. (Harper, 1942), p. 84. See also J. Quincy Hunsicker, "The Malaise of Strategic Planning," *Management Review,* 10 (March 1980), 8–14.
    4. Raymond Miles et al., "Organizational Strategy, Structure, and Process," *Academy of Management Review,* 3 (July 1978), 546–62; Charles Snow and Lawrence Hrebiniak, "Strategy, Distinctive Competence, and Organizational Performance," *Administrative Science Quarterly,* 25 (June 1980), 317–35. For a vivid illustration of this typology, see Robert Miles and Kim Cameron, *Coffin Nails and Corporate Strategies* (Prentice-Hall, 1982).
    5. "The Electronics Threat to Timex," *Business Week,* 18 August 1975, pp. 42–44; Arthur Thompson, Jr., and A. J. Strickland III, *Strategy Formulation and Implementation* (Dallas Business Publications, 1980), pp. 72–75.
    6. Henry Mintzberg, "The Manager's Job: Folklore and Fact," *Harvard Business Review,* 53 (July–August, 1975), 59.
    7. F. Scott Fitzgerald, *The Crack-Up,* ed. Edmund Wilson (New Directions Books, 1956), p. 69.
    8. Carl von Clausewitz, *On War,* trans. M. Howard and P. Paret (Princeton University Press, 1976).
    9. Bledstein, *Culture of Professionalism,* p. 33.
    10. Boorstin, *Americans: The National Experience,* p. 155.
    11. Max Weber, *On Universitites,* ed. and trans. Edward Shils (University of Chicago Press, 1974), p. 25.
    12. *Digest of Educational Statistics, 1981* (National Center for Education Statistics, 1981), p. 116.
    13. Ries and Trout, *Positioning: The Battle for Your Mind.* See also Larry Litten, "Marketing Higher Education: Benefits and Risks for the American Academic System," *Journal of Higher Education,* 51 (January–February 1980), 40–59.
    14. Leon Harris, "Marks and Spencer," *Gourmet,* 42 (September 1982), 104–5.
    15. See Quinn, "Managing Strategic Change," pp. 3–20, for a description of how some of the better executives carry out their strategies.
    16. Melville Dalton, *Men Who Manage* (Wiley, 1959), pp. 263–64.
    17. Chris Argyris, *Increasing Leadership Effectiveness* (Wiley, 1976), pp. 20–21.
    18. Ibid., p. x.
    19. Thomas Kuhn, *The Structure of Scientific Revolutions,* 2d ed. enlarged (University of Chicago Press, 1970).
    20. *Three Thousand Futures,* p. 9.
    21. Chandler, *Strategy and Structure,* p. 5.
    22. John Baldwin, *The Scholastic Culture of the Middle Ages, 1000–1300* (Heath, 1971), p. 22.
    23. Burton Clark, "The Organizational Saga in Higher Education," *Administrative Science Quarterly,* 17 (June 1972), 178–84.
    24. Berman and McLaughlin, "Implementation of Educational Innovation," pp. 345–70;

Haas, "Winning Acceptance for Institutional Research and Planning," pp. 539–54. According to Haas, "A first and elemental lesson from research on innovation is that new products that require dramatically different patterns of user behavior do not have a high probability of being adopted by the consumer."

25. David Webster, "Methods of Assessing Quality," *Change,* 13 (October 1981), 20–24; Jedamus and Peterson, *Improving Academic Management,* pt. 5.

26. *Post–Land Grant University,* p. xiii.

27. Robert Shirley and J. Fredericks Volkwein, "Establishing Academic Program Priorities," *Journal of Higher Education,* 49 (September–October 1978), 472-88.

28. Ewing, *Practice of Planning,* p. 78.

29. John Millett, "Relating Governance to Leadership," in Jedamus and Peterson, eds., *Improving Academic Management,* p. 501.

30. Ibid., p. 501.

31. Michael Kirst, "Crafting Policy Analysis for Decision Makers: An Interview with Lawrence Lynn," *Educational Evaluation and Policy Analysis,* 2 (May–June 1980), 86–87.

32. David Ewing, "The Time Dimension," in *Long-Range Planning for Management,* p. 445.

33. David Barton, Jr., ed., *New Directions in Higher Education: Marketing Higher Education* (Jossey-Bass, 1978); John Lucas, ed., *New Directions in Higher Education: Developing a Total Market Plan* (Jossey-Bass, 1979); Kotler, *Marketing for Nonprofit Institutions.*

34. Ries and Trout, *Positioning: The Battle for Your Mind,* p. 219.

35. Porter, *Competitive Strategy,* p. 4.

36. Drucker, *Management: Tasks, Responsibilities, Practices,* p. 675.

37. *Report to the President from the Committee to Study Consolidation of the Chicago Campus* (University of Illinois, 1981); also, *Appendix to the Report to the President.*

38. Porter, *Competitive Strategy,* pp. 41-42.

39. Richard Pascale and Anthony Athos, *The Art of Japanese Management* (Simon & Schuster, 1981).

40. Richard Chait, "Look Who Invented Japanese Management!" *AGB Reports,* 24 (March–April 1982), 3-7.

CHAPTER EIGHT: DIFFERENT CAMPUSES, DIFFERENT PROCESSES

1. Marvin Peterson, "Analyzing Alternative Approaches to Planning," in Jedamus and Peterson, eds., *Improving Academic Management,* pp. 113–63.

2. Max Weber, *The Protestant Ethic and the Spirit of Capitalism,* trans. Talcott Parsons (Scribner, 1958); G.W. F. Hegel, *The Philosophy of History,* trans. J. Sibree (Cooperative Publication Society, 1900), p. 30. An entrancing little Marxist essay of 1898 on this subject is George Plekhanov's *The Role of the Individual in History* (International Publishers, 1940).

3. Robert Hayes and William Abernathy, "Managing Our Way to Economic Decline," *Harvard Business Review,* 58 (July–August 1980), 67–77; Jordan Lewis, "Technology, Enterprise, and American Economic Growth," *Science,* 216 (5 March 1982).

4. Amitai Etzioni, *A Comparative Analysis of Complex Organizations* (Free Press, 1961), p. 83.

5. Lelong and Hinman, *Implementation of Formal Planning.*

6. William James, *Talks to Teachers* (Norton, 1958), pp. 111–12.

7. Edward Shils, *Tradition* (University of Chicago Press, 1981).

8. Hunsicker, "Malaise of Strategic Planning," pp. 8–14.

9. Robert Anthony, *Planning and Control Systems: A Framework for Analysis* (Harvard

University Press, 1965), pp. 8–14.

10. Fred Crossland, "Faculty Collective Bargaining: Impact on Planning," *Planning for Higher Education,* 5 (October 1976), unpaged.

11. King and Cleland, *Strategic Planning and Policy,* p. 273.

12. Michael Kami, "Planning: Realities vs. Theory," in David Ewing, ed., *Long-Range Planning for Management,* pp. 20–27.

13. Mortimer and Tierney, *The Three "R's" of the Eighties,* pp. 30–31.

14. Cyert, "Management of Universities of Constant or Decreasing Size," p. 345.

15. J. Victor Baldridge, "Managerial Innovation," *Journal of Higher Education,* 51 (March–April 1980), p. 124.

16. Charles Ping, "Bigger Stake for Business in Higher Education," *Harvard Business Review,* 59 (September–October 1981), 128.

17. Simon, "Job of a College President," p. 78.

CHAPTER NINE: TOMORROW'S PROFESSORS AND ADMINISTRATORS

1. Michael Cohen and James March, "Decisions, Presidents, and Status," in March et al., *Ambiguity and Choice in Organizations,* p. 189; Cohen and March, *Leadership and Ambiguity: The American College President.*

2. Veblen, *Higher Learning in America,* p. 209.

3. Peter Caws, "Design for a University," *Daedalus,* 99 (Winter 1970), 98. This is a vehement statement of the university as a community entirely devoted to intellection without cares about money and without authority. One is reminded of Friedrich Engels's views. Engels wrote, "Whoever mentions combined action speaks of organization. Is it possible to have an organization without authority? . . . Wanting to abolish authority in large-scale industry is tantamount to wanting to abolish industry itself." But three pages later Engels could also say, "All socialists are agreed that the political state and with it political authority, will disappear as the result of the coming socialist revolution" ("On Authority," in Lewis Feuer, ed., *Marx and Engels: Basic Writings on Politics and Philosophy* [Anchor Books, 1959], pp. 482–83, 485). Apparently all organizations for combined action require authority except the state—and the university.

4. David Truman, "The Academic Community in Transition," *NASPA Journal,* 8 (July 1970), 7.

5. J. B. Lon Hefferlin, *The Dynamics of Academic Reform* (Jossey-Bass, 1969), pp. 112–13.

6. Neustadt, *Presidential Power,* p. 114.

7. Mintzberg, *Nature of Managerial Work,* p. 37.

8. James, *Talks to Teachers,* pp. 34–35.

9. Alfred North Whitehead, *The Aims of Education and Other Essays* (Free Press, 1957), pp. v, 2.

10. Mary Parker Follett, *Dynamic Administration* (Harper, 1940), pp. 146–50.

11. Simon, *Sciences of the Artificial,* p. 167.

12. Bledstein, *Culture of Professionalism,* pp. 136–46.

13. Whitehead, *Aims of Education,* pp. 94–95.

14. Ibid., pp. 96–97.

REFERENCES

BOOKS

Abell, Derek. *Defining the Business: The Starting Point of Strategic Planning.* Prentice-Hall, 1980.

Abell, Derek, and Hammond, J. S. *Strategic Market Planning.* Prentice-Hall, 1979.

Ackoff, Russell. *Creating the Corporate Future.* Wiley, 1981.

Aldrich, Harold. *Organizations and Environments.* Prentice-Hall, 1979.

Allison, Graham. *Essence of Decision: Explaining the Cuban Missile Crisis.* Little, Brown, 1971.

Andrews, Kenneth. *The Concept of Corporate Strategy.* rev. ed. Dow Jones–Irwin, 1980.

Ansoff, H. Igor. *Corporate Strategy.* McGraw-Hill, 1965.

Anthony, Robert, and Herzlinger, Regina. *Management Control in Nonprofit Organizations.* rev. ed. Irwin, 1980.

Argyris, Chris, and Schon, Donald. *Organizational Learning.* Addison-Wesley, 1978.

Ascher, William. *Forecasting: An Appraisal for Policy-Makers and Planners.* Johns Hopkins University Press, 1978.

Ashby, Eric. *Adapting Universities for Technological Society.* Jossey-Bass, 1974.

Astin, Alexander, and Scherrei, Rita. *Maximizing Leadership Effectiveness: The Impact of Administrative Style on Faculty and Students.* Jossey-Bass, 1980.

Balderston, Frederick. *Managing Today's University.* Jossey-Bass, 1974.

Baldridge, J. Victor, et al. *Policy-Making and Effective Leadership: A National Study of Academic Management.* Jossey-Bass, 1978.

Bardach, Eugene. *The Implementation Game.* MIT Press, 1977.

Barnard, Chester. *The Functions of the Executive.* Harvard University Press, 1938.

Barzun, Jacques. *The American University.* Harper & Row, 1968.

Bell, Daniel. *The Reforming of General Education: The Columbia College Experience in Its Natural Setting.* Columbia University Press, 1966.

———. *The Coming of Post-Industrial Society: A Venture in Social Forecasting.* Basic Books, 1973.

Benezet, Louis; Katz, Joseph; and Magnusson, Frances. *Style and Substance: Leadership and the College Presidency.* American Council on Education, 1981.

Benjamin, Harold. *The Saber-Tooth Curriculum.* McGraw-Hill, 1939.

Bennis, Warren, and Beane, K. D. *The Planning of Change.* 3d ed. Holt Rinehart, 1976.

Benveniste, Guy. *The Politics of Expertise.* 2d ed. Boyd & Fraser, 1977.

Berdahl, Robert. *Statewide Coordination of Higher Education.* American Council on Education, 1971.

Berliner, Joseph. *The Innovative Decision in Soviet Industry.* MIT Press, 1976.

Blau, Peter. *The Organization of Academic Work.* Wiley, 1973.

Bledstein, Burton. *The Culture of Professionalism: The Middle Class and the Development of Higher Education in America.* Norton, 1976.

Blumberg, Arthur, and Greenfield, William. *The Effective Principal: Perspective on School Leadership.* Allyn & Bacon, 1980.

Boroff, David. *Campus U.S.A.: Portraits of American Colleges in Action.* Harper, 1960.

Breneman, David, and Finn, Chester, Jr., eds. *Public Policy and Private Higher Education.* Brookings Institution, 1978.

Brubaker, John, and Rudy, Willis. *Higher Education in Transition: A History of American Colleges and Universities, 1636–1976.* 3d ed., rev. Harper & Row, 1976.

Burke, Colin. *American Collegiate Populations.* NYU–Columbia University Press, 1982.

Burns, James MacGregor. *Leadership.* Harper & Row, 1978.

Capen, Samuel. *The Management of Universities.* Foster & Steward, 1953.

Caplow, Theodore, and McGee, Reece. *The Academic Marketplace.* Basic Books, 1958.

Cartter, Allan. *Ph.D.'s and the Academic Labor Market.* McGraw-Hill, 1976.

Chandler, Alfred, Jr. *Strategy and Structure: Chapters in the History of the Industrial Enterprise.* MIT Press, 1962.

———. *The Visible Hand: The Managerial Revolution in American Business.* Harvard University Press, 1977.

Cheit, Earl. *The New Depression in Higher Education.* McGraw-Hill, 1971.

Cleveland, Harlan. *The Future Executive.* Harper & Row, 1972.

Cohen, Michael, and March, James. *Leadership and Ambiguity: The American College President.* McGraw-Hill, 1974.

Cohen, Stephen. *Modern Capitalist Planning: The French Model.* rev. ed. University of California Press, 1977.

Coleman, James. *Youth: Transition to Manhood.* University of Chicago Press, 1974.

Conant, James. *Shaping Educational Policy.* McGraw-Hill, 1964.

Coombs, Phillip. *What Is Educational Planning?* UNESCO, 1970.

Corson, John. *The Governance of Colleges and Universities.* rev. ed. McGraw-Hill, 1975.

Cowley, W. H. *Presidents, Professors, and Trustees.* Jossey-Bass, 1980.

Cremin, Lawrence. *Public Education.* Basic Books, 1976.

Crozier, Michael. *Strategies for Change: The Future of French Society.* MIT Press, 1981.

Cyert, Richard, and March, James. *A Behavioral Theory of the Firm.* Prentice-Hall, 1963.

Daft, Richard, and Becker, Selwyn. *Innovation in Organizations.* Elsevier, 1978.

Dahl, Robert, and Lindblom, Charles. *Politics, Economics, and Welfare: Planning and Politico-Economic Systems Resolved into Basic Social Processes.* University of Chicago Press, 1976.

Dalin, Per. *Limits to Educational Change.* St. Martin's Press, 1978.

Dalton, Melville. *Men Who Manage.* Wiley, 1959.

Dressel, Paul. *Administrative Leadership.* Jossey-Bass, 1981.

Dror, Yezekiel. *Ventures in Policy Science: Concepts and Applications.* Elsevier, 1971.

Drucker, Peter. *The Effective Executive.* Harper & Row, 1967.

———. *The Age of Discontinuity: Guidelines to Our Changing Society.* Harper & Row, 1969.

———. *Management: Tasks, Responsibilities, Practices.* Harper & Row, 1974.

Easterlin, Richard. *Birth and Fortune: The Impact of Numbers on Personal Welfare.* Basic Books, 1980.

Emery, Frederick, and Trist, E. L. *Towards a Social Ecology: A Contextual Appreciation of the Future in the Present.* Plenum Press, 1973.

Etzioni, Amitai. *Modern Organizations.* Prentice-Hall, 1964.

Ewing, David. *The Human Side of Planning.* Macmillan, 1969.

———. ed. *Long-Range Planning for Management.* 3d ed. Harper & Row, 1972.

Galbraith, John. *The New Industrial State.* 3d ed. Houghton Mifflin, 1979.

Gardner, John. *Self-Renewal: The Individual and the Innovative Society.* Harper & Row, 1963.

Graham, Otis, Jr. *Toward a Planned Society: From Roosevelt to Nixon.* Oxford University Press, 1976.

Grant, Gerald, and Riesman, David. *The Perpetual Dream: Reform and Experiment in American Education.* University of Chicago Press, 1978.

Hage, Jerald. *Theories of Organizations: Form, Process, and Transformation.* Wiley, 1980.

Hall, Peter. *Great Planning Disasters.* Weidenfeld & Nicolson, 1980.

Hawkins, Hugh. *Between Harvard and America: The Educational Leadership of Charles William Eliot.* Oxford University Press, 1972.

Hennig, Margaret, and Jardim, Anne. *The Managerial Woman.* Doubleday, Anchor Press, 1977.

Henry, David. *Challenges Past, Challenges Present: An Analysis of Higher Education Since 1930.* Jossey-Bass, 1975.

Hipps, G. Melvin, ed. *Effective Planned Change Strategies.* Jossey-Bass, 1981.

Hirschman, Albert. *The Strategy of Economic Development.* Yale University Press, 1958.

——. *Exit, Voice, and Loyalty: Responses to Decline in Firms, Organizations, and States.* Harvard University Press, 1970.

Hofstadter, Richard, and Hardy, C. DeWitt. *The Development and Scope of Higher Education in the United States.* Columbia University Press, 1952.

Hopkins, David, and Massy, William. *Planning Models for Colleges and Universities.* Stanford University Press, 1981.

Jedamus, Paul, and Peterson, Marvin, eds. *Improving Academic Management: A Handbook of Planning and Institutional Research.* Jossey-Bass, 1980.

Jencks, Christopher, and Riesman, David. *The Academic Revolution.* Doubleday, 1968.

Karol, Nathaniel, and Ginsburg, Sigmund. *Managing the Higher Education Enterprise.* Wiley, 1980.

Katz, Daniel, and Kahn, Robert. *The Social Psychology of Organizations.* 3d ed. Wiley, 1978.

Kauffman, Joseph. *At the Pleasure of the Board: The Service of the College and University President.* American Council on Education, 1980.

Kaufman, Herbert. *The Limits of Organizational Change.* University of Alabama Press, 1971.

Kerr, Clark. *The Uses of the University.* 3d ed. Harvard University Press, 1982.

Kieft, R. N.; Armigo, F.; and Bucklew, N. *A Handbook for Institutional, Academic, and Program Planning.* National Center for Higher Education Management Systems (NCHEMS), 1978.

King, William, and Cleland, David. *Strategic Planning and Policy.* Van Nostrand–Reinhold, 1978.

Knoell, Dorothy, and McIntyre, Charles. *Planning Colleges for the Community.* Jossey-Bass, 1974.

Kotler, Philip. *Marketing for Nonprofit Institutions.* 2d ed. Prentice-Hall, 1982.

Kuhn, Thomas. *The Structure of Scientific Revolutions.* 2d ed. University of Chicago Press, 1970.

Lawrence, G. Ben, and Service, Allan, eds. *Quantitative Approaches to Higher Education Management.* AAHE/ERIC, 1977.

Lazarsfeld, Paul, and Sieber, Sam. *Organizing Educational Research.* Prentice-Hall, 1964.

Lee, Eugene, and Bowen, Frank. *Managing Multicampus Systems.* Jossey-Bass, 1975.

Lelong, Donald, and Hinman, Martha. *Implementation of Formal Planning: Strategies for the Large University.* Center for the Study of Higher Education, University of Michigan, 1982.

Levine, Charles, ed. *Managing Fiscal Stress: The Crisis in the Public Sector.* Chatham House, 1980.

Levinson, Harry. *Executive.* Harvard University Press, 1981.

Liebenstein, Harvey. *A New Foundation for Economics.* Harvard University Press, 1976.

Lindblom, Charles. *The Policy-Making Process.* Prentice-Hall, 1968.

Lindquist, Jack. *Strategies for Change.* Council for the Advancement of Small Colleges, 1978.

Lorange, Peter, and Vancil, Richard. *Strategic Planning Systems.* Prentice-Hall, 1977.

McGregor, Douglas. *Leadership and Motivation: Essays of Douglas McGregor.* MIT Press, 1966.

Machlup, Fritz. *Knowledge: Its Creation, Distribution, and Economic Significance,* vol. 1, 2. Princeton University Press, 1980, 1982.

Manuel, Frank, and Manuel, Fritzie. *Utopian Thought in the Western World.* Harvard University Press, Belknap Press, 1979.

March, James, et al. *Ambiguity and Choice in Organizations.* 2d ed. Bergen, Norway: Universitetsforlaget, 1979.

Marks, Walter, and Nystrand, Raphael. *Strategies for Educational Change.* Macmillan, 1980.

Maslow, Abraham. *Motivation and Personality.* 2d ed. Harper & Row, 1970.

Mayhew, Lewis. *Surviving the Eighties.* Jossey-Bass, 1979.

Meltsner, Arnold. *Policy Analysts in the Bureaucracy.* University of California Press, 1976.

Metzger, Walter. *Academic Freedom in the Age of the University.* Columbia University Press, 1961.

Michael, Donald. *On Learning to Plan and Planning to Learn.* Jossey-Bass, 1973.

Miles, Robert, and Cameron, Kim. *Coffin Nails and Corporate Strategies.* Prentice-Hall, 1982.

Miller, George. *The Psychology of Communication.* Basic Books, 1967.

Millett, John. *Planning in Higher Education: A Manual for Colleges and Universities.* Academy for Educational Development, 1977.

———. *Management, Governance, and Leadership.* AMACOM, 1980.

Mingle, James, ed. *Challenges of Retrenchment: Strategies for Consolidating Programs, Cutting Costs, and Reallocating Resources.* Jossey-Bass, 1981.

Mintzberg, Henry. *The Nature of Managerial Work.* Harper & Row, 1973.

Mortimer, Kenneth, and Tierney, Michael. *The Three "R's" of the Eighties: Reduction, Reallocation, and Retrenchment.* AAHE/ERIC, 1979.

Neustadt, Richard. *Presidential Power.* rev. ed. Wiley, 1980.

Nevins, Allan. *The State Universities and Democracy.* University of Illinois Press, 1962.

Ogburn, William. *Social Change with Respect to Culture and Original Nature.* new ed. Viking, 1950.

Olson, Keith. *The G.I. Bill, the Veterans, and the Colleges.* University of Kentucky Press, 1974.

Pace, C. Robert. *Measuring Outcomes of College.* Jossey-Bass, 1979.

Pascale, Richard, and Athos, Anthony. *The Art of Japanese Management.* Simon & Schuster, 1981.

Patton, Carl. *Academia in Transition: Mid-Career Change for Early Retirement.* Abt Books, 1979.

Perkins, James, ed. *The University as an Organization.* McGraw-Hill, 1973.

Peters, Thomas, and Waterman, Robert. *In Search of Excellence: Lessons from America's Best Run Companies.* Harper & Row, 1982.

Porter, Michael. *Competitive Strategy: Techniques for Analyzing Industries and Competitors.* Free Press, 1980.

The Post–Land Grant University: The University of Maryland Report. University of Maryland, 1981.

Potter, David. *People of Plenty: Economic Abundance and the American Character.* University of Chicago Press, 1954.

President's Research Committee on Social Trends. *Recent Social Trends in the United States.* 2 vols. McGraw-Hill, 1933.

Pressman, Jeffrey, and Wildavsky, Aaron. *Implementation.* 2d ed. University of California Press, 1979.

Pusey, Nathan. *American Higher Education, 1945–1970: A Personal Memoir.* Harvard University Press, 1978.

Quinn, James Brian. *Strategies for Change: Logical Incrementalism.* Irwin, 1980.

Richman, Barry, and Farmer, Richard. *Leadership, Goals, and Power in Higher Education.* Jossey-Bass, 1974.

Ries, Al, and Trout, Jack. *Positioning: The Battle for Your Mind.* McGraw-Hill, 1980.

Riesman, David. *On Higher Education: The Academic Enterprise in an Era of Rising Student Consumerism.* Jossey-Bass, 1980.

Riesman, David, and Stadtman, Verne, eds. *Academic Transformation.* McGraw-Hill, 1973.

Rivlin, Alice. *Systematic Thinking for Social Action.* Brookings Institution, 1971.

Rothschild, William. *Strategic Alternatives.* AMACOM, 1979.

Rourke, Francis, and Brooks, Glenn. *The Managerial Revolution in Higher Education.* Johns Hopkins Press, 1966.

Rudolph, Frederick. *The American College and University.* Knopf, 1962.

Sanford, Nevitt. *The American College.* Wiley, 1962.

Schendel, Dan, and Hofer, Charles, eds. *Strategic Management: A New View of Business Policy and Planning.* Little, Brown, 1979.

Schultz, Theodore. *Investing in People: The Economics of Population Quality.* University of California Press, 1981.

Schultze, Charles. *The Politics and Economics of Public Spending.* Brookings Institution, 1968.

Shirley, Robert; Peters, Michael; and El-Ansary, Adel. *Strategy Formulation.* 2d ed. Wiley, 1981.

Simon, Herbert. *Administrative Behavior,* 3d ed. Free Press, 1976.

———. *The New Science of Management Decision.* rev. ed. Prentice-Hall, 1977.

———. *The Sciences of the Artificial.* 2d ed. MIT Press, 1981.

Sloan, Alfred P., Jr. *My Years with General Motors.* Doubleday, 1963.

Slosson, Edwin. *Great American Universities.* Macmillan, 1910.

Sproul, Lee; Weiner, Stephen; and Wolf, David. *Organizing an Anarchy: Belief, Bureaucracy, and Politics in the National Institute for Education.* University of Chicago Press, 1978.

Steiner, George. *Pitfalls in Comprehensive Long-Range Planning.* The Planning Executives Institute, 1972.

———. *Strategic Planning: What Every Manager Must Know.* Free Press, 1979.

Stoke, Harold. *The American College President.* Harper, 1959.

Summer, Charles. *Strategic Behavior in Business and Government,* Little, Brown, 1980.

Thompson, Arthur, Jr., and Strickland, A. J. III. *Strategy Formulation and Implementation.* Dallas Business Publications, 1980.

Three Thousand Futures: The Next Twenty Years in Higher Education. Jossey-Bass, 1980.

Tinbergen, Jan. *Central Planning.* Yale University Press, 1964.

Van de Graaf, John, et al. *Academic Power: Patterns of Authority in Seven National Systems of Higher Education.* Praeger, 1978.

Vaughn, B. W. *Planning in Education.* Cambridge University Press, 1979.

Veysey, Lawrence. *The Emergence of the American University.* University of Chicago Press, 1965.

Whyte, William H., Jr. *The Organization Man.* Simon & Schuster, 1956.

Wildavsky, Aaron. *Speaking Truth to Power: The Art and Craft of Policy Analysis.* Little, Brown, 1979.

Wilensky, Harold. *Organizational Intelligence: Knowledge and Policy in Industry and Government.* Basic Books, 1967.

Wriston, Henry. *Academic Procession.* Columbia University Press, 1959.

Wyatt, Joe B.; Emery, James; and Landis, Carolyn; eds. *Financial Planning Models: Concepts and Case Studies in Colleges and Universities.* EDUCOM, 1979.

Zaltman, Gerald, ed. *Management Principles for Non-Profit Agencies and Organizations.* AMACOM, 1979.

ARTICLES

Aiken, Michael, and Hage, Jerald. "The Organic Organization and Innovation." *Sociology*, 5 (January 1971), 63–82.

Allison, Graham. "Implementation Analysis: 'The Missing Chapter' in Conventional Analysis." In *Benefit-Cost and Policy Analysis: 1974.* Aldine Publishing, 1975, 369–91.

Anderson, Richard. "A Financial and Environmental Analysis of Strategic Policy Changes at Small Private Colleges." *Journal of Higher Education*, 49 (January–February 1978), 30–46.

Andrew, Lloyd. "Involving Faculty in Planning." *Planning for Higher Education*, 7 (February 1979), 27–31.

Andrews, Kenneth. "To What Extent Should Corporate Strategy Be Explicit?" *Harvard Business Review*, 51 (May–June 1981), 18–20, 24, 26.

Ansoff, H. Igor. "Strategic Issue Management." *Strategic Management Journal*, 1 (April–June 1980), 131–48.

Archibald, Kathleen. "Three Views of the Expert's Role in Policymaking: Systems Analysis, Incrementalism, and the Clinical Approach." *Policy Sciences*, 1 (Spring 1970), 73–86.

Argyris, Chris. "The CEO's Behavior: Key to Organizational Development." *Harvard Business Review*, 51 (March–April 1973), 55–64.

Arns, Robert, and Poland, William. "Changing the University through Program Review." *Journal of Higher Education*, 51 (May–June 1980), 268–84.

Astin, Alexander. *When Does a College Deserve to Be Called "High Quality"?* Current Issues in Higher Education, no. 1. AAHE, 1980.

Bailey, Stephen. "Human Resource Development in a World of Decremental Budgets." *Planning for Higher Education*, 3 (Summer 1974), 1–5.

Balderston, Frederick. "Dynamics of Planning: Strategic Approaches and Higher Education." In *New Directions for Higher Education: Management Science Applications to Academic Administration.* Ed. J. Wilson. Jossey-Bass, 1981.

Baldridge, J. Victor. "Managerial Innovation." *Journal of Higher Education*, 51 (March–April 1980), 117–34.

Baum, Howell. "The Planner as Reluctant Scapegoat." Paper presented at the National Conference of the American Society for Public Administration, Detroit, Michigan, 12–15 April, 1981.

Behn, Robert. "Leadership for Cutback Management: The Use of Corporate Strategy." *Public Administration Review*, 40 (November–December 1980), 613–20.

Bell, Daniel. "Twelve Modes of Prediction." *Daedalus*, 93 (Summer 1964), 845–80.

Bennis, Warren. "The Sociology of Institutions, or Who Sank the Yellow Submarine?" *Psychology Today*, 6 (November 1972), 112–20.

Berman, Paul, and McLaughlin, Milbrey Wallin. "Implementation of Educational Innovation." *Educational Forum*, 40 (March 1976), 345–70.

Bok, Derek. "Business and the Academy." *Harvard Magazine*, 83 (May–June 1981), 23–35.

Boulding, Kenneth. "The Management of Decline." *Change*, 7 (June 1975), 8–9, 64.

Bourgeois, L. J. "Strategy and Environment: A Conceptual Integration." *Academy of Management Review*, 5 (January 1980), 25–40.

Bowen, Howard. "Systems Theory, Excellence, and Values: Will They Mix?" *NACUBO Professional File*, 9 (February 1977).

————. "Some Reflections on the Present Condition and Future Outlook for Higher Education." *Academe*, 66 (February 1980), 8–15.

Bowen, Howard, and Douglass, G. K., "Cutting Instructional Costs." *Liberal Education*, 57 (May 1971), 181–95.

Branscombe, Art. "The University of Denver." *Educational Record*, 62 (Summer 1981), 62–67.

Breneman, David. "Economic Trends: What Do They Imply for Higher Education?" *AAHE Bulletin*, 32 (September 1979), 1–5.

Cameron, Kim. "The Relationship between Faculty Unionism and Organizational Effectiveness." *Academy of Management Journal*, 25 (March 1982), 6–24.

Carbone, Robert. "What Professors Ought to Know about Presidents." *Academe*, 68 (January–February 1982), 19–21.

Caves, Richard. "Industrial Organization, Corporate Strategy, and Structure." *Journal of Economic Literature*, 18 (March 1980), 64–92.

Chait, Richard. "Look Who Invented Japanese Management!" *AGB Reports*, 24 (March–April 1982), 3–7.

Cheit, Earl. "The Management Systems Challenge: How to Be Academic though Systematic." In *Education and the State*. Ed. John Hughes. American Council on Education, 1975.

Child, John. "Organizational Structure, Environment, and Performance: The Role of Strategic Choice. " *Sociology*, 6 (January 1972), 1–22.

Clark, Burton. "Faculty Organization and Authority." In *Academic Governance*. Ed. J. Victor Baldridge. McCutchan, 1971, 236–50.

————. "The Organizational Saga in Higher Education." *Administrative Science Quarterly*, 17 (June 1972), 178–84.

Clark, Burton, and Trow, Martin. "The Organizational Context." In *College Peer Groups: Problems and Prospects for Research*. Ed. T. M. Newcomb and E. K. Wilson. Aldine, 1966.

Clark, David. "In Consideration of Goal-Free Planning: The Failure of Traditional Planning Systems in Education." *Educational Administration Quarterly*, 17 (Summer 1981), 42–60.

Cohen, David, and Garet, Michael. "Reforming Educational Policy with Applied Research." *Harvard Educational Review*, 45 (February 1975), 17–43.

Cohen, Kalman, and Cyert, Richard. "Strategy: Formulation, Implementation, and Monitoring." *Journal of Business*, 46 (July 1973), 349–67.

Cohen, Michael; March, James; and Olsen, Johan. "A Garbage Can Model of Organizational Choice." *Administrative Science Quarterly*, 17 (March 1972) 1–25.

Cope, Robert. *Strategic Planning, Management, and Decision Making*. AAHE/ERIC, 1981.

Corson, John. "The University: A Contrast in Administrative Process." *Public Administration Review*, 20 (Winter 1960), 2–9.

Crossland, Fred. "Faculty Collective Bargaining: Impact on Planning." *Planning for Higher Education*, 5 (October 1976), unpaged.

————. "Learning to Cope with a Downward Slope." *Change*, 12 (July–August 1980), 18, 20–25.

Cyert, Richard. "The Management of Universities of Constant or Decreasing Size." *Public Administration Review*, 38 (July–August 1978), 344–49.

Dill, William. "Environment as an Influence on Managerial Autonomy." *Administrative Science Quarterly*, 2 (March 1958), 409–43.

Dorsey, Rhoda. *Institutional Planning*, Booklet no. 11. Association of Governing Boards of Universities and Colleges, 1980.

Dresch, Stephen. "A Critique of Planning Models for Postsecondary Education." *Journal of Higher Education*, 46 (May–June 1975), 245–86.

Easterlin, Richard. "Implications of Recent Twists in Age Structure." *Demography*, 15 (November 1978), 397–432.

Elboim-Dror, Rachel. "Some Characteristics of the Educational Policy Formation System." *Policy Sciences*, 1 (Summer 1970), 231–53.

Enarson, Harold. "The Art of Planning." *Educational Record*, 56 (Summer 1975), 170–74.

Etzioni, Amitai. "Mixed Scanning: A Third Approach to Decision-Making." *Public Administration Review*, 27 (December 1967), 385–92.

———. "Human Beings Are Not Very Easy to Change After All." *Saturday Review*, 3 June 1972, pp. 45–47.

Feldman, Martha, and March, James. "Information in Organizations as Signal and Symbol." *Administrative Science Quarterly*, 26 (June 1981), 171–86.

Forester, John. "Questioning and Organizing Attention: Toward a Critical Theory of Planning and Administrative Practice." *Administration and Society*, 13 (August 1981), 161–205.

Frances, Carol. "Apocalyptic vs. Strategic Planning." *Change*, 12 (July–August 1980), 19, 38–44.

Fulton, Oliver, and Trow, Martin. "Research Activity in American Higher Education." *Sociology of Education*, 47 (Winter 1974), 29–73.

George, Alexander. "The Operational Code: A Neglected Approach to the Study of Political Leaders and Decisionmaking." *International Studies Quarterly*, 13 (June 1969), 190–222.

Gershuny, J. I. "Policymaking Rationality: A Reformation." *Policy Sciences*, 9 (June 1978), 295–316.

Glenny, Lyman. "Demographic and Related Issues for Higher Education in the 1980s." *Journal of Higher Education*, 51 (July–August 1980), 363–80.

Gross, Neal. "Organizational Lag in American Universities." *Harvard Educational Review*, 33 (Winter 1963), 58–73.

Haas, Raymond. "Integrating Academic, Fiscal, and Facilities Planning." *Planning for Higher Education*, 5 (October 1976), 2–5.

Hardin, Garrett. "The Tragedy of the Commons." *Science*, 162, 13 December 1968, 1243–48.

Harper, William Rainey. "The College President." *Educational Record*, 19 (April 1938), 178–86.

Hayek, Friedrich. "The Use of Knowledge in Society." *American Economic Review*, 35 (September 1945), 519–30.

Hayes, Robert, and Abernathy, William. "Managing Our Way to Economic Decline." *Harvard Business Review*, 58 (July–August 1980), 67–77.

Healy, Rose, and Peterson, Vance. "Who Killed These Four Colleges?" *AGB Reports*, 19 (May–June 1977), 14–18.

Herzlinger, Regina. "Managing the Finances of Nonprofit Organizations." *California Management Review*, 21 (Spring 1979), 60–69.

Hirschman, Albert. "The Principle of the Hiding Hand." In *Development Projects Observed*. Brookings Institution, 1967.

Hirschman, Albert, and Lindblom, Charles. "Economic Development, Research and Development, Policy Making: Some Convergent Views." *Behavioral Science*, 7 (April 1962), 211–22.

Hoenack, Stephen. "Direct and Incentive Planning within a University." *Socio-Economic Planning Sciences*, 11, no. 4 (1977), 191–204.

Hofer, Charles. "Research on Strategic Planning: A Summary of Past Studies and Suggestions for Future Efforts." *Journal of Economics and Business,* 28 (Spring–Summer 1976), 261–86.

Hollowood, James. "College and University Strategic Planning: A Methodological Approach." *Planning for Higher Education,* 9 (Summer 1981), 8–18.

Hosmer, L. T. "Academic Strategy: The Formulation and Implementation of Purpose at Three New Graduate Schools of Administration." Doctoral dissertation, Harvard Business School, June 1972.

Hunsicker, J. Quincy. "The Malaise of Strategic Planning." *Management Review,* 10 (March 1980), 8–14.

Jemison, David. "Organizational vs. Environmental Sources of Influence in Strategic Decision Making." *Strategic Management Review,* 2 (January–March 1981), 77–89.

Kast, Fremont. "Scanning the Future Environment: Social Indicators." *California Management Review,* 23 (Fall 1980), 22–32.

Keller, George. "The Search for Brainpower." *Public Interest,* no. 4 (Summer 1966), 59–69.

———. "Who's Running Our Colleges?" *Columbia College Today,* 15 (Winter 1967–68), 19–28.

———. "Women and the Future of Education." *Futures,* 7 (October 1975), 428–32.

———. "The Coming Revolution in Education." *University of Maryland Magazine,* 7 (Spring 1979), 15–17.

Kemeny, John. "What Every College President Should Know about Mathematics." *American Mathematical Monthly,* 80 (October 1973), 889–901.

———. "The University in a Steady State." *Daedalus,* 104 (Winter 1975), 87–96.

Kerchner, Charles, and Schuster, Jack. "The Uses of Crisis." *Review of Higher Education,* 5 (Spring 1982), 121–141.

Kerr, Clark. "Administration of Higher Education in an Era of Change and Conflict." In *Conflict, Retrenchment, and Reappraisal: The Administration of Higher Education.* University of Illinois Press, 1979.

Kolko, Gabriel. "Intelligence and the Myth of Capitalist Rationality in the United States," *Science and Society,* 44 (Summer 1980), 130–54.

Kotler, Philip, and Murphy, Patrick. "Strategic Planning for Higher Education." *Journal of Higher Education,* 52 (September–October 1981), 470–89.

Lawrence, Paul. "How to Deal with Resistance to Change." In *Organizational Change and Development.* Ed. G. Dalton, D. Lawrence, and L. Greiner. Dorsey Press, 1970.

Lee, Barbara. "Contractually Protected Governance Systems at Unionized Colleges." *Review of Higher Education,* 5 (Winter 1982), 69–85.

Levine, Charles. "Organizational Decline and Cutback Management." *Public Administration Review.* 38 (July–August 1978), 316–25.

Levitt, Theodore. "Management and the 'Post-Industrial' Society." *Public Interest,* no. 44 (Summer 1976), 69–103.

Light, Donald, Jr. "The Structure of the Academic Professions." *Sociology of Education,* 47 (Winter 1974), 2–28.

Lindblom, Charles. "The Science of 'Muddling Through.' " *Public Administration Review,* 19 (Spring 1959), 79–88.

———. "The Sociology of Planning." In *Economic Planning, East and West.* Ed. Morris Bornstein. Ballinger, 1975.

———. "Still Muddling, Not Yet Through." *Public Administration Review,* 39 (November–December 1979), 517–26.

Lipset, Seymour Martin. "The Limits to Futurology and Social Science Analysis." In *The Third Century: America as a Post-Industrial Society.* Hoover Institution Press, 1979.

Litchfield, Edward. "Organization in Large American Universities." *Journal of Higher*

Education, 30 (December 1959), 489–504.

March, James. "Footnoteş to Organizational Change." *Administrative Science Quarterly,* 26 (December 1981), 563–77.

Metzger, Walter. "The Academic Profession in 'Hard Times.' " *Daedalus,* 104 (Winter 1975), 25–44.

Miles, Raymond, et al. "Organizational Strategy, Structure, and Process." *Academy of Management Review,* 3 (July 1978), 546–62.

Miller, George. "The Magical Number Seven, Plus or Minus Two: Some Limits to Our Capacity for Processing Information." *Psychological Review,* 63 (March 1956), 81–97.

Mintzberg, Henry. "The Manager's Job: Folklore and Fact." *Harvard Business Review,* 53 (July–August 1975), 49–61.

———. "Patterns in Strategy Formulation." *Management Science,* 24 (May 1978), 934–48.

Mooney, Ross. "The Problem of Leadership in the University." *Harvard Educational Review,* 33 (Winter 1963), 42–57.

Murray, Edwin, Jr. "Strategic Choice as a Negotiated Outcome." *Management Science,* 24 (May 1978), 960–72.

Ogburn, William. "On Predicting the Future." In *William F. Ogburn on Culture and Social Change.* Ed. Otis Dudley Duncan. University of Chicago Press, 1964.

Ping, Charles. "Bigger Stake for Business in Higher Education." *Harvard Business Review,* 59 (September–October 1981), 122–29.

Porter, Michael. "The Contributions of Industrial Organization to Strategic Management." *Academy of Management Review,* 6 (October 1981), 609–20.

Quinn, James Brian. "Strategic Goals: Process and Politics." *Sloan Management Review,* 19 (Fall 1977), 21–37.

———. "Strategic Change: Logical Incrementalism." *Sloan Management Review,* 20 (Fall 1978), 7–21.

———. "Managing Strategic Change." *Sloan Management Review,* 21 (Summer 1980), 3–20.

Riesman, David. "Planning in Higher Education: Some Notes on Patterns and Problems." *Human Organization,* 18 (Spring 1958), 12–17.

Rogers, Everett. "The Communication of Innovations in a Complex Institution." *Educational Record,* 49 (Winter 1968), 67–77.

Rossi, Peter, and Wright, Sonia. "Evaluation Research: An Assessment of Theory, Practice, and Politics." *Evaluation Quarterly,* 1 (February 1977), 5–52.

Rubin, Irene. "Loose Structure, Retrenchment, and Adaptability." *Sociology of Education,* 52 (October 1979), 211–22.

Schlesinger, James. "Organizational Structures and Planning." In *Issues in Defense Economics.* Ed. Roland McKean. Columbia University Press, 1967.

Schmidtlein, Frank. "Decision Process Paradigms in Education." *Educational Researcher,* 3 (May 1974), 4–11.

Schumpeter, Joseph. "The Creative Response in Economic History." *Journal of Economic History,* 7 (November 1947), 149–59.

Shirley, Robert, and Volkwein, J. Fredericks. "Establishing Academic Program Priorities." *Journal of Higher Education,* 49 (September–October 1978), 472–88.

Shonfield, Andrew. "Thinking about the Future." *Encounter,* 32 (February 1969), 15–26.

Shuck, Emerson. "The New Planning and the Old Pragmatism." *Journal of Higher Education,* 48 (September–October 1977), 594–602.

Simon, Herbert. "The Job of a College President." *Educational Record,* 58 (Winter 1967), 68–78.

———. "Rational Decision Making in Organizations." *American Economic Review,* 69 (September 1979), 493–513.

Snow, Charles, and Hrebiniak, Lawrence. "Strategy, Distinctive Competence, and Organizational Performance." *Administrative Science Quarterly,* 25 (June 1980), 317–35.

Solebury, William. "Strategic Planning: Metaphor or Method?" *Policy and Politics,* 9 (October 1981), 419–37.

Terreberry, Shirley. "The Evolution of Organizational Environments." *Administrative Science Quarterly,* 12 (March 1968), 590–613.

Thackrey, Russell. "If You're Confused about Higher Education Statistics, Remember: So Are the People Who Produce Them." *Phi Delta Kappan,* 57 (February 1975), 415–19.

Thompson, Fred, and Zumeta, William. "A Regulatory Model of Governmental Coordinating Activities in the Higher Education Sector." *Economics of Education Review,* 1 (Winter 1981), 27–52.

Tinbergen, Jan. "The Use of Models: Experience and Prospects." *American Economic Review,* 77 (December 1981), 17–22.

Toll, John. "Strategic Planning: An Increasing Priority for Colleges and Universities." *Change,* 14 (May–June 1982), 36–37.

Traub, James. "Futurology: The Rise of the Predicting Profession." *Saturday Review,* 62 (December 1979), 24–32.

Trow, Martin. "The Expansion and Transformation of Higher Education." *International Review of Education,* 18 (February–March 1972), 61–82.

Unterman, Israel, and Davis, Richard Hart. "The Strategy Gap in Not-for-Profits." *Harvard Business Review,* 60 (May–June 1982), 30–36, 40.

Vaccaro, Louis. "Planning in Higher Education: Approaches and Problems." *College and University,* 51 (Winter 1976), 153–60.

von Hippel, Eric. "Users as Innovators." *Technology Review,* 80 (January 1978), 31–39.

Weathersby, George. "PPBS: Purpose, Persuasion, Backbone, and Spunk." *Liberal Education,* 57 (May 1971), 211-18.

———. "The Potential of Analytical Approaches to Educational Planning and Decision-Making." In *Proceedings of the 1976 National Assembly.* Ed. William Johnson. National Center for Higher Education Management Systems (NCHEMS), 1976.

———. "Scarce Resources Can Be a Golden Opportunity for Higher Education." *Change,* 14 (March 1982), 12–13.

Weick, Karl. "Educational Organizations as Loosely Coupled Systems." *Administrative Science Quarterly,* 21 (March 1976), 1–19.

Wildavsky, Aaron. "If Planning Is Everything, Maybe It's Nothing." *Policy Sciences,* 4 (June 1973), 127–53.

Wilson, Ian. "Socio-Political Forecasting: A New Dimension to Strategic Planning." *Michigan Business Review,* 26 (July 1974), 15–25.

Wyatt, Joe B., and Zeckhauser, Sally. "University Executives and Management Information: A Tenuous Relationship." *Educational Record,* 56 (Summer 1975), 175–89.

Yarmolinsky, Adam. "Institutional Paralysis." *Daedalus,* 104 (Winter 1975), 61–67.

Zalesnik, Abraham. "Power and Politics in Organizational Life." *Harvard Business Review,* 48 (May–June 1970), 47–60.

———. "Managers and Leaders: Are They Different?" *Harvard Business Review.* 55 (May–June 1977), 67–78.

Zemsky, Robert; Porter, Randall; and Oedel, Laura. "Decentralized Planning." *Educational Record,* 59 (Summer 1978), 229–53.

9, 12–15, 152; targets for, 68; at Teachers
College, 93; at Hartford, 51; at Wesleyan,
47
Etherington, Edwin, 45
Etzioni, Amitai, 114, 165
Ewing, David, 63, 67, 70, 112, 117, 155–56,
158
EXECUCOM, 91
Extension services, 22

Faculty: administration and, 28, 29, 33–34,
126–27; age of, 22–23; Anglophilic concept and, 31; antibusiness bias of, 34, 35;
Athenian concept and, 31, 33; autonomy
and, 32–33; Carnegie-Mellon strategy
and, 90; committees and, 24; communi-
cating with, 63; competition and raiding
of, 18; German *(Lehrfreiheit)* concept and,
32; at Goucher, 69; governance and, 33–
34, 37, 43, 61, 62, 86, 165; Hood strategy
and, 78, 79; inert knowledge and, 174;
information and, 131, 132; management
and, 43, 44–45, 55, 59, 126–27, 171–72;
managerial questioning and, 135; at
Milton, 4; part-time, 23–24, 36; power
and, 27, 29, 37; quality and, 135; salaries
of, 10, 23, 36, 45, 49, 78; statistics on, 9–
10, 22–23; strategy and, 177; strategy example and, 73; Teachers College strategy
and, 93–95, 96; tenure and, 64; turnover
of, 64; unions and, 23, 36–37; at Hartford,
49, 50, 51; at Wesleyan, 45, 46, 47, 48
Faculty senates, 33, 37, 126, 127
Fields, Emmett, 168
Finances: Barat strategy and, 84; computer
programs and management of, 53–54; endowments and, 152; forecasting and, 158;
Hood strategy and, 78; income squeeze
and, 11; information about, 133; management and, 59–61; outside aid and, 25; rating scheme and, 154–56; Rensselaer
Polytechnic strategy and, 82, 83; strategy
and, 168; Teachers College strategy and,
94; Hartford and, 49–51; Michigan strat-
egy and, 87–88; Wesleyan and, 45–49
Financial officers, 59–61
Finn, Chester, Jr., 65
Fisher, Homer, 23
Fitzgerald, F. Scott, 145
Follett, Mary Parker, 175
Folwell, William Watts, 175–76
Forecasting: areas concerned with, 157–58;
incrementalism and, 106; management
science and, 111; strategic planning and,
142
Foreign students, 9, 13. *See also* Students
Frazer, William, 59

Fringe benefits, 10
Functions of the Executive, The (Barnard), 41
Fund raising, 6–7; at Stanford, 138; at Wes-
leyan, 47
Future trends. *See* Forecasting

Galbraith, John Kenneth, 41
German *(Lehrfreiheit)* myth, 32
Giamatti, A. Bartlett, 176
Gibbon, Edward, 31
Gilman, Daniel Coit, 32
Goodman, Paul, 30–31
Goucher College, 69–70
Governance, 86; Anglophilic myth and, 31–
32; Athenian democracy myth and, 30–
31; external control and, 24–26; faculty
and, 33–34, 37, 43, 61, 62, 86, 165; fac-
ulty committees and, 24; German univer-
sities and, 32; management and, 61–62,
126–27; organizational change and, 175
Grants: students at Milton and, 4; Hartford
and, 50
Great Planning Disasters (Hall), 77
Grebstein, Sheldon, 85
Greene, Richard, 46, 47
Gross, Neal, 24
Guardo, Carol, 51

Hall, Peter, 77
Harper, William Rainey, 7
Harvard University, 52
Hass, Raymond, 86, 89
Hasselmo, Nils, 86
Hegel, Georg W. F., 165
Herzberg, Frederick, 41–42
Hesburgh, Theodore, 126
Heyman, Ira, 130
Higher Education Finance Research Insti-
tute, 53–54
Hirschman, Albert, 68, 107, 125
Hirschman's dilemma, 97
Hitch, Charles, 101, 148
Hodgkinson, Harold, 18
Hood College (Frederick, Md.), 77–80
Hoover, Herbert, 101
Hopkins, Ernest, 20
Horner, John, 156
Hornstein, Harvey, 95–96
Human resources. *See* People
Human Side of Planning, The (Ewing), 63
Hutchins, Robert, 126

*Identification of College and University Peer
Groups, An* (Elsass), 161
Incremental approach to organizations:
analysis of, 106–8; criticisms of, 111–15
Industrialists, founding of colleges and, 7